Rajendra A. Chitnis

Vladislav Vančura:
The Heart of the Czech Avant-garde

T0083507

RAJENDRA A. CHITNIS

VLADISLAV VANČURA:
THE HEART
OF THE CZECH AVANT-GARDE

Charles University in Prague
Karolinum Press 2007

Reviewed by Prof. PhDr. Jiří Holý, DrSc.
David Short

ISBN 978-80-246-1456-4

CONTENTS

ACKNOWLEDGEMENTS

This book was completed with the valuable help of an AHRC Research Leave grant.

I would like to thank staff at the Moravská zemská knihovna, Brno, and Univerzita Palackého, Olomouc, for their great help in locating materials used in this project, and library staff at Univerzita Tomáše Bati, Zlín, for allowing me to work in their reading room while the library was closed over the summer of 2006. I would also like to thank my parents-in-law, Liba and Martin, for accommodating us for long periods while I worked on the project, and for their help in sending books and materials I needed.

I am very grateful to David Short and Jiří Holý for their valuable, detailed comments on the manuscript. As ever, I am indebted to Robert Pynsent for his readiness to discuss the work in progress, and to my colleagues at the University of Bristol, especially Mike Basker and Derek Offord, for their support and encouragement in bringing this project to fruition.

This book is dedicated to Katka and to Filip, who arrived during its rather longer gestation.

VLADISLAV VANČURA:
A BRIEF BIOGRAPHICAL NOTE

Vladislav Vančura (1891–1942), the leading fiction writer of the Czech inter-war Avant-garde and arguably the greatest exponent of the Czech language in prose, was born in Háj u Opavy in Silesia, but spent most of his childhood and adult life on the middle Vltava near Prague. He studied medicine, graduating in 1921, and practised with his wife Ludmila in Zbraslav until 1929, when he devoted himself full-time to literature. During the inter-war period, Vančura worked not only as a published writer, but also as an editor, reviewer, theatre critic, press contributor and public speaker on literature and the arts, and occasional film director. He was the first chairman of the major Prague-based Avant-garde grouping Devětsil, established in 1920, which included the poets Jaroslav Seifert (1901–86) and (from 1922) Vítězslav Nezval (1900–58) and the leading Avant-garde theorist of the post-1918 generation, Karel Teige (1900–51), but had dissociated himself from the group by 1924. In 1929 he was expelled from the Communist Party, together with six other prominent writers, after they signed an address to workers, protesting at the take-over of the Party leadership by Klement Gottwald and his fellow-Stalinist supporters at the Fifth Party Congress. He nevertheless remained a prominent figure in left-wing cultural-political campaigns in the 1930s and during the German occupation of Bohemia and Moravia, he was active in the illegal Communist resistance, working particularly on models of cultural activity for the future Communist Czechoslovakia that was expected to follow liberation. In May 1942 he was arrested during the first wave of reprisals that followed the attempted assassination of the German Protector Heydrich and executed a few weeks later.

His major works, in order of publication, are (novels unless stated): the short story cycles *Amazonský proud* (The Amazonian current, 1923) and *Dlouhý, Široký, Bystrozraký* (Tall, Wide, Sharp-eyed, 1924), *Pekař Jan Marhoul* (Jan Marhoul the baker, 1924), *Pole orná a válečná* (Arable and battle fields, 1925), *Rozmarné léto* (A capricious summer, 1926), the plays *Učitel a žák* (Teacher and pupil, 1927) and *Nemocná dívka* (The sick girl, 1928), *Poslední soud* (The last judgement, 1929), *Hrdelní pře anebo Přísloví* (A capital case or Proverbs, 1930), *Markéta Lazarová* (1931), *Útěk do Budína* (Flight to Buda, 1931), the children's book *Kubula a Kuba Kubikula* (Kubula and Kuba Kubikula, 1931), the short-story cycle *Luk královny Dorotky* (Queen Moll's bow, 1932), the play *Alchymista* (The alchemist, 1932), *Konec starých časů* (The end of the old days, 1934), the play *Jezero Ukereve* (Lake Ukereve, 1935), *Tři řeky* (Three rivers, 1936), *Rodina Horvatova* (The Horvat family, 1938), the unfinished chronicle of Czech history *Obrazy z dějin národa českého* (Pictures from the history of the Czech nation, 1939 [Vol. 1], 1940 [Vol. 2], 1947 [fragments of Vol. 3]) and the play *Josefina* (1950). Of these, only two have been translated into English (for Czech publishing houses): *Konec starých časů* by Edith Pargeter as *The End of the Old Times* (1965) and *Rozmarné léto* by Mark Corner as *The Summer of Caprice* (2006).

INTRODUCTION:
FINDING A NAME FOR VANČURA

The most thought-provoking memoir about Vladislav Vančura, by the Catholic literary critic, Bedřich Fučík, is entitled: 'I cannot find a name for him.'[1] Fučík describes here the difficulties he has had in finding words that capture the essence of Vančura, as a writer and as a man. In the 1920s, despite their ideological differences, Vančura was, together with the Catholic Jaroslav Durych (1886–1967), the contemporary writer Fučík most admired.[2] After coming to know him personally in the late 1920s, as editor at the Melantrich publishing house he enabled Vančura to give up practising medicine and devote himself to his literary activities full-time.[3] For a time, around 1930, he, like his fellow Catholic Jan Čep thought he saw the stirrings of Catholicism in him.[4] Later, however, Fučík saw Vančura's apparent insistence on the pre-eminence of communism as a repeated stumbling block to the creation of a united front of anti-Fascist intellectuals.[5] Vančura emerges from Fučík's account as a complicated, elusive, but charismatic figure.

1) See B. Fučík, 'Hledám mu jméno' (dated 1973) in his *Čtrnáctero zastavení*, Prague, 1992, hereafter Fučík, *Čtrnáctero zastavení*, p. 121.
2) See, for example, B. Fučík, *Kritické příležitosti I*, Prague, 1998, hereafter Fučík, *Kritické příležitosti I*, p. 78.
3) See Fučík, *Čtrnáctero zastavení*, p. 124.
4) Both were encouraged by Vančura's possibly ironic comments in an interview, in which he declared: 'Catholicism has an old and wonderful tradition. The world-view of poets is complete. The order and interpretation of all phenomena is given. How nice for poets!' (Quoted in Fučík, *Kritické příležitosti I*, p. 335.) Responding specifically to the novel *Poslední soud*, Čep wrote: 'Believer or unbeliever (how can a poet be an unbeliever?), this creature will always be obsessed with a thirst for God.' (J. Čep, 'Vladislav Vančura' (1930) in his *Rozptýlené paprsky*, Prague, 1993, p. 51.)
5) See Fučík, *Čtrnáctero zastavení*, p. 130. In an article discussing who was at fault for the capitulation at Munich in 1938, Fučík claims that one such attempt in 1936, led by Vančura and Ivan Olbracht (1882–1952) collapsed when Catholics and the so-called 'moderate right' were excluded by the Party from the very first meeting. (See B. Fučík, 'Samomluvy nad křikem' (dated 1975) in his *Setkávání a míjení*, Prague, 1995, p. 251.)

Fučík's perception of Vančura contrasts with that of many commentators, who have preferred in their interpretations to emphasize the appearance of strength and clarity of thinking in his writing, especially in studies dating from the Communist period, when mainstream critical opinion was dominated by not so much aesthetic as political imperatives. In the 1920s, reviewers of his work like the Marxist Bedřich Václavek or socialist František Götz praised the 'masculinity' of his writing, while the Catholic Albert Vyskočil relished his 'manly, bullish [kančí] style'.[6] Götz comments: 'Vančura is a labouring man [dělník] of fiction [...] he writes prose with difficulty and tortuously, as when a sculptor works a shapeless, coarse piece of stone into a statue',[7] while in a similar vein A. M. Píša suggests that he creates his characters 'as though from a single piece with mighty blows of the chisel'.[8]

After the 1948 Communist take-over of Czechoslovakia, Vančura was claimed by the regime, though no significant new studies of his work were published until the late 1950s. In the politically compromised essays accompanying various volumes of the Československý spisovatel edition of his collected works (1951–61), Vančura's friend Jan Mukařovský accentuates, in the jargon of the period, his patriotism, his anti-Fascism, his optimism and his commitment to socialism, implicitly of the kind being instituted in Czechoslovakia. Mukařovský's argument was strengthened by the manner of Vančura's death, at the hands of the German occupiers.[9] Vančura was never, however, given the same mythicizing treatment accorded to the journalist and literary critic Julius Fučík, who was imprisoned in the same period but managed to delay his execution for over a year by feeding the Germans false information about illegal Communist

6) A. Vyskočil, 'Někdo a nic (Vladislav Vančura a A. C. Nor)' in his *Kritikova cesta*, Brno, 1998, p. 185.
7) F. Götz, *Jasnící se horizont*, Prague, 1926, p. 219.
8) A. M. Píša, *Dvacátá léta*, Prague, 1969, p. 326.
9) In a press release from June 1st 1942, Vančura, described as a doctor and writer, was named first on a list of people executed, having been found guilty of harbouring agents. (See B. Čelovský, *Řešení české otázky podle německých dokumentů 1933–1945*, Ostrava, 1995, p. 348.) Other than his prominence on the list, nothing suggests, as Mukařovský later claimed, that the Germans knew the significance of their victim and were carrying out the 'symbolic execution of a nation's culture' (J. Mukařovský, 'Řeč při tryzně' in his *Studie z poetiky*, Prague, 1982, p. 772.) Oleg Malevich, however, argues that he would have come to the attention of the authorities after his refusal to accompany a delegation of Czech cultural figures to Berlin in 1941 (see O. Malevich, *Vladislav Vanchura*, Leningrad, 1973, p. 177.)

activity. This distinction may be attributed not only to the attractiveness of Fučík's story and his reportage, gradually smuggled out of prison on scraps of paper, but also to Vančura's more complicated relationship with the Party in the inter-war period, and his frequent deviations from the prevailing ideological orthodoxy.

Milan Kundera's 1960 monograph continues to present Vančura as essentially a didactic writer, transforming Mukařovský's earlier, subtle description of Vančura's work as a 'journey towards the epic'[10] into a linear account of how, in his view, Vančura resolves the early twentieth century crisis of the novel in his fiction.[11] The apparent malleability of Vančura's work was further reflected in the attempt in 1964 by the new liberal journal *Tvář* to 'enlist' him in the campaign for a less rigidly ideological cultural policy through the re-publication of his 1931 essay 'O společenské funkci umění' (On the social function of art), in which he rejected the use of literature for political purposes and defended uncommitted literature.[12] In 1929 Vančura had written: 'One may not reject a book because of its tendentiousness, as long as this expands the artistic expression, as long as it is governed by the form, as long as both these things interconnect and are rooted in each other. If the idea of a book is incorrect, we may regret this or condemn the orientation, but not the work.'[13] In their foreword to the 1972 volume of Vančura's non-fiction cited, however, the editors Milan Blahynka and Štěpán Vlašín argued that Vančura later changed his mind on this issue, and that in any case the editors of *Tvář* had taken the essay out of the context of the vulgar use

10) Mukařovský, J., 'Vančurovská prologomena' in his *Studie II*, Prague, 2001, p. 511.
11) In one chapter Kundera even lists Vančura's 'latent artistic programme' point by point (see M. Kundera, *Umění románu: Cesta Vladislava Vančury za velkou epikou*, Prague, 1960, pp. 72–79.) In his review in *Tvář* a decade later, Jan Lopatka criticized what he saw as Kundera's efforts to construct a version of Vančura's development to fit a pre-existing model, rather than working from the author's texts (see J. Lopatka, 'Umění románu' in M. Špirit (ed.), *Tvář: Výbor z časopisu*, Prague, 1995, p. 525). This study belongs among those early works of Kundera which he later disavowed; in 1986 he sought to 'erase' it by publishing a new volume with the same title, *L'art du roman*, about his own work.
12) Vančura also played an indirect role in the liberalization of Czech Socialist cinema in the same period, with the release in 1967 of film versions of *Markéta Lazarová* (directed by František Vláčil) and *Rozmarné léto* (directed by Jiří Menzel). The films transformed Vančura's popularity among the wider public and the two novels have, perhaps unjustly, become his best known and most frequently re-published.
13) V. Vančura, *Řád nové tvorby*, Prague, 1972, hereafter Vančura, *Řád*, p. 69. He reiterated this position in his later 'Literární vyznání' (ibid., p. 171).

of literature by Czech nationalists and the First Republic establishment (but not, apparently, Marxists).[14]

This response shows how Vančura became caught up in the broader conflict between hard-line and pro-reform critics in this period. Writing in 1966, Vladimír Dostál, an opponent of liberalization and the leading ideologue of the subsequent so-called Normalization,[15] presents Vančura's first play *Učitel a žák* as a hard-line attack on the empty escapism of the Czech Poetist Avant-garde, commenting:

> The polemical confrontation of two kinds of romanticism, the [pupil's] romantic flight from an unpleasant reality and the [teacher's] romanticizing of work, guided by efforts to change reality, no doubt had something fundamental to contribute to the disputes within the artistic Avant-garde, which followed on from the Romantic tradition and was driven by the Romantic aesthetic.[16]

Dostál implicitly links this escapism with the 1960s reformers, augmenting his call for the play to be revived with the rhetorical question: 'Or do you think there is no one today on whom it might have an impact?'[17] Dostál's approach underpins subsequent efforts of mainstream critics to secure Vančura for the Normalization regime, which culminate in Blahynka's matchlessly comprehensive but ideologically marked 1978 monograph.[18]

For Blahynka, a key moment is Vančura's withdrawal from Devětsil in 1924, as the Czech left-wing Avant-garde grew increasingly divided between the Proletarian line, drawing on the tradition of, for example,

14) See Blahynka and Vlašín's introduction in Vančura, *Řád*, p. 27.
15) The Normalization was the name eventually given by the Czechoslovak Communist Party (which initially spoke of 'consolidation') to describe the period that followed the Warsaw Pact military intervention of August 1968 and the subsequent Moscow-supervised replacement of the reformist Party leadership in April 1969 with a regime that would, in their view, 'return society to normal'.
16) V. Dostál, *Slovo a čin*, Ostrava, 1972, p. 25.
17) Ibid.
18) This ideological bias is evident in Blahynka's rejection of Josef Galík's attempt to complicate Dostál's interpretation, published in 1970. Galík presents *Učitel a žák* as a criticism not only of Poetism, but of what Vančura presents as the feeble idealism of the Vitalist-influenced Karel Čapek (1890–1938) and Fráňa Šrámek (1877–1952). Blahynka, however, comments that 'such a one-sided interpretation can only be resisted' (M. Blahynka, *Vladislav Vančura*, Prague, 1978, hereafter Blahynka, *Vančura*, p. 144).

Slezské písně (Silesian songs, 1909) by Petr Bezruč (1867–1958), and influenced by cultural developments in post-revolutionary Russia, and Teige and Nezval's Poetism, which drew more on Avant-garde Paris and, by 1923, had come to dominate Devětsil.[19] Interpreting Vančura's withdrawal as an endorsement of Proletarianism, Blahynka uses it to claim Vančura for a notionally consistent Party line running from Proletarianism through Gottwald's Stalinist leadership to the Normalization regime. In consequence, deviations by Vančura from the prevailing Party line are presented as temporary misjudgements or superficial misunderstandings later corrected. This approach is exemplified by Blahynka's treatment of what he terms Vančura's period of 'crisis' (neatly coinciding for Blahynka with the international economic crisis), when he was expelled from the Party in 1929 for signing a pamphlet, later published in the social democrat paper *Právo lidu*, protesting against the new leadership.[20] Citing Nezval's memoirs, published in the 1950s, where the poet maintains that Vančura immediately regretted signing the offending document, Blahynka suggests that Vančura had simply been naively loyal to friends and really agreed with the Gottwald line all along.[21]

19) In his second 'Manifest Poetismu', Teige argues that through the work of the predecessors of the 1920s Czech Avant-garde: 'we joined with the rhythm of collective European art, a rhythm whose metronome [...] was Paris. Paris as the epicentre not of French, but of international artistic output, its metropolis and Babylon, the spiritual centre not only of artistic creation in the French language and the Latin tradition, but the successor of Italy and the predecessor of Moscow, in the way that spiritual hegemonies change in history according to changes in social and subsequently cultural systems'. (V. Nezval and K. Teige, *Manifesty Poetismu*, Prague, 1928, p. 16.)

20) The other writers expelled were Olbracht, Seifert, Josef Hora (1891–1945), Marie Majerová (1882–1967), Helena Malířová (1877–1940) and Stanislav K. Neumann (1875–1947). The writers presciently attacked what they saw as: 'the incompetent megalomania of comrades in the Party leadership, which has only words in common with Leninist doctrine, but to which the genuine Leninist spirit is entirely alien [...] May Communists be installed in the Party leadership who want the party to be united and to represent the masses, get rid of factional terrorism and restore the Party to a state where the masses of workers will once again have faith in themselves and in a leadership that they themselves have chosen.' ('Komunističtí spisovatelé o rozvratu KSČ' in Š. Vlašín (ed.), *Avantgarda známá a neznámá*, Vol. 3, Prague, 1970, pp. 47–8.) In a foretaste of the methods of the Communist regime that would take over under Gottwald in February 1948, the writers were subjected to sustained vilification in *Rudé právo*, led by the literary critic Julius Fučík (see F. Helešic, 'Komunističtí novináři 1921–38' in I. Koutská and F. Svátek (eds), *Politické elity v Československu 1918–48*, Prague, 1994, p. 200.)

21) See M. Blahynka, *Vladislav Vančura*, Prague, 1978, p. 158 and also V. Nezval, *Z mého života*, Prague, 1965, p. 101.

Vančura had already come into conflict with the Party in early 1926, after he published an article in the cultural journal *Tvorba* criticizing the dominance in the Czechoslovak Party of 'secretaries', lacking in skill or imagination. He writes:

in the Communist Party, membership of the working-class, expertise and style are worth nothing, just as elsewhere. All the abominations of democracy (dilettantisme, discussions, elections, parliamentary debating etc.) have found a place within a party whose duty is not to be a party, whose duty is to plan and implement a new system of work, to provide a scientific critique of the organization of power.[22]

In his response to this attack, Franz Carl Weisskopf regretted Vančura's decision to express his views publicly, but also noted: '[his] article in *Tvorba* is not merely uncritical, rebellious indiscipline, but an attempt to resolve the tangled complex of questions surrounding the problem of "the artist, society and collectivism."' In his view, 'the development of a new and revolutionary art will for a long time continue to travel along the road of "struggle" between the artistic individual and the social collective, between the more or less anarchistically minded artist and the bearer of the idea of collectivism'[23] before these two forces can be balanced.

Weisskopf's remark shows how dialectical patterns influenced the left-wing Avant-garde, who persistently confront opposites in their art in the hope of overcoming them in a new synthesis. Květoslav Chvatík, for example, notes the influence on Teige of the poet and theorist Guillaume Apollinaire (1880–1918) and his efforts to 'equalize the conflict between order and adventure, rationality and fantasy, logic and the imagination'.[24] All manifestations of this conflict may be said to reflect the struggle identified by Weisskopf to reconcile individual freedom with collective order. However, as, for example, Nezval's major 1920s poems show, this struggle takes place not only within the Avant-garde, but also within individual Avant-garde writers, anxious themselves to reconcile

22) V. Vančura, 'Proti sekretářům své strany' in Š. Vlašín et al. (eds), *Avantgarda známá a neznámá*, Vol. 2, Prague, 1972, p. 229.
23) F. C. Weisskopf in ibid., pp. 235–36.
24) K. Chvatík, 'Karel Teige jako teoretik avantgardy' in his *Od avantgardy k druhé moderně*, Prague, 2004, p. 64.

their advocacy of collectivism and rejection of bourgeois individualism with their wilful expression of artistic freedom. In a 1924 essay, expressing the typical position of the left-wing Avant-garde, Vančura states: 'all greatness, all art, every idea is necessarily founded on collectivism, in many cases, however, hidden and anonymous. We therefore do not declare collectivism a sign of modern art, but a sign of art in general and a sign of every successful piece of work.'[25] Interviewed in 1930, however, in reference to his expulsion from the Party, he comments:

> I conceive of communism as the old striving for fullness and happiness in life, which takes countless shapes and forms in keeping with the folk imagination (*lidová básnivost*). Marxism relies above all on economic conditions. These economic conditions are for me given by the situation of the nation. I have always thought of communism in this way and therefore in the Communist Party I have always rightly been considered an aberration.[26]

As I shall discuss in the context of Vančura's fiction, collectivism for him does not imply uniformity and conformity, but rather the protection and sustenance of an innately eccentric and aberrant humanity, reflected in his own broad, undogmatic, pluralist understanding of communism in the passage cited.

Bedřich Fučík characterizes Vančura in his memoir as 'a model of a personality heroically overcoming its own uncertainties with an implacable, unbending discipline'.[27] Though Blahynka goes further than previous critics in viewing Vančura's work as an examination of the conflicting positions within the Avant-garde, he presents this aspect more as a didactic commentary on the work of others, through which Vančura distances himself from Poetism, rather than an exploration of contradictory impulses within himself. Fučík's perception of Vančura finds a much stronger resonance in Jiří Holý's contention, in his 1990 study, that the emphasis in Vančura's writing repeatedly shifts between 'work' (*práce*) and 'poetic imagination' (*básnivost*), as these concepts are understood in Vančura's non-fiction. Holý writes:

25) Vančura, *Řád*, p. 56.
26) Ibid., pp. 330–31.
27) Fučík, *Čtrnáctero zastavení*, p. 133.

[Vančura's aesthetic projection of the world is epitomised by] on the one hand a precise, even cold, objective vision, purposefulness, striving for order, rational reflections, a sharp hierarchization in his perception of the world, an emphasis on the prose of life. [And] On the other [by] an emphasis on the poetry of life, an enchanted captivation by the world; a strong emotive involvement dynamizing the inner world of the human being, observing reality as flowing, open-ended activity with ever new horizons, a kind of creative chaos [...] His work is however a constant dialogue between these two elements, the objectively real and the poetic.[28]

Holý's study does not explore systematically the implications of this notion of dialogue for Vančura's fiction and drama, but rather traces the shifts of emphasis between 'work' and 'poetic imagination' in different periods of Vančura's writing, across both fiction and non-fiction and in the socio-political and cultural context. The meaning of the concepts is fluid in Vančura's writing, and one might not always agree with the way Holý distributes them. Nevertheless, his study offers a different framework in which to examine Vančura's work. Following its logic, one could say that Fučík's difficulty in finding a name for Vančura arises because there must, in effect, always be two names, in conflict with one another.

In Vančura's work, the desire to overcome these contradictions is consistently undermined by a desire to preserve the balance and equality of this dialogue, resisting premature, false resolutions. It is as though Vančura, until the late 1920s a practising doctor, views the ideal of life, epitomized by the healthy organism, as precisely a constant dynamic process sustaining equilibrium that contrasts with the static final order of death. As I shall describe in the next chapter, this perspective underpins Vančura's implicit characterization of the Avant-garde writer as a figure of transition, not of resolution, with the notion of life as movement towards an ideal challenged by a notion that preserving life as movement, as an endless transition, is the ideal. The conflict between these notions creates the fundamental dynamism in his work, and finds expression in any number of contrasting explicit and implicit metaphors. In the following chapters I explore this conflict through a series of pairs of 'names'.

28) J. Holý, *Práce a básnivost: Estetický projekt světa Vladislav Vančury*, Prague, 1990, p. 17.

The next chapter develops the medical parallel, examining the relationship between Vančura's understanding of the doctor-writer, as expressed in his theoretical writing and in *Nemocná dívka* and *Tři řeky*, and his use of language. Thereafter the study concentrates on his major works in more or less chronological order. In Chapter Three I turn to Vančura's response to the split between Proletarianism and Poetism in the Czech Avant-garde in his early cycles of short fiction, *Amazonský proud* and *Dlouhý, Široký, Bystrozraký*. In Chapter Four, with further reference to *Amazonský proud*, I focus on the recurring motif in his work of the 'current', which I associate with Bergson's notion of the 'current of life', the 'endless becoming' of life that contrasts with Marxism's teleological understanding of the movement of history. These two differing models are reflected in Vančura's approach to plot, which I discuss here in relation to *Hrdelní pře anebo Přísloví*. In Chapter Five I examine the conflict between collectivism and non-conformism in the context of *Pekař Jan Marhoul* and *Poslední soud*, and in Chapter Six I concentrate on the related tension between judgement and forgiveness in *Pole orná a válečná* and *Rozmarné léto*. In Chapter Seven I consider the widely acknowledged move towards more mainstream styles in the 1930s, and the conflict expressed in *Markéta Lazarová* and *Alchymista* between the expansive, self-confident perception of the human being associated in his work with the Renaissance and the diminished, timid perception of the human being that he associates with contemporary Bohemia. Finally, in Chapter Eight I concentrate on his unfinished chronicle, *Obrazy z dějin národa českého*, in which, I argue, Vančura brings the competing impulses in his writing together in the single figure of the chronicler.

The emergence of the doctor-writer is a striking phenomenon of Czech literature of the 1910s and 1920s, and given a cultural atmosphere in which the contemporary human being was seen as sickly, lacking in fibre, a shadow of his past and potential self, needing to be restored to health, it may be seen as more than a sociological coincidence. In an essay published in 1922 that had a strong early influence on the theories of the post-1918 Avant-garde, the Russian Il'ia Erenburg asserts that the 'new image of beauty is the healthy, developed individual. Gone are the Romantics' pale maidens and neurasthenic dreamers [...] the healthy human being loves joy, merriment and laughter'.[1] Writing in 1927, Jan Blahoslav Čapek argued that the common concern of Czech literature since 1918 was 'the dream of a new human being, free, unified, undissected, unmechanized, settled, incorporated, sunny. A human being no longer in turmoil. A human being who has blossomed again with spontaneous, organic strength'.[2] This quest for a renewed, liberating harmony of body and mind is most commonly associated with writers of the Marxist Avant-garde, like Vančura, or those close to it, such as Vladimír Raffel (1898–1967). However, it finds equal expression in Catholic writers like Durych, First Republic establishment figures such as František Langer (1888–1965) and social realist writers like Benjamin Klička (1897–1943), who all, like Vančura and Raffel, were doctors.

If the number of doctor-writers was new in Czech literature, the interest in regenerating the human being – and the intrinsically linked regeneration of literature – was not, and its inter-war manifestation may be seen on a continuum passing back through Masarykian Realism and the programmes of the Fin-de-Siècle even to the work of the nineteenth century 'revivalists'. In the 1920s, as in these earlier examples, what

1) I. Erenburg, *A vse-taki ona vertitsia*, Dresden, 1922, p. 58.
2) J. B. Čapek, 'Duchový obsah generace' in Š. Vlašín et al. (eds), *Avantgarda známá a neznámá*, Vol. 2, Prague, 1972, p. 391.

began as participation in a shared European concern for the human being narrows to a specific criticism of the Czech, a feature exemplified by Vančura's second play, *Nemocná dívka*. In the play, described by Dostál as a modern 'fairy tale about a sick princess',[3] the title character, Ida, describing her symptoms to medical staff, declares: 'není mi do zpěvu. Jsem mdlá, spala bych, a sotva usnu, již se probouzím, bojím se.'[4] As Blahynka argues, Vančura uses the story of how doctors combine collectively to treat her mysterious condition as a metaphor not only for 'the Avant-garde's efforts to return the human being to the fullness of life',[5] but also for the specific efforts of the Czech Avant-garde to restore feeble, timid Czech culture to health.[6] This use of the work of the doctor as a metaphor for the work of the writer, seeking not merely to diagnose but also to treat the condition afflicting contemporary humanity, occurs also in the later play *Jezero Ukereve* and possibly in the story 'Chirurgie' from the cycle *Luk královny Dorotky*, in which Vančura alludes directly to the effects of the contemporaneous economic depression. In *Jezero Ukereve*, efforts to cure sleeping sickness in Uganda function as an allegory of the writer's response to the spread of Fascism in Central Europe, while in 'Chirurgie', the story turns on the attempts of rival doctors in a provincial town to treat a labourer's dislocated shoulder.[7]

In *Nemocná dívka*, two young doctors, Křikava and Kolovrat, are set against one another, as indicated in the opening scene, in which the two are seen simultaneously debating and play-fencing in the laboratory. Křikava, whose rather negative-sounding name suggests 'screecher', is described in the *dramatis personae* as a 'fencer and experimenter', and in Nezval's programme notes for the first performance as a 'revolutionary'. Kolovrat, whose name, deriving from a prominent noble family, means 'spinning wheel' and may also allude to his desire to turn the

---

3) V. Dostál, *Slovo a čin*, Ostrava, 1972, hereafter Dostál, *Slovo a čin*, p. 31.
4) 'I don't feel like singing. I feel faint, I'd like to go to sleep, but scarcely do I fall asleep than I wake up again. I'm scared' (V.Vančura, *Nemocná dívka*, Prague, 1928, hereafter Vančura, *Nemocná*, p. 17).
5) M. Blahynka, *Vladislav Vančura*, Prague, 1978, hereafter Blahynka, *Vančura*, p. 146.
6) In support of this national interpretation Blahynka cites the melodramatic cry of Ida's landowner-father: 'Jde přece o království!' ('The kingdom is at stake!') (Vančura, *Nemocná*, p. 26.)
7) Blahynka writes: 'The story unwittingly alludes to the prevailing contemporary feeling that a time knocked out of joint was going mad...' (Blahynka, *Vančura*, p. 221.)

clock back, is described as a 'poet and adherent of palliative methods of treatment, turned towards the past, ceremonious', and for Nezval is the 'defender of traditions, the lover of miracles'.[8] Their qualities thus represent contrasting approaches to both medicine and writing, and perhaps, metaphorically, to the achievement of change.

Critical debate has centred on Vančura's attitude to each approach. At the end of the play, Křikava does not hesitate to plunge a needle containing the new serum into the sick girl's heart, but his action appears only to worsen the patient's condition and he is filled with self-recrimination. His method does not know how to deal with despair. Kolovrat, however, repeats Křikava's intervention and is successful. Dostál suggests that the conclusion represents balance, the 'combination of deed and poetry, of force and emotion, of the sword and the book', in which 'Křikava's self-confident decisiveness can bring as much benefit and cause as much harm as the wait-and-see timidity of Kolovrat'.[9] In Nezval's view, however, Kolovrat triumphs, while Blahynka favours Křikava, whose actions inspire Kolovrat.[10]

Křikava and Kolovrat reflect the conflict discussed in the introduction between a cold, practical rationalism and an empathetic, non-interventionist imagination. It is clear that these qualities compete within the doctor and within the writer, rather than distinguishing one from the other. Though, as he shows in *Amazonský proud* and *Pekař Jan Marhoul*, Vančura agrees that change can only be brought about by a combination of these qualities, his sympathies are ultimately with Kolovrat. His intervention, though inspired by Křikava, is decisive, as the emphasis in his final, suddenly assertive lines suggests: 'Není odvahy bez pochyb, není hrdinství bez bázně. Hřímejte, nízká nebesa, bude krásný den.'[11] The implied author's position is reflected in the contrasting designations for the groups of medical students who 'support' the two doctors during the operation. Křikava's fans are described as butchers, while Kolovrat's are, like Marhoul, bakers. Whereas the ultimately one-dimensional Křikava represents the impersonal march of science, Kolovrat represents a lovable, by nature imperfect humanity, as the cured girl indicates in the

8) V. Nezval, *Dílo* Vol. XXIV, Prague, 1967, pp. 194–95.
9) Dostál, *Slovo a čin*, pp. 36–37.
10) See Blahynka, *Vančura*, p. 147.
11) 'There is no courage without doubts, no heroism without fear. Thunder, low heavens, it's going to be a beautiful day'. (Vančura, *Nemocná*, p. 69.)

final line of the play: 'Děkuji vám, doktore Křikavo. Můj Kolovrate!'[12] As Vančura asserts most strongly in *Pekař Jan Marhoul*, it is in the name of that humanity that the revolution will be enacted.

One might argue that these medical metaphors reflect more a writer's perception of the doctor than a doctor's. Vančura only took up medicine as a slightly mature student, having failed to gain acceptance to art school and having abandoned law after a semester, and those who knew him suggest that he preferred writing to medicine, which he gave up in 1929.[13] The relationship between Vančura's work as a doctor and his writing is cursorily explored by Mukařovský, in an essay pondering how a writer's personality and biography are revealed in what he writes. For Mukařovský, the influence of Vančura's medical background may be seen most obviously in the fact that 'everything is within the human being: there is not a characteristic that he could not have, and every characteristic is at once light and shade [...] this is why at the very bottom of his being is the deep certainty of nature, of which the human being is part'.[14] However, according to Mukařovský, this feature might equally be attributed to the Protestant tradition in his family or to something else.

Vančura himself spoke about the relationship between his literary and medical careers in a lecture entitled 'Literární vyznání' (A literary profession of faith), dating from the mid-1930s and first published posthumously in 1947. At the end of the published version, Vančura suggests that 'it is beneficial for a writer to gain a specific view on the things of life'.[15] According to Blahynka and Vlašín, this assertion is followed in the manuscript by the remark that 'similar thinking had evidently once led

12) 'Thank you, Dr Křikava. My Kolovrat!' (Ibid.)
13) See L. Vančurová, *Dvacet šest krásných let*, Prague, 1974, hereafter Vančurová, *Dvacet šest krásných let*, p. 45 and J. Seifert, *Všecky krásy světa*, Prague, 1999, p. 111. Bedřich Fučík describes how, as editor at the Melantrich publishing house, he agreed a contract with Vančura for his collected works that enabled him to devote himself to literature full-time. He writes of Vančura's medical work: 'Vančura was undoubtedly a good and painstakingly conscientious doctor, who did not treat his civic profession as merely a job, even though he did not have enough of the "professional charm" that patients demand.' (B. Fučík, *Čtrnáctero zastavení*, Prague, 1992, p. 123.) He notes that Vančura's hidden compassion was revealed more in his willingness to charge patients according to their means, but recounts how patients calling at the Vančuras' home for a doctor always wanted to see his wife.
14) J. Mukařovský, 'Od básníka k dílu' in his *Studie z estetiky*, Prague, 1966, p. 292.
15) V. Vančura, *Řád nové tvorby*, Prague, 1972, hereafter Vančura, *Řád*, p. 173.

me to study medicine'.[16] 'Literární vyznání' draws heavily on the content of a 1935 lecture, 'Literatura, věda a život' (Literature, science and life), in which Vančura effectively develops the ostensibly rather banal statement contained in the unpublished section of 'Literární vyznání' that 'the content of both scientific and literary disciplines is life, or more precisely the human being'.[17] In 'Literatura, věda a život', he argues: '*everything* is nothing more than amorphous material that must be identified, classified, kneaded, mastered and organized into form [...] One must make the principle of form one's own to become familiar with the sphere of creation and of organic life.'[18] The work of the scientist and of the artist is united precisely in this activity of giving form to the amorphous material of life. In Vančura's view, however, someone wishing to become an artist would benefit from having studied natural sciences not because the method is the same, but because it is the opposite:

> Science strives to classify particular phenomena into a known system, that is, to automatize them. By contrast, the task of literature is to tear a particular phenomenon out of convention, to disturb known, everyday relationships and contexts and present it in a new light, even at the cost of deviation and violence against objective realities. This attempt, this violence is not, however, arbitrary, and just like science must capture the truth, only from a different angle and on a different level. [...] Science, then, [...] seeks to automatize, while art, using the means at its disposal, foregrounds [*aktualizuje*] a phenomenon as much as possible.[19]

In this context, the doctor-writer may be seen as a living embodiment of the unity to which the Avant-garde aspired, an unceasing, dynamic balancing of opposites, the repudiation of the split between art and science as methods of cognition and at least a faint reminder of the 'Renaissance man' who, for Vančura and so many of his contemporaries, constituted their ideal of the human being. However, as the label itself suggests, the doctor-writer more precisely represents a stage between the division of the present and the notional unity of the past and future, a quintessentially modernist figure of transition, embodying the competing impulses

16) Ibid., p. 583.
17) Ibid.
18) Ibid., p. 116.
19) Ibid., p. 108.

of the period to 'automatize' and to 'foreground' or 'defamiliarize', to establish and to resist the establishment of a final resolution and order. In this sense, the doctor-writer epitomizes the predicament of those writers of what Franco Moretti describes as 'modern epics', defined in his view by their revelation of and inability to overcome the 'discrepancy between the totalizing will of the epic and the subdivided reality of the modern world'.[20]

Writing from a linguistic perspective about the period when Vančura and his contemporaries entered literature, Mukařovský comments:

It was a time when the loosening of the relationships between the human being and reality, and therefore between the word and reality, had reached a critical point. The word is bound to reality for the European human being of the 1920s only through sensual indicators. The word smells of reality, it flickers with it and echoes with it, but it no longer expresses it as order, as something solid and binding.[21]

Vančura's writing, typically of the Czech inter-war Avant-garde, consistently expresses a yearning to overcome the 'subdivided reality' of the modern world, to resist the prevailing trend towards relativism and atomization and recover a unified, all-embracing perspective capable of giving form to the breadth of life. Mukařovský's description of Vančura's work as a 'journey towards the epic' seems to reflect this yearning.

In 'Literatura, věda a život', however, Vančura criticizes ideas contained in a volume of Maksim Gor'kii's essays, published in Czech in 1932, in which Gor'kii calls on literature to strive for greater generalization, typicization and clarity. Vančura objects ostensibly because Gor'kii appears to be demanding that literature abandon defamiliarization and instead function in the same way as science, as Vančura defines it. The lecture in essence defends the Formalist-Structuralist approach, which had come under increasing attack from hard-line Marxist critics who propounded the emerging model of Socialist Realism. As much as Vančura's writing resists relativism, it also resists becoming the servant of perspec-

---

20) Moretti, F., *Modern Epic*, London, New York, 1996, p. 5. Moretti's study includes analysis of such works as Goethe's *Faust Part II*, Wagner's *Ring*, Melville's *Moby Dick* and Joyce's *Ulysses*.
21) J. Mukařovský, 'Řeč při tryzně' in his *Studie z poetiky*, Prague, 1982, p. 778.

tives that lay false claim to being absolute, particular narrow doctrines or ideological positions that are no more than restrictive substitutes for the unified perspective to which he aspires. His writing therefore reflects the conflict between two opposed understandings of modernity implied by Moretti: one that seeks to embrace it, to capture the chaos of the present moment in all its uncertainty and incompleteness, and one that aspires to distance and control, a detached, ordering position.

Malevich maintains that Vančura only became acquainted at first hand with the work of the Russian Formalists in the late 1920s and 1930s, through his contacts with Mukařovský, Roman Jakobson and the Prague Linguistic Circle, at the time when key texts were first translated into Czech.[22] Ironically, as Malevich points out, Vančura's explicit advocacy of Shklovskii's ideas in his non-fiction comes as he moves away from overt defamiliarization in his fiction,[23] a change discussed in the final chapter. The conflict between the two contrasting notions of modernity, between the desire to 'automatize' and to defamiliarize is consequently most apparent in his approach to narration and language in his 1920s writing.

The aspiration in Vančura's writing for an ultimate, unifying perspective is reflected above all in the dominance of the narrating voice over the material he narrates. In his notes towards a study of Vančura's narrator, Mukařovský writes:

The text [in Vančura] is arranged in such a way that the reader never ceases for a moment to be aware that between him and the text stands a narrator, facing the reader as much as the situation and the characters about whom he is narrating to the reader. In Vančura the traditional hierarchy of narration is overturned. As a rule the fundamental, material relationship is created by the reality sensed behind the theme; in Vančura, however, the fundamental, material relationship is on the side of the

22) Malevich cites the sudden appearance of references to Viktor Shklovskii's theories in Vančura's sketches for lectures from this period and the apparent direct influence of Shklovskii's studies of de Maupassant and Chekhov and of *Tristram Shandy* on *Luk královny Dorotky* and the novel *Konec starých časů* respectively. (See O. Malevich, *Vladislav Vanchura*, Leningrad, 1973, pp. 126–27 and pp. 142–43). Vančura's earlier theoretical writings nevertheless reveal an affinity with Formalist ideas, which would have been common currency at the time among associates like Teige, Jakobson and others.
23) See ibid., p. 127.

narrator. The narrator never ceases to make clear to the reader that the narration in his hands.[24]

In his 1920s work, most strikingly perhaps in *Pole orná a válečná* and *Poslední soud*, all perspectives, characters, all events and episodes are absorbed into the narrative flow, a single, implicitly omniscient, omnipotent force, contrasting with the fractured weakness of the world it describes. Moreover, more ostentatiously than in his 1930s writing, the implicit claim of the narrating voice to be able to contain all life within itself, indeed to represent life, is mirrored in its implicit claim to contain all language within itself, to represent language as a living, developing organism.

For Kundera, Vančura's prose features 'perhaps the richest vocabulary that any Czech writer ever had; a vocabulary in which the language of all ages is preserved, in which words from the Kralice Bible and from modern argot stand humbly side by side'.[25] In an early attempt to characterize the heterogeneity of Vančura's writing, Václavek wrote:

> His language marks the regeneration of the degenerated language of poetic prose. On the one hand with his strictness and vigorous passion, which is not without healthily grotesque elements, he recalls the pure language of the old Czech bibles and medieval religious texts. On the other he refreshes many strong and graphic words that have already fallen out of use, and supplements his vocabulary with a supply of vernacular, ribald, supremely graphic and emotive words.[26]

Mukařovský notes also his use of specialist technical language, relating for example to particular trades or to medicine, and his use of poeticisms.[27] In addition, Vančura often chooses obsolete or old-fashioned morphological forms, notably for pronouns and noun endings, and makes extravagant use of participles and transgressives.

This approach may be seen in the context of the Avant-garde's challenge to Czech linguistic conservatism and the journalistic and neutral

24) J. Mukařovský, *Vančurův vypravěč*, Prague, 2006, hereafter Mukařovský, *Vančurův vypravěč*, pp. 63–64.
25) M. Kundera, *Umění románu: Cesta Vladislava Vančury za velkou epikou*, Prague, 1960, p. 22.
26) B. Václavek, *Od umění k tvorbě*, Prague, 1928, p. 139.
27) See Mukařovský, *Vančurův vypravěč*, p. 46.

realist prose styles favoured in the First Republic, which appear impoverished, unambitious and unartistic in the context of Vančura's prose.[28] Well before his fiction becomes overtly preoccupied with Czechness, his use of language constitutes an expression of the breadth and depth of Czech, its potency and potential, an implicit metaphor for what the Czech nation could be, but currently is not.[29] Above all, however, language as Vančura presents it, understood as a living, developing thing, encapsulates the dynamic, harmonious co-existence of the contradictory tendencies in the human being towards order and disorder, permitting both the playful freedom of the individual and the solemn endurance of the collective. In the conclusion of his study of Vančura's style Zdeněk Kožmín writes:

> For [Vančura], language is on the one hand entirely open to human interventions, an opportunity for the development of a totally autonomous structure that does what it wants with language, but on the other hand language means for him a collection of very strict laws that must not only be respected but exploited precisely as the sources of human freedom. The very essence of Vančura's style is founded on this dialectic.[30]

In Mukařovský's view, Vančura frequently places the emphasis of his narration on his 'choice of verbal expression', which becomes a device for drawing the reader's attention to the narrator. His choice, according to Mukařovský, is 'marked by some kind of deliberate approximation, a certain shift in relation to common usage'.[31] In other words, the path to 'automatization', to an ultimate unifying, ordering perspective, lies

---

28) In her memoirs, Vančurová recalls hearing how a school-teacher had declared that he would have given Vančura the lowest mark (*pětka*) for Czech language for his first novel and under no circumstances would he permit its inclusion in the school library (see Vančurová, *Dvacet šest krásných let*, p. 79). Defending the style of Vančura's early novels, F. X. Šalda intemperately rejected the prevalence of simple Czech sentences promoted by journalists and pedagogues: 'Czech prose has had the misfortune that its fate was decided by the semi-educated and idiots who forcibly reduced it to a mere communicative function: they charged it with the duty of being fluid, simple and natural. To hell with these negative virtues!' (F. X. Šalda, *Kritické glosy k nové poesii české*, Prague, 1939, pp. 305–06.)

29) In his 'Poznámka o románu' (1929), Vančura argued: 'but one gift falls into a poet's hands for which he is required to account. That is his mother tongue. Otherwise his choice is free and his sins forgiven'. (Vančura, *Řád*, p. 62.)

30) Z. Kožmín, *Styl Vančurovy prózy*, Brno, 1968, p. 155.

31) Mukařovský, *Vančurův vypravěč*, p. 48.

through defamiliarization. Defamiliarization in Vančura's writing does not constitute an end in itself, it is not 'art for its own sake' nor the destructive perpetuation of instability nor the nonchalant assertion of relativity, but a means of preventing partial perspectives taking hold, a means of wrenching the reader from a restrictive, normative apprehension of life in the interests of preserving the hope of attaining an all-embracing view. In his 'Literární vyznání', Vančura comments: 'the things of art pass into life and expand it [...] Art by itself is monstrous. Life is not only the starting-point, but also the goal of art.'[32] The defamiliarization of language functions as an instrument of persuasion, through which the narrator invites the reader to share his way of seeing. The reader must, however, be willing to cooperate, to work towards this synthesizing of perspectives. Through his challenging defamiliarization of reality, Vančura in effect expresses his view that the lot of the Avant-garde is hard labour and attention to detail, laying the foundations for the future, and seeks to engage the reader in that work.

Vančura seems to suggest that the task of the Avant-garde artist, the artist of transition, is to wait actively, to sustain the pursuit of 'automatization' through defamiliarization, and, in contrast to many of his contemporaries, to avoid slipping entirely into either the fragmentation implied by the total embrace of the present moment, or the didacticism of almost god-like detachment. The difficulty of maintaining this position is demonstrated by the example of his Central European contemporary, the Hungarian Marxist, Georg Lukács. In his influential *Theory of the Novel*, dating from 1915, Lukács develops Hegel's account of the epic, describing the novel as 'the epic of a world abandoned by God', an attempt to restore the Utopian unity of life and meaning of the classical epic that must by definition fail 'until the world itself has been transfigured, regenerated'.[33] Following the 1917 Bolshevik Revolution, however, Lukács repudiated the pessimism of his *Theory of the Novel*, apparently persuaded that the means of achieving that regeneration had been found.[34] Vančura seems to fall between the positions of Lukács in 1915 and after 1917, striving to avoid such oscillation in favour of an intermediate position – between false certainty and optimism and debilitating uncertainty and pessimism – perhaps most suited to both the writer and the doctor.

32) Vančura, *Řád*, p. 168.
33) G. Lukács, *Theory of the Novel*, London, 1971, p. 88.
34) See 'Preface' (1967) in ibid., p. 12.

Vančura's work thus epitomizes the view of those in the post-1918 Avant-garde who saw themselves as part of the transition, but not necessarily of the outcome, a view the Avant-garde inherited from the Decadents. Writing in 1921, Píša argues:

> The revolutionary poet must not settle for the thunder of words, the bombast of slogans and battle-cries, he must learn much, get to know much and renounce much. He must study the collective human being as he passes from darkness to the light, he must accompany him on every step of his struggle. But at the same time today's artist, infected despite all good will with the sickness and feebleness of the past, can never penetrate to the depth of the new world, incarnated in the revolutionary human type, he will never comprehend his spiritual cosmos, never attain his singularity and order. Such is the tragedy of his lot [...] his life is burdened with eternal yearning and constant struggle [...] To the poets of today returns the great original task, to be John the Baptists, messengers of wisdom, givers of order, labourers, fighters and prophets.[35]

Characters called Jan recur in Vančura's work, bearing, in Blahynka's words, 'the burden of Vančura's dreams, opinions, thoughts and experiences on their shoulders'.[36] Though they differ significantly from each other, the name is always given to children or child-like characters (reflected in the common use of diminutive forms of the name) who undergo literal or metaphorical journeys from the idealism and freedom of childhood to the straitening realities of modern bourgeois society. This confrontation seems to be at the heart of the implied author's identification with these characters, with Vančura repeatedly questioning, most notably in *Pekař Jan Marhoul*, whether the idealism and freedom of childhood is merely illusory, and whether the realities of modern bourgeois society are the only possible reality. Each Jan is essentially judged on the extent to which they capitulate to those realities (like the pupil in *Učitel a žák*) or retain an awareness of their child-like ideals. The name Jan serves

---

35) A. M. Píša, 'K orientaci nejmladších tvůrčích snah' in Š. Vlašín (ed.), *Avantgarda známá a neznámá*, Vol. 1, Prague, 1970, p. 192.
36) Blahynka, *Vančura*, p. 107. These characters include Jeník in 'Cesta do světa', Janek the bear in 'Poslední medvěd na Šumavě' (The last bear in the Šumava) from *Amazonský proud*, the title character in *Pekař Jan Marhoul*, and the central characters in *Učitel a žák*, *Tři řeky* and *Rodina Horvatova*.

to assert their ordinariness, the potential universality of their journey, and according to Blahynka had personal connotations for Vančura.[37] However, since it marks the character chosen by Vančura to bear his message, the name may also be seen to reflect the Avant-garde writer's sense of being chosen to bear witness, an allusion both to the 'voice of one crying in the wilderness', as suggested by Píša, or the author of the Book of Revelation, both figures on the threshold between the old and new worlds.

This relationship between the writer and the collective human being described by Píša may be compared to the work of a doctor striving to restore a patient to health. That, at least, is the metaphor used by Vančura in *Tři řeky* in his account of the relationship between the central character, Jan Kostka, and the local doctor, Hugo Mann. From the moment of his birth, Mann watches over Jan, often from a distance. He performs an emergency section when Jan's mother dies giving birth to him, continues to check regularly on the sickly child and once saves him from drowning. Later he teaches the adolescent Jan about Socialism, unaware that at the same time Jan is having an affair with his wife. During the First World War, stricken with frostbite on the eastern front, Jan encounters a surgeon who studied with Mann. He ensures that Jan's legs are not amputated. Subsequently, in Russia in 1917, Jan witnesses the ideological defeat of another medical colleague of Mann, who favours the gradualist social democratic line.

Mann is described by the narrator as 'mladý, veselý a rozkřičený',[38] qualities of which Vančura always approves, yet we are also told that, as a young man 'se neměl k světu. Ležel v knížkách a smál se jen věcem, které lze podařeně vypravovat'.[39] This bookishness and vicarious enjoyment of the adventures of others may be said, throughout Vančura's writing, to represent the 'sickness and feebleness of the past'. Without wishing to exaggerate the identification between Mann and Vančura, one might nevertheless note that Vančura openly acknowledged that he drew on the accounts of others for his depiction of Russia in the novel,[40] and

---

37) See Blahynka, *Vančura*, pp. 107–8.
38) 'young, jolly and inclined to shout' (V. Vančura, *Tři řeky*, Prague, 1958, hereafter Vančura, *Tři řeky*, p. 10).
39) 'he was not equipped for the world. He had his head buried in books and only laughed at things about which a good yarn could later be spun' (Ibid.).
40) See K. Nový, 'Rozhovor', *Panorama*, 14 (1936), 4, p. 57.

similarly had no direct experience of the front, having apparently made himself ill to avoid conscription.[41]

Jan, by contrast, makes the literal and metaphorical passage from sickness to health in the novel through his unthinking preference for unmediated experience, fostered in him in early childhood by the tramp, Černohus, and the Gipsy, Filomena. Mann's role is more that of guardian angel than teacher, and many of his contributions to the shaping of Jan are unwitting. As elsewhere in his fiction, Vančura seems to suggest that the patient's recovery is very much in his own hands. At the end of the novel, when Jan returns from Russia, Mann, now old, looks at Jan's hands: "'ta solená ruská kuchyně dělá divy. Myslil jsem si do té chvíle, že mám největší ruku." "A myslil jste si," prohodí Jan Kostka, "že je také nejkrásnější? V tomto případě byste byl dvakráte poražen.'"[42] Implicitly, Jan's hands are beautiful because they are calloused, reflecting the experience of their owner, who wanted to be a doctor or a writer, but has grown big, beautiful and self-confident through physical labour and is now ready to work, perhaps still as a doctor or writer, for the radical change for which Mann has always yearned. Reflecting the time of transition, the novel's ending is in fact a beginning, Mann's temporary defeat not precluding the promise of eventual victory.[43]

In *Tři řeky*, Vančura identifies with both the flawed, slightly comical, well-intentioned Mann, whose time is going as Jan's is coming, and with Jan, whose fate may nevertheless ultimately mirror Mann's. This passing of the 'Avant-garde' burden from one generation to the next recurs in Vančura's 1930s writing, for example in the bond in *Rodina Horvatova* between the old socialist, Eduard, and his niece Robina. In *Alchymista*, the wiser, if still youthful Italian alchemist leaves Bohemia having possibly inspired other characters to share his idealism and ambition. Though one senses Vančura's increasing identification with the 'older' characters, this feature does not so much imply Vančura's resignation as it emphasizes

---

41) See Vančurová, *Dvacet šest krásných let*, pp. 46–7.

42) "'that salty Russian cooking works wonders. I thought till this moment that my hand was the biggest." "And did you think," interjected Jan Kostka, "that you also had the most beautiful? In that case you would be beaten twice.'" (Vančura, *Tři řeky*, p. 264.)

43) The ending echoes that of 'Cesta do světa', in which the two central characters return to the stagnant Bohemian countryside having worked on the land, protested and fought against Fascism in northern Italy. Transformed from boys into men, they are ready to begin the work of transforming their homeland.

the notion of a prolonged transition, during which the flame of hope is kept burning until the day it is realized.

The doctor-writer in Vančura's case serves as a metaphor for his paradoxical efforts to overcome division and recover wholeness, and to resist the imposition of false unities, partial perspectives that curtail the possibility of progress towards the ultimate goal. Vančura sees only honour in maintaining a position that others, including those critics who seek to rob him of it, might view as impossible, self-contradicting, even hopeless. In 'Literatura, věda a život' he writes:

> Of poets it is said that they pay for their work with their lives; of doctors it is true. Sooner or later you finish your studies and, full of enthusiasm and full of learning, you find yourself practising. Practising and perhaps immediately in a situation where you cannot refer to the page of any text-book. At this point you may feel depressed and helpless either because of the uselessness of what you have at your disposal or because of a lack of understanding. At a moment like this everything fails except one thing, nobility, a feeling of human solidarity, an optimistic, elevated feeling that all facts, all realities, all opposites, in short everything is mutually co-dependent. Nothing is irreplaceable, but nothing of value proves worthless. If it dies, it is only so that it can renew itself in new lives and realize evolution [vývoj]. Evolution is the most important thing that I can say.[44]

This perception of success even in failure, of the temporariness of defeat, underpins his writing throughout the 1920s and 1930s, and one cannot but wonder whether it also sustained him at the time of his death.

44) Vančura, *Řád*, p. 112.

Vančura's first book publication was *Amazonský proud* (The Amazonian current, 1923), a very short collection of fourteen pieces, many of which had appeared in journals between 1918 and 1923, and some of which were revised for the volume. Compared to the reaction that would greet Vančura's first novel, *Pekař Jan Marhoul*, a year later, the cycle did not make a dramatic impact on Czech critics, and according to Pavel Fraenkl it had been all but forgotten by the time *Rozmarné léto* was published in 1926.[1] Also writing later in the 1920s, Václavek described the cycle as 'preliminary studies for a subsequent great epic composition, as though [the author] was learning to carve out the foundations for a future structure'.[2] As will become clear in the following discussion, Vančura would 'return' throughout his subsequent work to *Amazonský proud* for plots and motifs, and in a similar way it may serve as a source of his most fundamental ideas.

In their response to the collection, critics initially emphasized what they saw as the fragmentation of narrative in the modern world, even the death of narrative prose. Šalda, reflecting either a desire that Czech literature should also produce a work of radical modernism, or his misunderstanding of the term, described it as 'Dada [...] arising from an artistic form that has lost its meaning and purpose because it has nothing to bear in today's life and irrelevant world, from the hoarse, contentless "content" of that world and has therefore, in popular parlance, gone nuts'.[3] Václavek wrote in relation to the cycle: 'The referential function, giving testimony about the world, has been taken away from prose above all by cinema and journalism, which perform it better. Prose is nearing the abandonment of epic, of logically developing action; only

---

1) See P. Fraenkl, 'Rozmarné léto', *Rozprávy Aventina* II (1926–27), p. 143.
2) B. Václavek, *Od umění k tvorbě*, Prague, 1928, hereafter Václavek, *Od umění*, p. 129.
3) F. X. Šalda, *Kritické glosy k nové poesii české*, Prague, 1939, p. 99.

an emotional, poetic function remains.'[4] Miloš Pohorský later followed the line of the inter-war critics, comparing Vančura's approach to that of a Cubist painter, radically destroying the conventions of Czech prose.[5] He links *Amazonský proud* to the stylistically heterogeneous collection of prose pieces that makes up *Krakonošova zahrada* (Krakonoš's garden, 1918, pieces published separately 1908-1912) by Karel Čapek and Josef Čapek (1887-1945) and to *Měsíc* (Moon, 1920) by Vančura's second cousin Jiří Mahen (pseudonym of Antonín Vančura, 1882-1939). The latter more directly inspired the Devětsil writers with its opening playful, stylized history of Czech literature, in which the Bohemian kingdom is scornfully characterized as the 'land of the Single Idea' and the narrator advocates the poetry of 'pure imagination'.[6]

Like Mahen's collection, however, Vančura's *Amazonský proud* is not only or even mainly about disintegration or destruction, but about loosening hardened notions of language and structure, setting them in motion. In his study of Vančura's style, Kožmín writes:

> He wanted to create a technique that would be capable of capturing the growing complexity of relationships in the twentieth-century world and be true to the fast rhythm of the time, but would at the same time retain the capacity to react to the eternal values of life. He consciously created his narrative technique as a synthesis of tradition and modernity.[7]

Kundera rightly rejected the association of *Amazonský proud* with Dadaism, arguing that Dada had no positive purpose,[8] and subsequent studies by Kožmín, Blahynka and Holý have concentrated on the 'constructive' meaning of the cycle.

These contrasting critical viewpoints indicate how *Amazonský proud* captures the decisive shift in balance between constructive and destruc-

---

4) Václavek, *Od umění*, p. 130. Writing in 1924 in Devětsil's periodical *Pásmo* (named after Čapek's translation of Apollinaire's poem 'Zone'), Karel Schulz had provocatively asserted: 'The future of prose lies in the lyric. The epic belongs to cinema and the papers.' (K. Schulz, 'Próza' in Š. Vlašín (ed.), *Avantgarda známá a neznámá*, Vol. 1, Prague, 1970, hereafter Vlašín (ed.), *Avantgarda 1*, p. 528.)
5) M. Pohorský, *Portréty a problémy*, Prague, 1974, p. 212.
6) See J. Mahen, *Měsíc*, Brno, 1997, p. 14.
7) Z. Kožmín, *Styl Vančurovy prózy*, Brno, 1968, hereafter Kožmín, *Styl*, p. 150.
8) See M. Kundera, *Umění románu: Cesta Vladislava Vančury za velkou epikou*, Prague, 1960, p. 65.

tive elements in the Czech post-1918 Avant-garde compared to slightly earlier European Avant-garde movements. Matei Calinescu, for example, comments how, in European Avant-garde art, the human being is dehumanized by 'distorting or eliminating man's image, disrupting his normal vision, dislocating his syntax'.[9] In his view the 'avant-gardiste', 'hypnotized by his enemy, forgets about the future which can take care of itself when the demons of the past are exorcised'.[10] In an important early essay, however, Teige, distances the post-1918 Avant-garde from earlier movements: 'Are vague, run-of-the-mill Expressionism and headless Dadaism not the last remnants of the old art and its collapse? Artistic civilism led to emptiness and nothingness, it became a desert and tedium'.[11] For Teige, the task of the Avant-garde is 'building a new world. No one comes any more with proposals for modern art, but with plans for a new life, a new organization of the world'.[12] The purpose of Avant-garde art is, in his view, to prefigure this new way of living.

At the same time, as both Blahynka and Holý argue, *Amazonský proud* also reflects the emerging split in the Czech Avant-garde between Proletarianism and Poetism. This dispute typifies the division that Calinescu sees arising between the 'political avantgarde', who believe that 'art should submit itself to the requirements and needs of the political revolutionaries', and the 'artistic avantgarde', who believe in the '*independently* revolutionary potential of art' [Calinescu's italics].[13] The most vocal representative of the former position in post-First World War Czechoslovakia was Stanislav K. Neumann, whose earlier collection of

9) Calinescu, M., *Five Faces of Modernity*, Durham, 1987, hereafter Calinescu, *Five Faces*, p. 125.
10) Ibid., p. 96.
11) K. Teige, 'Obrazy a předobrazy' in Vlašín (ed.), *Avantgarda* 1, p. 99. Ironically, hardline Marxist criticism would in time take the same view of Poetism. Writing in praise of Jiří Wolker's commitment to Proletarian art, Julius Fučík declared of the Poetists: 'They inherit the tradition, they continue in the production of these decadent trifles that are charming and playful and with which they amuse or provoke us, the inheritors of bourgeois taste and culture; they make these useless and increasingly pointless things that we call art. Old men revolt against them – entirely in keeping with tradition – just as the experiments of new generations of poets have always been revolted against – and the new generation of poets in return provokes them – entirely in keeping with tradition – just as old men have always been provoked. And art – in keeping with tradition – heads towards catastrophe like the class for which it works'. (J. Fučík, 'Likvidace Wolkrova kultu' in his *Stati o literatuře*, Prague, 1951, pp. 41–42.)
12) K. Teige, 'Obrazy a předobrazy' in Vlašín (ed.), *Avantgarda* 1, p. 97.
13) Calinescu, *Five Faces,* p. 104.

essays, *Aťžije život!* (Long live life!, 1920, written 1913-14) had done much to inspire Vančura and his comrades. In an editorial addressed to poets in his journal *Kmen* in 1920, Neumann wrote: '[from the next issue] we are ceasing to publish verse by young poets if (1) it is not clear in form and comprehensible to the average reader and (2) it does not consciously and directly through its content declare itself ideologically in favour of the Socialist world and Socialist revolution.'[14] By contrast, writing in early 1921, Teige rejected the use of contemporary industrial, technological and urban imagery, instead promoting by example Mahen-like chains of intoxicating exotic imagery that seek to capture the spirit and abundance of the world to come (and prefigure the Surrealism that he, Nezval and others would formally adopt with the establishment of the Surrealistická skupina in 1934). The '*independently* revolutionary potential of art' is expressed in his assertion that 'the way of young art cannot be false. It is determined by an unfailing faith in the human being and love of life and the desire to raise the human soul from its orphanhood and isolation, to bear it from the prison of a narrow individual life to an incarnated inter-relationship with society and with all things'.[15]

For a time the Avant-garde seemed to be seeking a synthesis of these perspectives, as Wolker suggested in his 1922 essay 'Umění všední či nedělní?' (Art of the everyday or of Sunday?), in which he questions 'whether proletarian art should be for the worker a weapon for the struggle or a soothing bandage for his wounds?'[16] Wolker criticizes schematic, sentimental social novels that remind the worker of his everyday drudgery, and understands why workers are drawn to escapist art featuring heroic figures from higher social classes, but argues that art that is 'only for Sundays' is too idyllic. His conclusion seems to point to an art that is uplifting while remaining embedded in the real world, sustaining the struggle while retaining the promise of victory:

> [The worker] wants a concrete change to concrete reality. His every festive moment is closely linked with his most difficult hours, which brought him to that moment and will also take him from it. This human being is pursuing something and wants to achieve it. Sunday and the working day seem completely separate for him, and yet they interpenetrate one another so

14) S. K. Neumann, 'Básníkům' in Vlašín (ed.), *Avantgarda* 1, p. 75.
15) K. Teige, 'Obrazy a předobrazy' in ibid., p. 97.
16) J. Wolker, 'Umění všední či nedělní?' in ibid., p. 217.

much. They are for him an allegory of his struggle and his triumph. Just as once festive happiness carried people away somewhere to the heavens and was for them a means of forgetting this world, so today the holiday is the supreme recognition of that world.[17]

Wolker contributed to the first Devětsil anthology, *Revoluční sborník Devětsilu* (The Devětsil revolutionary miscellany, 1922), which as a disparate whole reflects the tensions between Proletarian and proto-Poetist approaches, but he subsequently broke with the group, unhappy with Teige's increasing hostility towards social content and ideological tendentiousness in art and his espousal of 'Sunday art', an art inspired by traditional and modern popular entertainment.[18] In a manifesto from 1924, Teige argued:

The beauty of poetry is without intentions, without great phrases, without deep purposes, without postulates. A game of beautiful words, a combination of imaginings, a web of images, perhaps even without words. It requires the free spirit of a juggler, which does not seek to apply poetry to rational lessons and infect it with ideology; modern poets are more clowns, dancers, acrobats and tourists than philosophers and pedagogues.[19]

Holý sees in *Amazonský proud* a 'bi-polarity' between the Proletarianism of Josef Hora (1891–1945) and Jindřich Hořejší (1886–1941) and the nascent Poetism of Teige and Nezval.[20] He shares Blahynka's perception that the cycle reflects Vančura's growing doubts about the direction being taken by Devětsil and constitutes a warning against the drift away from practical activity into the imagination: 'the poetic can obscure the real proportions of the world. It is not dreaming, not beautiful imaginary visions, not abstract projects, but daily active work that will transform the face of the reality in which we live.'[21] However, this assessment seems more unequivocal than Vančura proves to be. Rather than reflecting a

17) Ibid., p. 218.
18) Teige explicitly linked Poetism with the day of rest, quoting the Czech Symbolist Otakar Březina (1868–1929): 'After six days of work and building the world, beauty is the seventh day of the soul.' (Teige, K., 'Poetismus' in ibid., p. 556.)
19) Ibid.
20) See J. Holý, *Práce a básnivost: Estetický projekt světa Vladislav Vančury*, Prague, 1990, hereafter Holý, *Práce a básnivost*, p. 59.
21) Ibid., p. 61.

shift in Vančura's work towards Proletarian art, the cycle seems to exemplify the early aspirations of the Czech left-wing Avant-garde to find a synthesis between, in Wolker's terms, the 'art of the everyday' and the 'art of Sunday'.

The 'extremes' of these two notions of art may be seen in the pieces that frame the cycle, the parody cosmogony 'Ráj' (Paradise), a playful, eccentric expression of the creative imagination, and 'Býti dělníkem' (To be a worker), a thunderous call for workers of the world to unite and end the tyranny of capitalism. However, as Blahynka points out, the order of the pieces does not correspond to the order in which they were first published in periodicals, and therefore does not represent a straightforward chronological account of Vančura's artistic or ideological development.[22] Blahynka instead argues that pieces in the collection are paired on the basis of common themes that either complement or contrast with one another, echoing Kožmín's suggestion that at times the author explores the 'confrontation of antithetical phenomena', while at others he 'aims more for their harmonisation'.[23] Rather than the final piece constituting a repudiation of the first, 'Býti dělníkem' serves as a counterweight to 'Ráj'. At a time when the Avant-garde seems to be moving apart, Vančura seems to assert the need for a dynamic co-existence between the spontaneous imagination and organized revolutionariness.

In the cycle, and consistently in Vančura's subsequent work, the debilitating separation of these aspects is presented as a crisis of imagination and a crisis of masculinity. Holý notes how characters in the cycle like the postman in 'Slapská pošta' (The Slapy post), the young bear, Janek, in 'Poslední medvěd na Šumavě' and the playfully named Teige, the tailor in 'Čižba' (Fowling), are depicted as living in harmony with the universe, close to nature and enchanted by the whole world around them and within them.[24] For Holý, these characters, precursors of the baker Jan Marhoul, represent an approach to life that Vančura sets against the pragmatic utilitarianism of the modern world, with which they show little interest in dealing. The tendency of these characters – and others in the cycle – to engage in a creative relationship with the world around them marks them out as metaphors for a particular under-

22) See M. Blahynka, *Vladislav Vančura*, Prague, 1978, hereafter Blahynka, *Vančura*, p. 76.
23) Kožmín, *Styl*, p. 16.
24) Holý, *Práce a básnivost*, p. 60.

standing of the writer with which Vančura sympathizes. Their tendency to drift into dreams and fantasies reflects, however, the alienation of their imaginations from the real world. As he would again in *Pekař Jan Marhoul*, Vančura questions whether it is the men or the world they live in that has failed.

Throughout the cycle, the characters' imaginations offer nothing more than a fleeting illusion of escape or a temporary source of comfort from a difficult reality. In 'Slapská pošta', Široký the postman loves to rattle along noisily in his cart, lost in his dreams, in harmony with his surroundings, until one day he comes across a dead man hanging from a tree: 'civí na něho mrtvá tvář a oko obrácené k smrti.'[25] His dreaming and rattling serve to drown out the inevitability of death; he turns from the horror and rattles on. In 'Čižba', Teige prefers to go catching birds, which he immediately releases, rather than work as a tailor in the company of his nagging wife. Later, in the trenches of the First World War, his anxieties about her fidelity are assuaged by imagining that she has come to love fowling.

The activity of the imagination is foregrounded above all in the contrasting pair of pieces 'Vzpomeň si na něco veselého' (Remember something happy) and 'Samotný chlapec' (A boy alone). In the first, a rough older man, a drinker, stands at an urban window at night trying to recover his childhood self and become a dreamer again. Here, Vančura's favouring of the marginalized imagination is unequivocal: 'Odvaha a dovednost sloužívá, avšak uvažování, jež tvoří, bláhovost a nejšťastnější láska jsou zneuznanými pány světa.'[26] In the subsequent piece, the boy of the title, Josef, has come from the countryside to take up an apprenticeship in a factory in Libeň, a tough industrial suburb of Prague. Prefiguring 'Cesta do světa', the narrative shows how he filters his dispiriting experiences through his imagination, a chaos of fantasies, fragments of Jules Verne and fairy-tales and images of the America of skyscrapers and of Red Indians, bringing colour and hope to the bleak reality of his new life: 'Dým nad městem se stahuje v zlověstný mrak.

25) 'staring at him was a dead face and an eye turned towards death' (V. Vančura, *Amazonský proud – Pekař Jan Marhoul – Pole orná a válečná – Poslední soud*, Prague, 2000, hereafter Vančura, *Amazonský proud etc.*, p. 24).
26) 'Courage and skill are always of service, but thinking that creates, folly and the happiest love are the unrecognized masters of the world' (ibid., p. 36). This sentiment underpins the contrast discussed later between Josefina Marhoulová and her husband in *Pekař Jan Marhoul*.

Vkročiv v ně chlapec svírá pevněji svůj uzlík, neboť všechny obličeje před ním jsou apačské.'[27] Like the Poetists, he prefers the comedy of popular theatre to the implicit tragedy of the proletarian pub.

As the title indicates, the key element of Josef's plight is that he is on his own, able to commune only with himself: 'blátivý břeh, smutné domečky a dělníci jdoucí do práce – není nová podívaná. Hledám neobvyklé věci a kéž bych je nalezl nikoliv sám, ale s ostatními chlapci.'[28] All these characters discussed here share a sense of isolation and a yearning for collectivity. In *Amazonský proud*, Vančura describes a crisis of the human imagination that, in the modern capitalist world, has become fragmented, humbled and neutered, but nevertheless for the implied author represents humanity's greatest strength, the capacity to embrace the whole world, to bring together, to empathize and to transform. This crisis of imagination mirrors – or indeed serves as a metaphor for – the crisis of masculinity. Vančura's dreamers are all men who are forced to live in their imaginations because they are denied the opportunity to realize themselves in life, they are passive, helpless, incapable of change and of action.

The most transparent metaphor for the plight of the contemporary artist is Janek the bear in 'Poslední medvěd na Šumavě', whose name is both a diminutive of 'Jan' and also, in Czech, suggests 'wild, untamed'. As a young bear, Janek is not so much wild as playful; the opening sentence – 'celý les je mláděti ke hře'[29] – encapsulates his attitude to the world. Then his mother is shot by a hunter, he is sold to a bear-trainer and becomes a performing bear in travelling side-shows and circuses. His instinctively playful, creative relationship with the world is reduced to cheap entertainment, though he proves unsuited to the task: 'Dobromyslný pochybovač, s představivostí působivější nad skutečnost, neznaje rozdílu pomyslu a věcnosti, nevzdělal se ve smyslu užitečného umění. Planě moudrý, šlechtěn k nepochopení, spával na výsluní od výprasku do výprasku.'[30]

27) 'The smoke above the city draws together into an ominous cloud. Having stepped into it the boy grips his knapsack more tightly, for all the faces before him are Apache' (ibid., p. 39).
28) 'the muddy river bank, the sad little cottages and the workers walking to work is not a new spectacle – I am looking for unusual things, and I wish I could find them not on my own, but with the other boys' (ibid.).
29) 'the whole forest was there for the bear-cub to play' (ibid., p. 12).
30) 'a kindhearted doubter, with an imagination more potent than reality, ignorant of the difference between invention and materiality, he was not educated in the sense of useful

The reference to circuses may be taken as an allusion to Devětsil's love of clowns and acrobats, prefiguring the later implicit equation of the Poetists with the travelling showman in *Rozmarné léto*. However, even in this first collection, Vančura's ambitions seem to extend beyond parochial aesthetic differences. Significantly the narrator notes that Janek, who is taken by his trainer as far as Bavaria, forgets about the Carpathian forest and the ways of the wild. Nearly twenty years later, at the beginning of the first volume of his *Obrazy z dějin*, Vančura describes how the Czechs, having encountered Frankish traders, move from this same place of trees and bears into the land they will make their home. Janek may in this context be seen as the wild, eastern Czech bear rendered impotent and comical by long living in the west. This notion recurs most obviously in the contrasting of Ruthenians and Praguers in *Poslední soud* and Czech robbers and German nobles in *Markéta Lazarová*.

In the foreword to *Amazonský proud*, signed Devětsil, the authors quote Vančura's 1921 essay 'Západ a východ' (West and east), in which he characterizes the east as a place of origin, wholeness and timeless values, epitomized by the simplicity and unity of a Chinese painting, while the west appears as a geometrically fragmented place, epitomized by Cubism, which borrows for sale, exploitation and disposal:

> Not for no reason is it said that paradise was in the east. Even today these places are closer to heaven and miracles, for things and characteristics kept close to the origin have retained the sheen of birth, their need is for inter-relatedness and cause, while the west churns out all manner of goods for the purpose of consumption. The means of expression for eastern wholes is the sign, in which is incarnated the image of an absolute value; the west covers things in planes and lines, whose harmony exists for its own sake. The question of creation is broken in two: how and what. If everything were divided into method and content, what would be left?[31]

This assertion of the unity of form, understood as an intuitive expression of the experience of life is echoed by Janek the bear, who, responding

art. Wise in a homespun way, raised so as to understand nothing, he used to sleep in the sunshine from one whipping to the next' (ibid., p. 13).

31) The last two sentences might be read as a paraphrase of lines in Neumann's essay 'Ať žije život!' Neumann writes: 'We already know all too well that in art *how* (or more correctly *how what*) is always decisive, not *what* [Neumann's italics]' (S. K. Neumann, *Stati a projevy IV*, Prague, 1973, p. 30).

to his trainer's 'Western' criticism that his dreaming lacks form, argues: 'Proudí, vece medvěd a sveden řečí, těžce se zamyslí. Tvaru nelze odděliti od pojaté myšlenky, dí po úvaze.'[32]

Vančura yearns in his writing for the Czechs to recover their 'easternness'. In the title story of *Dlouhý, Široký, Bystrozraký*, contradicting the popular idea of Bohemia as an ideal synthesis of east and west, the mediocrity of Bohemia seems encapsulated in Dlouhý's comment: 'Vím, že západ a východ není na malé zemi.'[33] In his 1921 essay, the east appears to mean the Orient proper. In *Pole orná a válečná*, however, the east is explicitly revolutionary Russia. In an inversion of Decadent images of barbarians descending on the ruins of Western civilization, Vančura sees the promise from the east of a new, genuine civilization coming to replace the barbarity of Western ways; at one point the narrator calls to a fleeing crowd: 'Prchejte! Pospěšte! Na východě zdvihla se země a západ se octl v propastech.'[34] In an article written after visiting Russia in 1927, he naively contrasts what he perceives as the natural unity of spirit evident at a workers' gathering in Moscow with the 'hideous dilettantism' of similar amateur events in Bohemia.[35] In *Konec starých časů*, Vančura ambiguously contrasts the pallid, superficial adoption of aristocratic ways by the First Republic nouveaux riches with the perhaps genuinely aristocratic White Russian refugee, Megalrogov. In the subsequent *Tři řeky*, timid Jan is shaped by his experiences in Russia during the First World War. On crossing a river into Russian territory, a fellow soldier, struggling to put his boots on his soaked feet, says to him: '"Sotva se člověk dotkne Ruska [...] už povyroste ze svých střevíců."'[36] Taken captive, he hopes to join a Czechoslovak regiment fighting on the Russian side, but is sent to southern Russia to work in fields, where he becomes involved in local fighting as the country falls into revolution and civil

32) 'It flows, quoth the bear and seduced by language, he fell into deep thought. Form cannot be separated from the idea conceived, he said after some consideration' (Vančura, *Amazonský proud etc.*, p. 13).
33) 'I know that there is no west and east in a small country' (V. Vančura, K. Konrád, J. J. Paulík, *Poetistická próza*, Prague, 2002, hereafter Vančura et al., *Poetistická próza*, p. 52.)
34) 'Flee! Make haste! The earth has risen up in the east and the west finds itself in the abyss' (Vančura, *Amazonský proud etc.*, p. 260).
35) See V. Vančura, *Řád nové tvorby*, Prague, 1972, hereafter Vančura, *Řád*, pp. 59–60.
36) 'No sooner does a man touch Russia [...] than he grows out of his boots' (V. Vančura, *Tři řeky*, Prague, 1958, p. 175).

war. Though he finds comradeship and love, the Russians remain alien to him, as the father of the woman he loves suggests: '"Jdi, prchni ze země, které nerozumíš! Vrať se! Vrať se do svých Čech [...]".'[37]

The awakening of this 'easternness' forms the subject of the rest of 'Poslední medvěd na Šumavě'. Perhaps in a reference to crumbling western civilization, the narrator points out that the circus tent is falling apart but the tame, westernized Janek shows no great desire to escape: 'Celý stan čpí a mokvá jako jedovatá houba. Medvěd si stáhl důmyslně obojek a našlapuje opatrně na špičky, nikoliv na celou plosku, projde stavbou [...] Zkusiv nepevnost stanu, Janek je téměř na svobodě, leč neodchází.'[38] His behaviour contrasts with the furious she-bear's in a neighbouring cage, whose roaring 'awakens a dark vision of unfettered strength'. She finally inspires him to make his escape, and together they flee to the Šumava. Janek, however, does not fit in: 'zdála se Jankova vzdělanost divočejší dravosti a byl velmi obáván.'[39] The title suggests that such wildness cannot be sustained in this timid Bohemian environment. Similarly the she-bear's rebellious spirit fades with motherhood, and she becomes the first of many wives in Vančura who grow sour, trapped in the monotonous existence of family life. In the last line, recalling nostalgically her time as a performing bear, she says: 'ach, jaké je divadlo krásné!'[40] The comment reflects the enduring separation of art from life in bourgeois society, compartmentalized as entertainment and escapism, and the inability of the feeble Czech bourgeois to overcome it.

As the she-bear's inspirational fury indicates, the force that can resolve the crisis of idle imagination, of idle masculinity and impotent, Westernized Bohemia is feminine. Blahynka points out that the title of the collection, which the reader might initially associate with the penultimate piece, 'Proud amazonský', describing the hunting down of a Sioux on the banks of the Amazon, is a play on words alluding to a

---

37) 'Go, flee from this country that you do not understand. Go back! Go back to that Bohemia of yours!' (ibid., p. 245).

38) 'The whole tent stank and dripped like a poisonous toadstool. The bear ingeniously pulled off his collar and stepping carefully on tiptoes, not on the flat of his paws, he walked through the structure [...] Having tested the instability of the tent, Janek was almost free, but he did not leave' (Vančura, *Amazonský proud etc.*, p. 14).

39) 'Janek's educatedness seemed wilder than his savagery and he was greatly feared' (ibid., p. 16).

40) 'Oh, isn't the theatre lovely!' (Ibid.) This wistful ending is echoed in a similar context in *Rozmarné léto*.

very different Amazonian current. In the opening piece, 'Ráj', Vančura offers an alternative creation myth, suggesting that male and female, including a boy and girl, were initially kept apart from one another in separate paradises, which they share with angels. Vančura describes an atmosphere of growing restlessness, reflecting the frustrated potential strength and vigour of the males, expressed in pointless bellowing or meaningless savagery: 'Macku, řekl hoch tygru, jenž později utekl do Bengálska, proč máš tak veliké zuby. Přestaň, vidím červeně, mluvíš-li o tom. Ta barva je teplá jako můj dech. Duše zvířat pohnula se jako křídla. Jeleni ržou, kozlům pučí rohy a levhart, lev a pardál zadávili po pěti andělech. V tu dobu přišlo první rajské jaro.'[41] The females too, in their orchard, appear to be waiting for something to happen, but are sleepy and scattered: 'Navzdory mladosti bylo tu vše malátné a změtené. Psice nebyly ve smečkách, laně ve stádech, všechna zvířata chodila sama a příhody nikdy nestaly se zkušeností. Sad vzdoroval jaru, byl unylý a bez pohnutí.'[42]

In this context the serpent's tempting is a positive influence, calling for the virgin to be bold: 'Odvahu, a vaše štěstí je hotovo!'[43] She climbs the tree in the centre of the paradise, prompting the beasts to rush the wall separating them, and bringing them face to face with our 'colourless' world, where they once again hesitate. Blahynka writes that the 'Amazonian current begins' at this moment: 'Panenská mysl proudí, není opatrná. Vstaň a vyjdi rozvalenou zdí! Otevřená krajina budí bázeň, ale panna se nevrátí, ó andělé! Když zvířata a děvče vnikly do obory, objaly se ráje. Samci se prali a muž porazil strom na palivo. Andělé byli na holičkách.'[44] The Amazonian current is a powerful creative force that

---

41) 'Big Tom, said the boy to the tiger, who later ran away to Bengal, what big teeth you have. Stop it, I see red when you talk about it. That colour is warm on my breath. The soul of the animals twitched like wings. The stags bellow, the billy goats sprout horns, the cheetah, the lion and the leopard killed five angels each. At this moment came the first spring in paradise' (ibid., pp. 10–11).

42) 'Despite their youth, everything here was feeble and confused. The she-dogs were not in packs, nor the deer in herds, all the animals walked about alone and adventures never became experience. The orchard resisted the spring, it was languid and motionless' (ibid., p. 11).

43) 'Courage, and happiness is yours' (ibid.).

44) 'The virgin's thought flows, she is incautious. Rise and pass through the ruined wall! The open country arouses fear but the virgin will not return, o angels! When the animals and the maiden had broken into the enclosure, the paradises embraced. The males fought and the man cut down a tree for fuel. The angels were left dangling' (see M. Blahynka, *Vladislav Vančura*, Prague, 1978, hereafter Blahynka, *Vančura*, p. 57).

unites and makes action possible, banishing the feeble, child-like and childish angels of 'sterile' imagination.

The early pieces in the cycle repeatedly feature bold, rebellious, spontaneous females who, like the virgin and the she-bear, challenge the male characters' inactivity. In the satirical 'Starosta a báby' (The mayor and the old women), beggar-women band together to take playful revenge on a corrupt, miserly mayor by setting fire to his pile of manure; he loses the next election. The dynamic character of the female is captured in the title of 'Houpačka' (The swing), in which a cooper's wife persuades her husband to make her a swing, declaring, 'miluji pocit závrati a dlouhé cestování mezi nepohnutými trámy'.[45] This remark soon becomes a clear allusion to her infidelity, with both her husband and her lover thus compared to planks of wood. The piece opens with an image of potent masculinity, a lion depicted on an ancient well, a symbol of early human communal life all but buried amid centuries of urbanization. The lion roars in a vain effort to rouse the downtrodden to action, foregrounding the link between marginalized imagination and marginalized labour: 'Otylé město, nestav znamení síly do louže!'[46] As later, in his account of the medieval commercialization of Prague in Volume Two of the *Obrazy z dějin*, Vančura expresses scorn for those who do not manufacture but merely profit from the work of others, writing: 'Měšťanstvo obchoduje a slouží. Ušlechtilá řemesla, všechna odvětví výroby a nádeničina jsou pomíjeny. Soudní obuvníci, tesaři, krejčí a novotářští dělníci pracují zneuznáni. Jim straní lev.'[47]

Throughout Vančura's subsequent writing, nearly all his most unambiguously positive characters are female. Young women like Anna in *Rozmarné léto*, Anna in *Učitel a žák*, Jana in *Útěk do Budína*, Ljubov in *Tři řeky*, Robina (whose real name is Anna) in *Rodina Horvatova* and the title character of his last play, *Josefina*, embody an unthinking spontaneity, vitality, optimism, ability to empathize and to love. Towards the end of *Amazonský proud*, however, this type of female character is replaced by embittered, frustrated wives, in keeping with Holý's observation that

45) 'I love the sensation of dizziness and the long journeying between motionless beams' (Vančura, *Amazonský proud etc.*, p. 17).
46) 'Flabby city, do not cast the sign of strength into the mire' (ibid., p. 16).
47) 'The burghers do deals and serve. The noble trades, all branches of manufacture and hard labour are as of no account. Wise shoemakers, carpenters, tailors and innovative workers work without recognition. The lion takes their part' (ibid., p. 17).
48) See Holý, *Práce a básnivost*, p. 58.

the mood in the cycle darkens.[48] Vančura's focus shifts from the playful but impotent imagination to the struggle of the working man in a world which, as *Pekař Jan Marhoul* and especially *Pole orná a válečná* reflect, the female element as characterized in *Amazonský proud* is virtually absent. The final piece, 'Býti dělníkem' posits its return in the form of revolution, which is motivated by and imbued with anger and love: 'hněv je rudý a láska je rudá.'[49]

In the piece, the revolution will be carried out by those unthinkingly aware of the unity of life against those who have created division by trying to make life measurable: 'Neměřte světa prostorem, ani časem, ani váhou. Co víte o velikosti? Letící bouře, stmi se nad Greenwichem, padni na hvězdárnu a sval ji!'[50] Prefiguring his scathing, sarcastic and angry treatment of the First World War in *Pole orná a válečná*, in 'Býti dělníkem', Vančura uses the construction of the Panama Canal, described as 'netvorný záměr příliš prospěšný',[51] as a grotesque hyperbole of the capitalist exploitation of the worker and its waste of human ingenuity and effort: 'Jen pro rychlost a bezpečí kupeckého zboží činíme křivé rovným a ostrostí cest protínáme zemi'.[52] Its grotesqueness culminates in the allegation that, more than once, the canal company deliberately allows the site to flood, causing the deaths of hundreds of workers, to obtain insurance money. However, at the same time, rather as Wolker suggests that the worker's present defeat contains the intimation of his ultimate triumph, Vančura implies that the effective enslavement of workers from all over the world might be transformed into its opposite and become the international solidarity of the proletariat. The apocalyptic storm and flood prefigures the final destruction of a way of life and the coming of a new, just and peaceful world, for which the narrator repeatedly calls. Blahynka notes how Vančura re-uses motifs from the first piece.[53] However, their re-use is not so much a recontextualization as a recognition of the interrelationship between the two pieces. Where 'Ráj' describes the awakening and liberation of the creative imagination

49) 'Anger is red and love is red' (Vančura, *Amazonský proud etc.,* p. 45).
50) 'Don't measure the world by area, time or weight. What do you know about size? Storm in flight, darken over Greenwich, fall on the observatory and bring it down!' (ibid., p. 42).
51) 'a monstrous plan that was too rewarding' (ibid., p. 43).
52) 'Just for the speed and safety of merchants' goods we make the curved straight and cut through the earth with the sharpness of roads' (ibid., p. 45).
53) See Blahynka, *Vančura,* pp. 76–77.

through the metaphor of sexual awakening, 'Býti dělníkem' calls for the concomitant awakening and liberation of the working man, sealing the mutual relationship between the crisis of the imagination and of masculinity that pervades the collection.

The problems of the idle imagination and idle men are again intertwined in Vančura's second book, the volume of three stories, *Dlouhý, Široký, Bystrozraký* (Tall, Wide, Sharp-eyed), published in 1924, by which time Vančura, like Wolker, had left Devětsil. Compared with *Amazonský proud*, the volume lacks the feminine element. It contains more explicit social satire and possesses a more sarcastic tone, as Kožmín points out of the first story, 'Cesta do světa'.[54] It also focuses more sharply on the shortcomings of Czech society. Perhaps for these reasons, Blahynka and Holý both interpret it again as a criticism of the romantic illusions of Poetism and an assertion of the 'hard labour' of Proletarianism. However, if we look particularly at the organization of the volume, Vančura's preoccupation still seems more about the synthesis of 'everyday' and 'Sunday' art than the unequivocal adoption of one or other. Somewhat as he uses 'Ráj' and 'Býti dělníkem' to frame *Amazonský proud*, in *Dlouhý, Široký, Bystrozraký* he foregrounds the split between the Proletarian and Poetist approaches through the stylistic contrasts between the first and last of the three stories in the volume.

Vančura had originally contributed 'Cesta do světa' to the *Revoluční sborník Devětsilu* in 1922, a decision that might well be seen as an attempt by the author to distance himself from the proto-Poetist direction which Teige was developing, since it is Vančura's most overtly Proletarian piece in its themes and in its relative stylistic simplicity. In the story, a homeless boy, Jeník, and the son of a Jewish shop-keeper, Ervín, filled with a wide-eyed desire for the exotic and adventure, band together to run away and seek their fortunes, first in a sordid, hostile, capitalist Prague and then in Austria and northern Italy. Throughout, Vančura uses motifs that contrast dynamism and stasis. At the beginning Jeník, described as tired, sad and alone, calls across the Vltava to Ervín, asking for a boat to help him across. Neither, however, can hear the other: 'Hoch na druhém břehu vykřikl, ale jeho hlas spadl doprostřed řeky a potopil se.'[55] Vančura draws attention here to the weakness of the individual, emphasizing the

54) See Kožmín, *Styl*, p. 145.
55) 'The boy on the other bank cried out, but his voice fell into the middle of the river and sank' (Vančura et al., *Poetistická proza*, p. 9).

need for the weak to join together to change their lot. After Ervín has ferried Jeník across the river, the narrator comments: 'Ticho, jež je vozem a lodí objevitelskou, neslo oba hochy.'[56] This silence, collective, dynamic and full of promise, contrasts with the helpless, dispiriting silence of loneliness. The image of a boat on a river recurs in the story, symbolizing movement forward, in keeping with the inexorable forward movement of time. In the context of the story, the opening may be understood to show how each boy is stuck until they come together and provide one another with the necessary momentum. The encounter gives meaning to Jeník's limitless but empty freedom and offers Ervín a way to free himself from his limited petty bourgeois existence.

The boat imagery is contrasted in the story with images of imprisonment. The four walls of the barn where Ervín lets Jeník sleep is described as 'žalářní krychle';[57] by contrast, when the boys run away, the previously more confident Ervín loses heart without the security of his home, and little Jeník has grown into Jan: 'Zlé kouty našeho stavení, obklopte mne, jsem slabý a nikam nedojdu, myslil si, řka Janovi: Vraťme se!'[58] Ervín's family is implicitly also a prison – he matters to his father only because he is the heir to the mill his father has established by putting a workers' cooperative out of business – as is Bohemia itself: 'Čechy jsou nedobrodružná země, prošel jsi třemi okresy a víš to.'[59] Later, when the boys are caught and briefly returned to Ervín's home village, the narrator says of the sympathetic local rabbi who goes to collect them from the police: 'chtěl říci osvobozující slovo, ale není ho v naší mateřštině'.[60] Ervín describes Prague as a 'city on a dead river', foreshadowing *Poslední soud* and also the depiction, for example in *Rozmarné léto* and the story 'Usmívající se děvče' from *Luk královny Dorotky*, of staid, insipid Bohemian towns standing on the shallowest, calmest stretches of rivers: 'Ervín věděl, že tímto řečištěm teče zlý proud'.[61]

Similarly to the boy in 'Samotný chlapec', Jeník and Ervín possess

---

56) 'Silence, which is the cart and ship of discovery, carried both boys' (ibid., p. 10).
57) 'a cube-shaped prison' (ibid., p. 13).
58) 'Evil corners of our building, surround me. I am weak and will not get anywhere, he thought, saying to Jan: Let's go back' (ibid., p. 22).
59) 'Bohemia is an unadventurous land, you have walked three districts and know it' (ibid., p. 17).
60) 'he wanted to say a liberating word, but there is none in our mother tongue' (ibid., p. 29).
61) 'Ervín knew that an evil current flowed through this river bed' (ibid., p. 31).

the potential to free themselves because of their imaginations. Jeník, who is favoured by the implied author because he is a vagabond and has a closer relationship to nature, the countryside and tradition, filters his experience of the world through fairy-tales, authentic stories he has been told that imply the collectivity of oral retelling. By contrast, the more modern Ervín's imagination is dominated by imported westerns he has read. In his second essay entitled 'Nové umění', published in 1924, Vančura, contradicting the Poetist view, rejected borrowing models of sensational literature like detective stories or westerns from abroad.[62] In 1926, however, he published the never realized screenplay for a parody, *Nenapravitelný Tommy* (Incorrigible Tommy), set in the United States.[63] It might be argued that, in *Markéta Lazarová*, he attempted to write a 'Czech western', in which, like the Indians in many westerns, the robbers are more noble in defeat than their aristocratic conquerors. Ervín's less immediate, less bold relationship to life is reflected later in the fact that, in Prague, Jeník, who is not interested in books, plans to become a ship's cook and travel the world, while Ervín, somewhat prefiguring Dr Mann in *Tři řeky*, hopes to become a geography teacher.

The boys' imagination contrasts with the lack of imagination of a third boy, František Mestek, who belatedly follows them to Prague, where he catches syphilis from a chambermaid. When they move on, they leave him because he seems quite happy in the city, the immoral materialism of which is encapsulated in the vile Hotel Gent, compared by the narrator to a dying whore. Ten years later, they return from Italy, where they have been 'working in vineyards and harbours, building roads, railways and tunnels, demonstrating, leading strikes and shooting at Fascists',[64] to discover that Mestek has become the local policeman. As the title suggests, their journey has taken them away from their fantasies into the real world; they have surrendered the stasis of utopia for the dynamism of the struggle for a better world, implicitly the essence of real life. Jeník says to Ervín: 'Všechno, co se nám líbilo, bylo nahoře, ale teď jsme staří jako všichni dělníci. Záře nad světem není jeho sláva, ale rudost boje'.[65] The alternative to this struggle is to stagnate and decay like the bour-

62) See Vančura, *Řád*, p. 57.
63) See Blahynka, *Vančura*, p. 141.
64) Vančura et al., *Poetistická proza*, p. 46.
65) 'Everything we liked was up above, but now we are old like all workers. The glow over the world is not its glory, but the redness of the struggle' (ibid., p. 45).

geois world of Mestek; the last word of the story, printed separately in the centre of the final line, is 'tabes', the degenerative disease caused by untreated syphilis, from which Mestek dies.

In total contrast to this first story, the third story in the volume, 'F. C. Ball', is one of Vančura's least accessible, with its parodically chaotic, elliptical structure and style and its 'in-joke' allusions to his contemporaries, and may be seen as a burlesque of Poetist, or indeed broader Avant-garde modes of expression.[66] For Blahynka, the story of a football team founded in a pub that becomes for a time the most fabulous in the world constitutes a satirical account of the story of Devětsil.[67] Alena Hájková reads it as a more general commentary on the European Avant-garde, of which Devětsil, Vančura playfully suggests, is the glorious culmination, the team to beat all others.[68] In the story, Vančura seeks simultaneously to express and cast doubt on the allure of endless innovation.

His use of social satire, self-parody and in-joke, his thematic exploitation of popular culture and the frenetic narrative style at once imitate and parody the techniques of the Czech artistic Avant-garde, to the point where it is difficult to judge how far Vančura deliberately intended the piece to be a bravura performance that, in its content and impact, is ultimately ephemeral and superficial. This, however, appears to be his message about the Avant-garde's preoccupation with being modern. F. C. Ball is a collective that cannot last; it becomes a victim of its own success and, in what Blahynka considers a canny prediction of the eventual commercialization of the Avant-garde, the team are sabotaged by a bourgeois *rentier* who engineers, and then profits from, their demise. The last line of the story, somewhat echoing the last line of 'Poslední medvěd na Šumavě', reflects with genuine ambiguity on the passing beauty of this kind of artistic creation: 'jest prý krásnější to, co již není, a biograf jest novou skutečností.'[69]

66) Holý attempts to decode a few of the allusions in his commentary to the edition cited here (see ibid., p. 587).
67) See Blahynka, *Vančura*, p. 97.
68) See A. Hájková, *Humor v próze Vladislava Vančury*, Prague, p. 1972, hereafter Hájková, *Humor*, p. 18. The title – and indeed the idea for the story – may even be derived from a play on words based on the name of the German Expressionist and co-founder of Dadaism, Hugo Ball (1886–1927).
69) 'They say that nothing is lovelier than what is no more, and the cinema is the new reality' (Vančura et al., *Poetistická próza*, p. 95).

Stylistically and thematically, Vančura would not repeat the ironic embrace of modernity of 'F. C. Ball', and it might equally be argued that he would not write another work as schematic and didactic as 'Cesta do světa' until *Tři řeky*. In the context of the Avant-garde 'adoption' of styles, it may be an over-simplification to read 'Cesta do světa' as the advocacy of a particular literary method and 'F. C. Ball' as the rejection of an another. Rather, the solemnity and seriousness of 'Cesta do světa' merely reflect the style of writing, just as self-undermining parody belongs to the style of 'F. C. Ball'. The two stories represent extremes of seriousness and playfulness that Vančura continues to seek to reconcile, as emphasized by the other story in *Dlouhý, Široký, Bystrozraký*, which, significantly, occupies the centre of the volume and gives it its name.

The story appears divided between Poetist and Proletarian perspectives, describing the spectacular dream journey around the globe of four unemployed men who can find no other way of realizing themselves in First Republic Prague than by meeting every day in their local pub. Hájková describes how its 'comic effect emerges mainly through the intertwining of two layers of reality, the fantastic and the concretely historical'.[70] This intertwining is established by the title, which is borrowed from a Czech fairy tale, but in the story refers to three of the men, while the name of the fourth, Havraní Křídlo (Raven Wing), appears to come more from westerns. The fact that he is the character who inspires the action perhaps indicates how the western has supplanted the fairy tale in the modern imagination. The 'fantastic' narrative layer, described by Mukařovský as a 'game of semantic associations', recounts their search for a donkey that has apparently been stolen from Havraní Křídlo, and is seen by Blahynka as a criticism of the unrealistic exoticism of the Poetists. At the end of the story, back in the pub, Bystrozraký (whose name means 'sharp-eyed', but whose eyesight is failing) notices that the donkey is in a book, at which point, to Havraní Křídlo's embarrassment, the donkey leaps from the pages and rushes into Prague.[71] Havraní Křídlo explains:

70) Hájková, *Humor*, p. 19.
71) Bystrozraký's eyes have apparently been damaged by his work as a photographer. The narrator remarks sarcastically: 'Každý muž má na svém těle znaky práce: pekař křivé nohy, spasitel rány, buržoa břicho' (Every man has on his body the marks of work: a baker his crooked legs, a saviour his wounds, a bourgeois his gut) (Vančura et al., *Poetistická proza*, p. 51). The narrator notes that he is turned to face the east, implying that he 'sees' more imaginatively than those who face the west.

'Vzpomněl jsem si, [...] že jsem kdysi napsal básničku o oslici. Pitomé ženské ji kdákaly, jako by byla pro ně, a tlustý spisovatel mi ji ukradl. Tu básničku jsem napsal na památku jednoho správného filmu u Ponrepa. Nebylo to zvíře trefené a nebylo jako živé?'[72]

For Zdeněk Pešat, given that the imaginary journey has been inspired by a film, the story constitutes a 'parody of old fairy tales, whose tricks are surpassed by modern technology, which can evoke an imagination even richer than fairy tales'.[73] The pace of the 'dream sequence' and the characters' ability to cross continents in moments may therefore be seen as an attempt to mimic in prose the power of cinema, the one aspect of modern technology that Vančura admires.[74] The replacement of literature by cinema is posited, perhaps ironically, in the final line of 'F. C. Ball' and the volume. This doubt about the purpose and future of literature is also noted by Hana Kučerová, who argues that 'the story of three fairy-tale heroes, one human being and a lost donkey who can only be found in a book, seeks to emphasize that it is *precisely* no more than literature, which unfortunately cannot replace life and on the other hand cannot even be compared to it'.[75]

Blahynka sees the treatment of escapism that unites the stories in the volume as a criticism of the Poetist attitude to literature, but in all three, Vančura seems to sympathize with escapism, to reflect sadly on the prevailing gap between reality and the imagination, between the world as it could be and the world as it is. In this context, 'Cesta do světa' may be read not as an allegory of the writer who learns to abandon his escapism in favour of the hard work of building revolutionary consciousness, but as a self-conscious criticism of those who write in favour of those who learn to act intuitively, in harmony with life, without the mediation of text. In this interpretation the volume becomes Vančura's

72) 'I remembered [...] that I had once written a little poem about a donkey. Stupid women clucked it as though it were for them, and a fat writer stole it from me. I had written the poem in memory of one good film at the Ponrepo [cinema]. Didn't I get the animal just right and didn't it seem as though it was alive?' (ibid., p. 59).
73) Z. Pešat, 'Vladislav Vančura a počátky socialistické literatury: Příspěvek k analýze literární avantgardy', *Česká literatura*, IX (1961), 4, p. 484.
74) This attempt to replicate the cinematic in prose recurs in Vančura's writing. Holý notes particularly the imitation of cutting in the constant switching from short scene to short scene in *Tři řeky* (see Holý, *Práce a básnivost*, p. 151).
75) H. Kučerová, 'Vančurův umělecký vývoj v prvních letech poválečných', *Česká literatura*, XX (1972), 6, p. 484.

strongest expression of the Avant-garde's desire to eliminate the distinction between art and life and to end artistic creation as it is understood in bourgeois society.

More than assert the Proletarian approach, in *Dlouhý, Široký, Bystrozraký* Vančura seems to question the activity of writing, to express the enduring gap between the artistic aspirations of the Avant-garde and reality, and the widening gap within the Avant-garde over how those aspirations might be realized. By making 'Dlouhý, Široký, Bystrozraký' the centrepiece and title story, Vančura seems to emphasize that the 'hard work' of the writer rests in remaining faithful to the original aspirations of the Avant-garde. That means striving to maintain the notional unity of the artistic and ideological Avant-garde, and consistently reflecting the conflict between the individual and the collective, the separation of art and life and the division between intellect and intuition that mark the present, while seeking their reconciliation in a new order. Perhaps the hardest aspect of this work is resisting the drift into either Poetist, proto-Surrealist linguistic play or nascent Socialist Realist didacticism and not falling into either despair or illusory utopianism. As a reflection of this resistance, each story in *Dlouhý, Široký, Bystrozraký*, ends, as Píša suggests it must for the Avant-garde writer, on a note of temporary defeat.

Beginning with the title of Vančura's first book, the notion of *proud* – current or flow – is central to Vančura's writing. Mukařovský notes that 'the river is [...] one of the most frequent motifs, indeed heroes of Vančura's fiction', and points to the fact that Vančura spent most of his life on the Vltava, which, explicitly or fictionalized, forms the setting for nearly all his works.[1] At the same time, however, Vančura's attraction to the metaphor of the current invites comparison with Henri Bergson's notion of the 'courant de la vie'. In *Evolution créatrice*, Bergson, whose ideas had a significant influence on Czech writers in the 1910s and 1920s, writes:

> At a certain moment, in certain points of space a visible current has taken rise; this current of life, traversing the bodies it has organized one after another, passing from generation to generation, has become divided amongst species and distributed amongst individuals without losing anything of its force, rather intensifying in proportion to its advance.[2]

Vančura makes no direct reference to Bergson in his own theoretical writing, but he more than once acknowledges a debt to Neumann's *Ať žije život!*, in which Bergson is highly praised. In the 1913 essay that gives the collection its title, Neumann establishes key tenets of the post-1918 Czech Avant-garde, rejecting the dualism of philosophers and theologians in favour of the 'sense of the unity of all life' experienced by ordinary people, and attacking the 'real enemy' (especially in his view in Czech culture) of 'aestheticism', which 'calls hypochondria culture'. According to Neumann, 'Bergson [...] with his sense for the flow of life,

1) J. Mukařovský, 'Od básníka k dílu' in his *Studie z estetiky*, Prague, 1966, p. 292.
2) H. Bergson, *Creative Evolution*, translated by Arthur Mitchell, London, 1911, hereafter Bergson, *Creative Evolution*, p. 27. The echo of Bergson's 'courant de la vie' in Vančura's writing is noted by Holý in his monograph (see J. Holý, *Práce a básnivost: Estetický projekt světa Vladislav Vančury*, Prague, 1990, pp. 30–32).

for the internal connectedness of phenomena in time, at last leads us onto the right path'.[3]

In the period after the First World War, by which time Neumann had moved towards Russian Proletarianism, the importance of Bergson was most strongly asserted by leading figures in the Literární skupina, a Brno-based Avant-garde grouping. Constituted a few weeks after Devětsil, it soon came under attack from its Prague counterpart for its woolly Marxism and vague use of terms like socialism and expressionism. In an essay published in March 1921, its leading spokesman, František Götz, claimed that Bergson, the psychologist William James and the anthropologist Emil Durkheim were the three leaders of contemporary intellectual life. Writing the same year, Píša, at the time associated with the Literární skupina, alludes to Bergson in his description of how the contemporary poet

> captures a machine or other phenomenon of modern civilization in the dynamism of its functions, in the flowing current of all its forms and all the potency of its existence; the phenomenon here has not become independent, but is one of the forms into which the fluid activity of life has incarnated itself, flowing through it and absorbing it into its unbroken continuity and vibrant rhythm.[4]

References to 'flowing', 'coursing' and 'current' are widespread in descriptive criticism of Vančura's work at the time and subsequently, in a not always conscious reflection of the significance of this metaphor for him.[5]

In *Evolution créatrice*, Bergson criticizes the belief that the rational approach of science – the use of the intellect alone – is capable of reaching

3) S. K. Neumann, *Stati a projevy IV*, Prague, 1973, hereafter Neumann, *Stati IV*, p. 25.
4) A. M. Píša, 'K orientaci nejmladších tvůrčích snah' in Š. Vlašín (ed.), *Avantgarda známá a neznámá*, Vol. 1, Prague, 1970, hereafter Vlašín (ed.), *Avantgarda* 1, p. 179.
5) The metaphor is scarcely unique to Vančura, however, but, like Bergson, reflects the way of seeing of the period. Miroslav Rutte, writing in 1919, comments of contemporary Czech literature: 'an active, dynamic conception of reality emerges to counter its static conception. There are no longer isolated things finite in themselves and among them is no longer a human being alienated from everything through the deception of his senses. On the contrary, everything is a constantly moving unity in diversity, an endless row of billowing and falling waves, that together all make up that majestic, inscrutable sea – the activity of life' (M. Rutte, *Nový svět: Studie o nové české literatuře 1917–19*, Prague, 1919, p. 44).

a true understanding of the whole of life. In his view, the attempt to break life down into systems (and the accompanying proliferation of sub-divisions of science) is erroneous and leads to the omission of those aspects that cannot – or cannot yet – be systematized, which in Bergson's view might be the most essential:

> That life is a kind of mechanism I cordially agree. But is it the mechanism of parts artificially isolated within the whole of the universe, or is it the mechanism of the real whole? The real whole might well be, we conceive, an indivisible continuity. The systems we cut out within it would, properly speaking, not then be *parts* at all; they would be *partial views* of the whole. And, with these partial views put end to end, you will not make even a beginning of the reconstruction of the whole.[6]

In *Amazonský proud* and *Dlouhý, Široký, Bystrozraký*, Vančura's criticism of those living partial lives concerns men who are active only in the solitude of their imaginations, but unable to act in the world around them. This criticism later extends in his work to 'ivory-tower' intellectualism, to those in the thrall of religion or superstition and to merchants and businessmen preoccupied only with profit. His hostility in 'Býti dělníkem' to those who measure clearly resonates with Bergson, but translated from a criticism of scientific method to a criticism of the withering effect on human life of contemporary materialism.

Bergson aspires to a new method of grasping life as a whole, understood as a continuous, unending creative flow, in which individual life forms are merely the 'excretions' of this flow, or 'buds' on the 'tree of life'. Having rejected the detachment of the intellect as a means of comprehending this flow, he turns to intuition, which he equates with sympathy:

> [Intelligence] goes all round life, taking from outside the greatest possible number of views of it, drawing it into itself instead of entering into it. But it is to the very inwardness of life that intuition leads us – by intuition I mean instinct that has become disinterested, self-conscious, capable of reflecting upon its object and of enlarging it indefinitely.[7]

6) Bergson, *Creative Evolution*, p. 32.
7) Ibid., p. 186.

In the piece 'Proud amazonský', a Sioux who has murdered a member of another tribe is chased by two Indians from that tribe to the banks of the Amazon, where he collapses with exhaustion. The piece is pervaded by intuition, a capacity not completely lost by more 'primitive' people, as Vančura will later reiterate in his depiction of the Ruthenians in *Poslední soud* and the robbers in *Markéta Lazarová*. Seeing that the Sioux is on the verge of death, his pursuers do not kill him, but in his last moments become aware of what unites them, and give him something to drink. Only two words are spoken. The encounter has a mystical quality for the narrator, but – like the sense of harmony with the universe experienced by other characters in the cycle – merely as a pale intimation of the reconciliation he believes can one day be realized: 'Nebe bylo až dole u země, ale nestal se zázrak, neboť tři nejsou zástup. Smír neklenul se jako stan o třech stěnách nad mrtvým tělem. Položili dlaň na mrtvolu a teplota smrti a živých těl se mísily.'[8] In the last paragraph of the piece, in a very Bergsonian way the individual existence of the Sioux seems almost nothing compared to the great continuity of life, embodied by the unbroken flow of the Amazon: 'Bez zastavení plyne veliká Amazonka a potrvá do konce světa. Bůh tohoto proudu je bůh zástupů a bůh hojnosti; jen veliké věci vládnou. Tvůj zločin, siouxský Indiáne, tvoje smrt a přátelství, před koncem uzavřené, je unášeno bouří dějů jako vzdech.'[9] Vančura reiterates this idea in the passage quoted at the end of Chapter One about the role of the doctor in the face of death.

This perception of life does not imply an indifferent attitude to the existence of the individual. Rather, given the commonness of death in Vančura's work, one might argue that, where science seeks to distance

8) 'Heaven was right down close to the earth, but no miracle happened, for three is not a crowd. Reconciliation did not arch like a three-sided tent over the dead body. They put the palm of a hand on the corpse and the warmth of death and living bodies merged' (V. Vančura, *Amazonský proud – Pekař Jan Marhoul – Pole orná a válečná – Poslední soud*, Prague, 2000, hereafter Vančura, *Amazonský proud etc.*, p. 41).
9) 'Without stopping the great Amazon flows and will endure until the end of the world. The god of this current is the god of crowds and the god of abundance; only great things rule. Your crime, Sioux Indian, your death and the friendship sealed before the end is borne away by a storm of events like a sigh' (ibid., p. 42). Blahynka notes that, had the collection ended here, it would have ended with an image of reconciliation, but Vančura chooses instead to end the collection with the call to revolution of 'Býti dělníkem' (see M. Blahynka, *Vladislav Vančura*, Prague, 1978, hereafter Blahynka, *Vančura*, p. 77). This suggestion of a writer torn between reconciliation and revolution pervades Vančura's work.

death, religion seeks to diminish it and superstition derives from fear of it, Vančura acknowledges its central place in life. In the piece 'Nenadálá smrt' (An unexpected death), one of a group of raftsmen transporting wood on the Vltava drowns trying to jump from the river-bank to the raft with a partridge they have ensnared. The narrator emphasizes the men's closeness to nature and their intuitive understanding of the river, a reflection of their intuitive approach to life, of which for them death is an inalienable part: 'Řeko, jsi tak malá, změní tvoje rychlosti a ovládnou tě jako děvče v tanci. Plaviti se široširým mořem na bečce? Pokoušet živel? Nač? říká Dudek, ručím za vor a plavba je zápas. Svedu plť všemi vrátky, znám řeku, úplavy mělčiny i kameny v řečišti'.[10] Vančura tells of the death before telling of the events that lead up to it, giving the reader something of the same experience of the suddenness of death amid the flow of life that the men go through. As in 'Proud amazonský', the gathering of the men in silence around the body suggests that death reminds human beings of their shared fate and might – especially in the case of Řeka's in *Pole orná a válečná* – inspire the resurrection of that harmonious co-existence.

Neumann is most interested in Bergson's ideas to the extent that they serve to inspire a creative rather than scientific method: 'art can best recreate its language to correspond to the feeling of the symphonic unity of life.'[11] According to Neumann, 'we can best evoke a vision of things and events in their internal truth and interconnectedness with life through the most disparate images, running together towards the same goal, but not pushing into each other'.[12] This approach is closely reflected in Vančura's writing. Bergson writes: 'The impetus of life [...] consists in a need of creation. It cannot create absolutely because it is confronted with matter [...] But it seizes upon this matter, which is necessity itself, and strives to introduce into it the largest possible amount of indetermination and liberty.'[13]

In Vančura's writing this understanding of the 'impetus of life' corresponds to the activity of language, or perhaps more precisely of form, which Mukařovský describes as the 'energy sustaining the unity of all

10) 'River, you are so small, they change your speeds and master you like a girl in a dance. Sail over widest sea in a barrel? Tempt the element? Why? says Dudek. I vouch for the raft and sailing is a struggle. I'll guide the raft through all the gates. I know the river, the runs of shallow water and the stones in the river bed' (Vančura, *Amazonský proud etc.*, p. 25).
11) Neumann, *Stati IV*, p. 25.
12) Ibid., p. 28.
13) Bergson, *Creative Evolution*, p. 265.

elements of the work, flowing unbroken through time'.[14] Understood like this, form may be seen to give rise to the work as the 'current of life' gives rise to organisms. Indeed, the part of 'Západ a východ' quoted in the foreword to *Amazonský proud* ends: 'What was, is and will be, without causal relation in sheer being accumulates and from a hidden store the fluidity of events derives form: crystals, organisms and the work of art.' As I have described, in his 1920s fiction, language seizes hold of its material, imbuing it with dynamism, drawing everything into the flow of narration. For example, in *Poslední soud* the narrator describes a dog emerging from the Vltava, implicitly linking language and the river as metaphors for this ennobling 'current of life':

Kdyby městské okresy byly označeny jménem zvířat, vládl by na nábřeží pes. Pes, který se vynořuje z vody maje tvář obrácenu k horlivému slunci, ocas zaťat v kruh a proslulé dřívko, či hůl, napříč v hubě. Pes, jehož škodlivost a neužitečnost byla zjištěna ve věci střevních parazitů, pes na okamžik volný a vděkuplný,jenž ve skvrnách ticha se ohlašuje štěkotem a nezná mezí v hopkování, když stihl zem.[15]

Vančura does not view the activity of language as some totally random force, but a perfect symbiosis of order and freedom. Language is in effect presented in Vančura's work as Bergson views life, as 'hidden order', a 'process of becoming', a 'reality which is making itself as a reality is unmaking itself'. This description may be compared to Jakobson's dialectical model of the linguistic system. Peter Steiner writes that in this model:

language is not a harmonious, symmetrical whole but an ongoing struggle between revolutionary tendencies aiming to alter the status quo and their conservative counterparts set on preserving it. At any moment the system is both balanced and imbalanced; it is simultaneously a state and a muta-

14) J. Mukařovský, 'Tradice tvaru' in his *Studie II*, Prague, 2001, p. 562.
15) 'If the city districts were marked with the names of animals, a dog would reign on the embankment. A dog that emerges from the water with its face turned to the ardent sun, its tail fixed in a circle and the fabled piece of wood or stick held crosswise in its mouth. A dog whose harmfulness and uselessness has been established on the basis of intestinal parasites, a dog for a moment free and full of gratitude, who in the patches of silence announces himself with a bark and whose frolicking, when it reaches land, knows no bounds' (Vančura, *Amazonský proud etc.*, p. 317).

tion. The ruptures in previous equilibriums coexist with the equilibriums that mended these ruptures and all of them point to consequent changes that will redress this situation in the future.[16]

Once again Vančura expresses this idea through the metaphor of the river. In the 1918 version of 'Ráj', the narrator comments: 'Srovnejte i říční proud; při rozdílu rovin se ustaluje, pohybem vody směřuje jako neklidné vahadlo k rovnováze.'[17] We see here how Vančura is drawn more to a constant, perhaps unending process of maintaining balance, rather than to the ultimate reconciliation or synthesis envisaged by the Hegelian-Marxian teleological conception of the 'process of becoming'.

In Vančura the 'revolutionary' elements in the system tend to be older, almost forgotten forms that might mistakenly be thought to be fossilized or 'conservative', but actually serve to reveal the superficiality of contemporary norms, most obviously in his weaving of folk sayings and proverbs into the novel *Hrdelní pře*. Jiří Opelík writes of Vančura's method:

> He chose mainly proverbs which worked as autonomous poetic images and by amending them he bared their metaphoric roots or heightened their expressivity. Through the use of a suitable context he then as it were degraded some from generally provocative images into eternal messages, to create a situation from which the proverbs freely sprouted or sometimes returned the proverbs to their pre-proverbial state, recalling the act of their birth and in this way more generally the act of creation.[18]

Kožmín additionally points out that certain statements acquire the quality of proverbs, though they are not. Jakobson saw the attraction of

---

16) P. Steiner, *Russian Formalism,* Ithaca, London, 1984, hereafter Steiner, *Russian Formalism,* p. 220.

17) 'Consider the river current; given a variety of levels it stabilizes itself, through the movement of water it aims, like a restless weigh-beam, towards equilibrium' (V. Vančura, 'Ráj' (1918) in Blahynka, *Vančura,* p. 349).

18) According to Opelík the proverbs were drawn mainly from the two-volume collection *Česká přísloví* (Czech proverbs, 1911, 1913) by Václav Flajšhans (1866–1950) and the seven-volume *Česko-německý slovník zvláště grammaticko-fraseologický* (Czech-German dictionary, particularly grammatical and phraseological, 1878–93) by František Kott (1825–1915). (See J. Opelík, 'Kapitola nultá anebo Předmluva...' in V. Vančura, *Hrdelní pře anebo Přísloví,* 1979, hereafter Vančura, *Hrdelní pře,* pp. 14–15.)

the proverb in its metanarrative function, like Biblical language, shaping, explaining and echoing the experience of life, not only or so much in its content as in its resonance, its sound and rhythm.[19] In the novel, the effect of the interweaving is to contrast this intuitiveness with the empty babble of the characters.

Vančura's use of the setting of the middle Vltava (fictionalized or explicit) in so many of his works may be seen not only to reflect where Vančura the man considered to be his home, but also to express the endlessly evolving intermediacy of life that corresponds to the place of transition where Vančura the writer makes his home. Vančura shares Bergson's hostility to the efforts of science to divine retrospectively teleological models, which imply that life has aims that it works to achieve. Bergson writes:

> To speak of an end is to think of a pre-existing model that has only to be realized [...] It is to believe that life, in its movement and in its entirety, goes to work like our intellect, which is only a motionless and fragmentary view of life and which naturally takes its stand outside of time. Life on the contrary progresses and endures in time. Of course, when once the road has been travelled, we can glance over it, mark its direction, note this in psychological terms and speak as if there had been pursuit of an end [...] But, of the road which was going to be travelled the human mind could have nothing to say, for the road has been created pari passu with the act of travelling over it, being nothing but the direction of this act itself.[20]

Vančura generally resists resolution in his endings. His works frequently end with beginnings, or, as in *Pole orná a válečná, Poslední soud* or *Rodina Horvatova*, with a shift of plane from contemporary reality to dreams or visions of the future seen by characters as they die.

Mukařovský writes: 'Vančura's experimentation (if it can be so called) is not experimenting without hypotheses or even driven by an attempt to evade all hypotheses, but is the constant search for a new form of narration, subject to but at the same time freed from the bonds of regressive motivation.'[21] Mukařovský means here the type of narra-

---

19) See Steiner, *Russian Formalism,* p. 206.
20) Bergson, *Creative Evolution,* p. 54.
21) J. Mukařovský, 'Vančurovská prologomena' in his *Studie II,* Prague, 2001, hereafter Mukařovský, 'Vančurovská prologomena', p. 547.

tive in which, once the outcome is known, it can be explained by what preceded it. Bergson writes: 'the present moment of a living body does not find its explanation in the moment immediately before [but rather] all the past of the organism must be added to that moment, its heredity, in fact the whole of a very long history.'[22] This quotation offers an attractive way of interpreting Vančura's efforts in *Obrazy z dějin* to trace the heredity of the 'organism' of the Czech nation, but his sympathy with this view can also be seen elsewhere in his writing. Mukařovský argues that Vančura's heroes do not develop, but that this is not the same as saying that they do not change. He points to *Tři řeky*, Vančura's only attempt to write a *Bildungsroman*, a novel type theoretically predicated on a teleological model of existence. Near the end, Doctor Mann asks Jan whether he has finally decided what he is going to be. Jan replies: 'Tím, čím jsem'.[23] The exchange may be characterized as one between intellect and intuition, reflecting the limitations of the cuckolded, sheltered doctor, who is ultimately surpassed by his protegé in his ability to grasp life.

Perhaps the most obvious example of Vančura's rejection of the search for regressive motivation, however, is *Hrdelní pře anebo Přísloví*, a parody detective novel in which four men, a retired judge, a doctor, a teacher and a writer (the narrator) attempt to solve a murder case that the judge, Skočdopole, had tried some years before. The outcome then was the apparently false imprisonment of one Jiří Půlpytel, the victim's brother-in-law. The professions of at least three of the men point to characters who favour the use of the intellect in solving problems. Early on, indeed, Skočdopole alludes to what Mukařovský terms 'regressive motivation', presented as an irritating habit he, like most human beings, is unable to break: '"To ví ďas, proč se mi od dvou měsíců nelení poslouchati zmatené příběhy a vymýšleti k nim začátek."'[24] Vančura's attitude to the men and their approach to life is actually encapsulated in the opening chapter, in which they abjectly fail in their efforts to kill a pig, foreshadowing how they will botch the investigation and perhaps indicating the mess that their generation has made, in Vančura's view, of Czech society and culture.

22) Bergson, *Creative Evolution*, p. 21.
23) 'What I am' (quoted in Mukařovský, 'Vančurovská prologomena', p. 549).
24) 'The devil knows why two months [after I have retired] I can still be bothered to listen to confused stories and think up a beginning to them' (Vančura, *Hrdelní pře*, p. 25).

In his idiosyncratic foreword to the third edition of the novel, Opelík suggests that Vančura was motivated by the public's vicarious enjoyment of court reports: 'Criminal cases might perhaps become the national game and the search for a killer a sport.'[25] In another indication in Vančura that women are closer to the 'truth' than men, this view is supported in the novel by the crucial intervention of Lucie, the victim's sister, who is possibly dying of pneumonia.[26] As the investigation proceeds, the details of the case grow ever murkier and the prospects of identifying the killer ever slimmer, until she finally speaks up: '"Chtěla jsem poprositi, abyste toho již nečinili a zanechali své hry. "Hry?" řekl Skočdopole. "Což se domníváš, že je to kratochvilné?" "Bojím se, že je tomu tak," odpověděla.'[27] The men's investigation, a metaphor for their life's work, is not real living but on the contrary distracts them from the 'current of life', revealed to Lucie, the other characters and the reader by the threat of death that she apparently faces.

The target of Vančura's satire is not, however, so much people's failure to take death seriously, as their tendency to take too seriously – to invest their whole lives in – what the implied author presents as the pointless search for truth, which will provide them with happiness and satisfaction in life. Though, as in *Rozmarné léto*, the implied author expresses some affection for the camaraderie among the friends, the novel makes fun of the First Republic establishment, in particular its views on truth, justice and literature, and perhaps specifically as they are embodied in Karel Čapek's hugely popular collections of detective stories, *Povídky z jedné a z druhé kapsy* (Stories from one pocket and Stories from the other pocket, 1929), which, Hájková points out, were published the year before *Hrdelní pře*.[28]

At one point Půlpytel, Vančura's spokesman in the novel, mocks the judge's fixation with the truth in terms that present Čapek's fascination with the relativity of truth as a banality and closely resonate with Bergson's view of contemporary science: 'Pozbyl jste klidu, neuvěřiv

25) Ibid., p. 12.
26) Opelík notes that the proverbs chosen for inclusion in the novel are generally polite about women. (See ibid., p. 20.)
27) '"I wanted to ask you to stop doing this and give up your games." "Games?" said Skočdopole. "Do you mean to say that you think that this is entertainment?" "I'm afraid that that is the case," she replied' (ibid., p. 145).
28) See A. Hájková, *Humor v próze Vladislava Vančury*, Prague, p. 1972, p. 33.

na prosté věci, vy hledači pravdy příliš lidské, vy hlupáčku, který jste nepochopil, že holé skutky jsou nepostižitelné. Nechte své snahy, neboť vše, co známe, je deformováno k určitému obrazu.'[29] Čapek's advocacy of perspectivism in the search for truth is parodied in the structure of the investigation and the transparently schematic characterization, and rendered absurd when, just as the reader is expecting the revelation of the truth, Půlpytel has an epileptic fit. With wonderful irony, this image of meaninglessness does in one sense equate with the truth, since it provides an alternative explanation for why he was found shortly after the murder of his sister-in-law in a dishevelled state, unable to remember where he had been.

Půlpytel's proximity to the implied author is further confirmed by his exchanges about language and literature with the teacher, Vyplampán, whose views may be seen as a parodic reflection of the reaction of establishment critics to Vančura's work. The passages may indeed be directed specifically at Ferdinand Peroutka, whom Bedřich Fučík characterizes as the self-styled 'spokesman for progressively [pokrokově] ordered bourgeois taste'.[30] In a 1930 review condemning what he perceived as the gratuitously over-stylized language of *Poslední soud*, Peroutka might be said to have tried and convicted Vančura of murdering Czech literature.[31] At one point Půlpytel, prefiguring the tone of Vančura's alchymist, asserts: 'Mě, který vyznávám boha a ostříhám svoji duši, okouzluje krev. Krev, která jako nové víno uvodí bouřlivý sen.'[32] This implicit criticism of the bloodlessness – and therefore lifelessness – of contemporary Czech bourgeois culture was a central theme of the Czech Avant-garde. In Vančura the restoration of blood is often literal, most obviously in his next novel, *Markéta Lazarová*, in which the narrator's addresses to a squeamish female reader may even be taken as a slight on the manliness of the implied First Republic reader. In Vyplampán's reply, as in his other speeches, Vančura burlesques the predilections and pompous style of establishment critics:

29) 'You have lost your sense of calm, having refused to believe simple things, you seeker of a truth all too human, you silly fool who has not understood that raw acts cannot be apprehended. Leave your striving, for all that we know has been deformed into a particular image' (Vančura, *Hrdelní pře*, p. 48).
30) B. Fučík, *Čtrnáctero zastavení*, Prague, 1992, p. 126.
31) See F. Peroutka, *Sluší-li se býti realistou*, Prague, 1993, pp. 80–89.
32). 'I, who acknowledge God and care about my soul, am enchanted by blood. Blood which like a new wine ushers in a stormy dream' (Vančura, *Hrdelní pře*, p. 38).

Oh vy rozvrátníku, vaše řeč je jakžtakž podobná naší mateřštině, ale to, co povídáte, je odporné. [...] Chcete-li mluviti česky, vypravujte, jak jste ve vší slušnosti strádal a jak vás napravila některá pokrokářská věta. Jářku, ať je v tom ušlechtilost, kterou pociťuji, ať jsou v tom lidé, jak je znám a jak je snáším! Ať je v tom láska dobře větraná, palcát, dudy a něco ze statečnosti legionářů! A mluvte jazykem úřadů a středních škol, mluvte, jak mi narostl zobák, nebo vás vykleštím.[33]

In the novel, the modern human being's preoccupation with 'knowing' in a positivist sense is set against the perspective of humour, which Vančura considers the timeless expression of superior, intuitive knowledge, inherent in proverbs. Early on, the narrator comments: '[Skočdopole] mívá v hlavě všelijaké žerty [...] Je však mnoho čápů a málo žab. Zazaboucha, Vyplampán a já se rovněž snažíme o žerty, ale věc se vždy nedaří. Bohužel, neboť smáti se je lépe věděti'.[34] Opelík notes the importance of this last assertion for Vančura, which also appears in his 'Poznámka o humoru' (A note on humour). As Hájková points out, Vančura's views on humour are close to Teige's, as expressed in his 1928 book *Svět, který se směje* (A world that laughs, 1928), in which he also distinguishes between superficial physical comedy and humour as a way of seeing. For Vančura, humour is above all about balance, it is 'the elevated stand-point of poets [...] it is control over emotions, colours and moods, it is an expanse in which all is balanced out, it is a scale-beam that can raise up every sorrow'.[35]

---

33) 'Oh you seditious element, your language is more or less like our mother tongue but what you say is disgusting... If you want to speak Czech, tell us how you with all due respect suffered and how you were set on the right path by a progressive thought. Mark you, let there be in it a nobility that I can feel, let there be in it people as I know them and can stand them! Let there be in it well aired love, a mace, bagpipes and something of the courage of the [Czech foreign] legionaries. And speak in the language of the authorities and secondary schools, speak in plain Czech or I shall castrate you' (ibid., p. 39).

34) '[Skočdopole] tends to have all kinds of jokes in his head [...] There are, however, many storks and few frogs. Zazaboucha, Vyplampán and I also try to make jokes, but they are never successful. Sad to say, for to laugh is better than to know' (ibid., p. 25).

35) V. Vančura, *Řád nové tvorby*, Prague, 1972, hereafter Vančura, *Řád*, p. 75. In his 'Poznámka o humoru', Vančura's affection for what he perceives as the all-embracing, intuitive, equalizing, 'tolerantly loving' early modern world-view of Rabelais, Cervantes and Shakespeare is very clear. There are allusions to the early novel in *Hrdelní pře* in, for example, the characters' onomatopoeic, expressive names and the sentences instead of

In his essay on laughter, Bergson argues that its function is corrective, to expose 'a certain mechanical inelasticity, just where one would expect to find the wideawake adaptability and the living pliableness of a human being'.[36] In Vančura, laughter ironizes and subverts the mechanical clumsiness of the human mind manifest when it tries to dissect reality, freeing it to return the broader apprehension of a reality in a constant process of becoming. For example, the original version of 'Ráj' begins with a description of scholars debating the truth about paradise:

Někteří asyriologové, katoličtí exegeti a mnoho školometů se vadí, hádá a pře se o ráj. „Ta krásná zahrada," praví jedni, „byla na arménské vysočině. Píšon vykládá se na Kur, Gichon na Aras – starý Araxes." – „Jakže?" dí F. Delitzsch, „to je zpozdilé tvrzení, ať se propadnu, nebyl-li Gichon průliv arachtuský!" „Ratata! ratata!" uvádí, pěkně křiče, dobráček Brůno svoje důvody, „vy šejdíři! mrzcí mluvkové!, Ó, ho-ho-ho! Ó, ty-ty-ty!" Když všechny řádně usadí, řekne mna si ruce: „Jen mi dej pánbůh dobrého zdraví!"

Vy, čtenáři, chcete-li s užitkem čísti, vězte, že byly ráje dva [...].[37]

Brůno's interruption not only restores the balance between mind and body, bringing everyone back to the living reality around them, but also, by creating the space for Vančura's narration, asserts the pre-eminence of the playful, creative approach over pedantic positivism as a means of penetrating life's essence.

chapter titles, ostensibly summarizing their content. However, attempts by Hájková and others to compare Vančura to Rabelais seem misplaced, since Vančura's writing is never as grotesque, fantastic, vulgar or witty as the French writer.
36) H. Bergson, *Laughter: An Essay on the Comic*, translated by Cloudesley Brereton and Fred Rothwell, London, 1911, p. 10.
37) 'Some assyriologists, Catholic exegetes and many pedants were wrangling, quarrelling and squabbling over paradise. 'That beautiful garden,' said some, 'was in the Armenian highlands. Pishon is thought to be at Kur, Gichon at Aras – old Araxes'. 'Where do you get that from?' quoth F. Delitzsch, 'that is a preposterous assertion, I'll be damned if Gichon was not the Arachtus Channel!' 'Bang-bang-bang! Bang-bang-bang!' good old Brůno announced his conclusions, not half shouting, 'You cheats! Wretched chatterboxes! Ho-ho-ho! Tut, tut, tut!' When he had properly shut everyone up, he said, rubbing his hands: 'I'll be happy if the Lord grants me good health!' If you, dear reader, want to benefit from your reading, you should know that there were two paradises [...]' (Vančura, V., 'Ráj' (1918) in Blahynka, *Vančura*, p. 349.)

PEKAŘ JAN MARHOUL AND POSLEDNÍ SOUD:
THE COLLECTIVIST NON-CONFORMIST

Brůno's intervention typifies Vančura's fondness for subversion and non-conformism that, as I noted in the introduction, apparently contradicts his advocacy of collectivism. This fondness is reflected in his choice of characters, who, as we have already seen in *Amazonský proud* and *Dlouhý, Široký, Bystrozraký*, are frequently drawn from those who are not only marginalized by society but who also exclude themselves through their natures, their often unthinking refusal to accept the limitations of society. Kožmín writes:

> the vast majority of characters in Vančura's novels [...] are socially déclassé, people who are poor or have become poor, people who do not develop according to bourgeois taste and style [...] These characters are, for him, not only an indictment of the unjust social order, but also the true representatives of life's virtue despite everything, bearers of the resilience of life and faith in the human being.[1]

Kožmín points out that Vančura does not draw his characters from the industrial proletariat; they come instead from what might be viewed as a more traditionally and timelessly Czech cast of artisans, peasants, tramps and street-entertainers and aristocrats, landowners and burghers. He thus depicts not so much a Marxist class conflict as a conflict between those degraded by money and those who refuse to be. In these misfits, substantially excluded from the degeneration of bourgeois society, he perceives the embodiment of human life in all its fullness and freedom, the potential for revolution and the pre-figuring of a collective that, if realized, might form the basis of a better world. Mukařovský comments: 'Alongside the other characters these [unconventional] characters as catalysts: they constantly set the world in

1) Z. Kožmín, 'Jazyková charakteristika postav v díle Vladislava Vančury' in *Sborník vědeckých prací vyšší pedagogické školy v Brně, 5: O literatuře*, Prague, 1958, p. 172.

motion, transforming their relationships with the world and with things and thus also intervening, usually unwittingly, in the fates of their environment.'[2]

The archetypal example of this character type in Vančura is the baker, Jan Marhoul. The novel *Pekař Jan Marhoul* effectively describes the process through which this type of character becomes marginalized and, in Marhoul's case, ultimately destroyed by society's refusal to tolerate him and his own refusal to adapt to society's expectations. In the novel, Marhoul, who has a wife Josefina and son Jan Josef, is declared bankrupt after inadvertently offending the council administrator and loses his bakery on the town square in Benešov. He rents a disused mill from a nobleman on a remote estate, but despite putting the mill back in working order and selling his bread from a cart pulled by dogs and later a sledge he pulls himself, he is unable to pay the rent. The nobleman therefore rents out the mill to a wealthy miller, complete with Marhoul and his family. They are thrown out by the miller after Marhoul castigates him for his exploitative terms of work, and return to Benešov, where Marhoul is given work by a master baker, who has to sack another assistant to make room. However, Marhoul soon sickens with a spinal infection and, unable to afford hospital treatment, dies.

The reader is encouraged to focus on the character of Marhoul not only by the title and his dominance in the text, but also by the constant judgements passed on him by the narrator and other characters, who criticize what they see as his passivity in the face of oppression, his blinkered optimism and his refusal to learn from his mistakes. Pešat comments: 'his character is made up of several striking features: on the one hand love for work, a craftsman's dexterity and a worker's skill, limitless kindness and lack of guile, on the other naivety, dreaminess and total helplessness in his dealings with the world, or, in the words of the narrator, angelic stupidity and folly.'[3] Critics have tended to share the narrator's view. The hard-line Marxist Edo Urx articulated what many saw as the essential shortcoming of Marhoul's character: 'Jan is a passive fellow who, despite all his disappointments believes constantly in his work (which is good), but he is not able to realize that his work is not free and does not try in

2) J. Mukařovský, 'Vančurovská prologomena' in his *Studie II*, Prague, 2001, hereafter Mukařovský, 'Vančurovská prologomena', p. 514.
3) Z. Pešat, 'Vladislav Vančura a počátky socialistické literatury: Příspěvek k analyze literární avantgardy', *Česká literatura*, IX (1961), 4, p. 486.

any way to fight for freedom for his work.'[4] Writing in 1929, František Halas commented: 'Marhoul is more a socially harmful type because of his passivity and lack of rebelliousness. His contentedness with the world is of such a kind that if he were not so rare a phenomenon, he would be dangerous.'[5] Comparing Marhoul to Dostoevsky's 'holy fool', Myshkin, whom Vančura discusses in 'Literatura, věda a život', Holý argues that Marhoul 'lacks something necessary' to survive in the world in which he finds himself.[6] Blahynka, who sees in Marhoul a metaphor for the writer, suggests that Marhoul represents the flawed approach of the Devětsil poet:

> Marhoul is not just any poet from any time. With his playfulness, his child-like naivety, his dreaminess and lack of practicality he is the personification of the peculiar features of the poets from that wave of Czech poetry that staked everything on love, fantasy and kindness of heart. In the fate of the baker, whose kindness, conviviality, industriousness and professional skill Vančura admires, is also Vančura's judgement of his poet contemporaries. Like them, Marhoul has a beautiful, joyful and energetic conception of life, but does not know how to enforce it [...][7]

For these critics, the novel combined an account of what Kundera calls the 'process of proletarianization' in capitalist society with a criticism of the lack of revolutionary consciousness in the contemporary proletariat.[8] Václavek argued that with the novel Vančura 'repaid his debt to Proletarian art',[9] while Josef Hora similarly felt that the work owed more to Wolker than Teige.[10]

The process whereby the proletarian comes to consciousness of his revolutionary role is described by Lukács in an essay also written in the early 1920s. Lukács argues that, in the market economy, 'a man's activ-

---

4) E. Urx, 'Moderná próza' in his *Básník v zástupe*, Bratislava, 1961, hereafter Urx, 'Moderná próza', p. 118.
5) F. Halas, 'Vladislav Vančura' in his *Imagena*, Prague, 1971, p. 319.
6) J. Holý, *Práce a básnivost: Estetický projekt světa Vladislav Vančury*, Prague, 1990, hereafter Holý, *Práce a básnivost*, p. 68.
7) M. Blahynka, *Vladislav Vančura*, Prague, 1978, hereafter Blahynka, *Vančura*, p. 111.
8) M. Kundera, *Umění románu: Cesta Vladislava Vančury za velkou epikou*, Prague, 1960, hereafter Kundera, *Umění románu*, p. 30.
9) B. Václavek, *Od umění k tvorbě*, Prague, 1928, hereafter Václavek, *Od umění*, p. 132.
10) See J. Hora, *Poesie a život*, Prague, 1959, p. 360.

ity becomes estranged from himself, it turns into a commodity'.[11] The human being thus finds himself objectified like any other commodity; according to Lukács:

> By selling [his labour], his only commodity, he integrates it (and himself; for his commodity is inseparable from his physical existence) into a specialized process that has been rationalized and mechanized, a process that he discovers already existing, complete and able to function without him and in which he is no more than a cipher reduced to an abstract quantity, a mechanized and rationalized tool.[12]

The collective is replaced by what Marx terms the 'isolated individual'. For Lukács, as for Proletarian writers, the proletarian, by becoming aware of his objectification, takes the first step to understanding the 'profound irrationality that lurks behind the particular rationalistic disciplines of bourgeois society'.[13] In this way, according to Lukács, the 'isolated individual' is abolished and the proletariat emerges as a class that comprehends both history as a process leading to the overthrow of bourgeois social relations and its role in that process:

> Man must be able to comprehend the present as a becoming. He can do this by seeing in it the tendencies out of whose dialectical opposition he can make the future. Only when he does this will the present be a process of becoming that belongs to him. Only he who is willing and whose mission it is to create the future can see the present in its concrete truth.[14]

In his study of the novel, Grygar notes the repetition of Marhoul's encounters with more powerful men, arguing that 'all those scenes in which Marhoul negotiates with those in authority and the mill-owner form a connected order. They do not constitute, however, a mere variation on a single humbling moment in life, but sharply rising phases in Jan's cognition and his coming to his senses'.[15] Few other critics would

---

11) G. Lukács, *History and Class Consciousness*, translated by Rodney Livingstone, London, 1971, p. 87.
12) Ibid., p. 166.
13) Ibid., p. 178.
14) Ibid., p. 204.
15) M. Grygar, *Rozbor moderní básnické epiky: Vančurův* Pekař Jan Marhoul, Prague, 1970, p. 14.

agree, however, that Marhoul attains the consciousness described by Lukács. Given the outer circle of narrative that frames the work, depicting Marhoul on his death-bed, the repeated encounters with powerful figures may rather be seen as circles through which Marhoul descends from the place of human warmth of his own bakery to what is explicitly described as the 'hell' of another man's bakery.[16]

His only act of revolt constitutes not an acknowledgement, but a futile denial of his objectification. When the wealthy miller takes over the mill, he installs alongside Marhoul a consumptive former soldier, Durdil, as a co-worker. When Durdil dies, the miller tells Marhoul that he must run the mill unaided, with no increase in wage, and accuses Marhoul of stealing grain from him to feed his pig. Marhoul, in whom a vague sense of injustice has been growing, turns on him: 'Kdo jste, že mi chcete rozkazovati? Kdo to neví? Kdo vás nezná? Jste pouhý šibal a lichvář, jenž vládne svými pytli, ale nikoliv lidmi, nikoliv lidmi!'[17] At the end of the argument, he shows a complete lack of understanding of his situation by demanding rhetorically: 'Což jsem tak bídný, abych nemohl říci svého mínění, což jsem se prodal za pět chlebů.'[18] For Kučerová, his inability to recognize himself for what he has become is encapsulated in the episode at the end of the novel when he cruelly mocks the Jewish lemonade-seller, Rudda, who, together with the road-mender Deyl, has constantly tried to help him find work and see sense.[19] It might be argued that he similarly fails to recognize his own plight in the fate of Durdil, or even of his own aging dog, no longer strong enough to pull the bread-cart. On the other hand, however, perhaps Marhoul does not recognize himself in them because he is not like them.

The criticisms of Marhoul, like the critical remarks of the narrator that essentially pre-empt the attitude of the implied reader, come from the perspective of the present world and concern Marhoul's incapacity either to survive in that world or be an active agent of change. At the

16) See V. Vančura, *Amazonský proud – Pekař Jan Marhoul – Pole orná a válečná – Poslední soud*, Prague, 2000, hereafter Vančura, *Amazonský proud etc.*, p. 138.
17) 'Who are you that you think you can order me about? Who does not know? Who does not know you? You are a mere rogue and a money-lender who rules over his sacks but not over people, not over people!' (ibid., p. 118).
18) 'What, am I so poor that I cannot express my opinion, have I sold myself for five loaves of bread?' (ibid., p. 119).
19) See H. Kučerová, 'Vančurův umělecký vývoj v prvních letech poválečných', *Česká literatura*, XX (1972), 6, p. 517.

same time, however, the narrator saves his strongest invective for the town and people who destroy Marhoul. Rather than a sympathetic but critical account of Marhoul's approach to life, the novel might also be read as an anti-didactic form of revolutionary writing, in which Vančura calls on the reader to overturn his or her thinking, to see the discrepancy between Marhoul and the world not as a failing of Marhoul, but as a failing of that world. He is one in a line of literary *ingénus*, holding up a mirror to the society in which they find themselves. Píša sees Marhoul as a 'passive revolutionary, shaking today's moral concepts with the infinite holiness of his heart, untouched by the iron, though severely rusted logic of the social order and apparently self-evident customs'.[20] For the implied author, Marhoul represents the goal, not the means of achieving it, the unfettered ideal of what Václavek terms 'pure humanity', freed from centuries of degradation. This contrast is encapsulated in the descriptions of his handwriting, as he makes a note of all the money he owes, and that a few pages later of the notary authorizing the seizure of Marhoul's property. Of Marhoul the narrator writes: 'psal způsobem dávno již vyšlým z obyčeje a krásným.'[21] Of the notary, he says: 'slova plynula ze skřípajícího hrotu jako z koktavých úst.'[22]

For Václavek, Marhoul's 'pure humanity, passive in its endless goodness, is a sort of folly in today's world. Incongruous to the present environment and conditions of life, it is dada'.[23] By contrast, perhaps reflecting how Vančura's writing strives to sustain the common ground within the Avant-garde, Holý links the novel not with Dada, but with the militant wing of German Expressionism and 'utopian dreams of society's transformation on the basis of the "pure heart".'[24] At one point the narrator notes of Marhoul: 'Chodíval za rakvemi ubožáků a zoufalců, někdy nepřipraven a skrývaje zástěru v pase složenou, ne aby plakal, ale protože byl podoben všem lidem a všichni lidé byli trochu jím samým.'[25] This

---

20) A. M. Píša, *Dvacátá léta*, Prague, 1969, hereafter Píša, *Dvacátá léta*, p. 148.
21) 'he wrote in a way that had long since gone out of practice and that was beautiful' (Vančura, *Amazonský proud etc.*, p. 56).
22) 'the words flowed from the scraping nib as though from stammering lips' (ibid., p. 64).
23) Václavek, *Od umění*, p. 133.
24) Holý, *Práce a básnivost*, pp. 66–67.
25) 'He used to walk behind the coffins of poor, miserable wretches, sometimes not properly dressed and hiding his apron tucked into his waist, not to weep but because he was like all people and in all people was a little of him' (Vančura, *Amazonský proud etc.*, p. 52).

passage not only draws attention to Marhoul's unconscious awareness of the collective identity he embodies, but also evokes an early example of modern Czech social literature, 'O měkkém srdci paní Rusky' by Jan Neruda (1834–91). That story describes a widow who fills her days attending funerals and gossiping about the deceased until, having upset the local petty bourgeoisie, she is forbidden by the police from attending any more. Neruda challenges the reader to see the widow not merely as a comical eccentric, but as the only person at the funerals with a real understanding of human life and its loss. In the same way, in *Pekař Jan Marhoul*, through the ambiguousness of his narrator, Vančura challenges the reader to recognize that this 'pure humanity' is not madness, but rather that a world which systematically seeks to efface that humanity is mad. The reader is complicit in this effacement to the extent that he or she demands from Marhoul adaptation and compromise.

In the first chapter, Marhoul is depicted as an unthinkingly hard-working, selfless, sociable, peaceable and compassionate man: 'Nezastavoval se od rána do večera, tu pracoval v dílně a opět v krámě a doma. Robil na zahradě i ve včelíně, hřebelcoval koně ve stáji a nespěchával. Jeho dny byly dlouhé a vždy měl dosti času, aby vycházel. Býval v hospodách i v židovské kořalně a stoje na náměstí poslouchal dlouhá vypravování bab.'[26] He thrives on collective existence, encapsulated by his almost compulsive desire to talk: 'Často uprostřed práce přepadala Jana potřeba řeči.'[27] He fosters an ideal collective among his rough assistants: 'Pekařští pomocníci poslouchali mistra, aniž ustali v práci; byli účastni všech výhod tohoto domu. Pracovali s Janem, tlachali s ním a nikdo z nich neskrýval nic před ostatními.'[28] It is precisely his love of talking and his unthinking openness, however, that leads him to tell the council administrator in the pub what others have been saying about him, setting in motion the chain of events that ruin him.

26). 'He did not stop from morn till night, he worked in the workshop and then in the shop and at home. He worked in the garden and at the apiary, he curried the horses in the stable and never hurried. His days were long and he always had enough time to go out. He was often in the pubs and in the Jewish liquor shop and standing on the square he would listen to the long tales of the womenfolk' (ibid., p. 53).
27) 'Often in the midst of his work Jan was overcome by the need to speak' (ibid., p. 57).
28) 'The assistants listened to the master baker without ceasing their work; they were party to all the benefits of the house. They worked with Jan, they gossiped with him and none of them hid anything before the others' (ibid.).

Again early in the novel, the narrator describes how he is easily cheated by customers and swindlers who come begging for charity. A key aspect of his humanity is his refusal to impose hierarchies on what surrounds him; he treats all things equally and his compassion extends even to a lame stray dog that wanders into his bakery. He is forced away from this community into literal isolation, leavened briefly by an improbable encounter with navvies that somewhat exposes Vančura's idealism. Unlike the selfish, malicious townspeople, these navvies appear intuitively to understand Marhoul and do not steal his bread, though they could: 'Protože se svěřil s celým svým majetkem do jejich zlodějských rukou a neřekl nic mimo to, že potřebuje peněz, bratránci, jako by uhadovali jeho výjimečné obchodování, zaplatili mu, zůstávajíce dlužní jen za dva chleby.'[29] Marhoul is incapable of violence or vengeance, or of taking satisfaction from his enemies' misfortunes. Turning on the chairman of the small loans company who seals Marhoul's fate, the narrator declares: 'Dobytku, který ze všech pohrom a revolucí doveds vynésti svůj bachor neporušen, již kráčí ti, kdo tě zdrtí [...] Kdyby se Marhoul dočkal tvé porážky, plakal by pro tebe, ale bude již mrtev, až se to naplní.'[30]

Throughout the novel, as in his others, Vančura's language frequently has a biblical or liturgical resonance, which serves to create a tension between the characters being described and the words used to describe them. Discussing Vančura's use of low colloquial and high literary registers, Mukařovský notes how 'fallen, scorned, morally or intellectually inferior' characters are often depicted in his work using 'high-style' language.[31] This feature might be viewed as a linguistic enactment of Christ's blessings in the Sermon on the Mount, which is sarcastically paraphrased in *Pekař Jan Marhoul*. In this novel, however, biblical allusions also function as negative symbols, dissociating Marhoul from any identification with Christ. Whereas in his next novel, *Pole orná a válečná*, Vančura encourages the reader to associate the primitive, dim-witted, ostensibly repellent Řeka with Christ, in *Pekař Jan Marhoul*, he encourages

29) 'Because he had entrusted all his goods to their thieving hands and said nothing save that he needed money, his brothers, though they had seen through his extraordinary manner of trading, paid him, owing in the end for just two loaves' (ibid., p. 98).
30) 'You swine, who has managed to carry his gut untouched through every catastrophe and revolution, those who will crush you are already on the march. If Marhoul lived to see your defeat, he would weep for you, but by the time it is accomplished, he will already be dead' (ibid., p. 64).
31) Mukařovský, 'Vančurovská prologomena', p. 483.

the reader to view Marhoul as the embodiment of not Christ-like and other-worldly, but essentially human qualities. In the final line of the novel – 'Zemřel a třetího dne byl pohřben'[32] – Vančura subtly alters the lines of the Creed referring to Christ's death and resurrection: 'passus et sepultus est, et resurrexit tertia die.' As well as reaffirming Marhoul's mortality, the line implicitly indicates that any redemption of human life must take place in this world.

Perhaps the most fundamental biblical allusion is, however, kept implicit and relates to the passage from Deuteronomy, quoted by Christ in the Gospels of Matthew and Luke: 'man doth not live by bread only, but by every word that proceedeth out of the mouth of the Lord doth man live.'[33] At the beginning of the novel, bread embodies both material and spiritual nourishment, the essence of life. The reader is drawn away from the silence and isolation of the opening scene, at Marhoul's death-bed, back to the time, fourteen years before, when he was his own master, to images of a vibrant, abundant, joyful and harmonious collective existence:

Jeho dům stál na jížní straně náměstí a štít, obrácený k lidem, zněl z jeho zdi jako zvon z věže kostelní: Chléb, chléb, chléb. Oheň plápolal v peci, bujní koně hryzli udidla. Přebytek radosti podobal se plameni a vodám, trýskajícím z nitra skal a hlomoznému kolu, jež okřídleno nese veselého boha. Otevřenými dveřmi vanula vůně pečeného chleba a košíky byly plny žemlí, housek a rohlíků. [...] Marhoul stál před domem s rukama složenýma pod zástěrou a naslouchal hlasům svého domu. V poschodí zpívala si žena, dílna se ozývala smíchem a na dvoře kdosi klel, zřejmě nikoliv proto, aby zlořečil. [...] Marhoul zůstával venku. Šli mimo lidé a pozdravovali ho.[34]

32) 'He died and on the third day was buried' (Vančura, *Amazonský proud etc.*, p. 151).
33) Deuteronomy 8:3. In his scathing description of the town, the narrator, referring to one character's attempt to sell books, comments: 'i kdyby tyto knihy byly dobré, benešovští by jich nekoupili, neboť nebyli živi slovem' (even if those books had been any good, the folk of Benešov would not have bought them, for they did not live by words; ibid., p. 61).
34) 'His house stood on the south side of the square and the shop-sign, turned to face people, rang out from its wall like a bell from a church tower: Bread, bread, bread. A fire crackled in the oven, exuberant horses champed at their bits. The surplus of joy resembled a flame and water gushing from the heart of rocks and a clattering wheel that, winged, bears a merry god. Through the open doors wafted the scent of baked bread and the baskets were full of loaves, buns and rolls. Marhoul stood in front of his house with his

During the novel, however, mirroring Marhoul's fate, bread loses all these connotations and is reduced to a commodity.

In the first chapter, the narrator describes Marhoul making dough, an implicit depiction of how work should be, a harmonious, intuitive process with the whole human being at its centre, in which the finished product as a commodity is all but incidental. The beginning of the passage, recalling Christ's prophecy of Peter's denial, typifies the way biblical allusions are used stylistically in the novel:

Dříve než kohout podruhé zakokrhá, Jan Marhoul na všechno zapomene. Teď mísí chléb a jeho pět smyslů pracuje jako pětiruký bůh. Tu vládne dřevěnou kopistí, podobuje se plavci, jenž přemáhá divoké moře. Tytam jsou peněžní starosti, je mlád jako všechny děti a nemyslí, jako děti nemyslívají na nic, leda na to, co se jim právě hýbe v rukou. Jeho zručnost stávala se zázračnou v práci, jež byla více hrou než robotováním; tím lépe, že takto dobýval chleba.[35]

It is this kind of work that Vančura has in mind when, notably in his 1924 essay on the new art, he seeks to identify the work of the writer with that of the worker. He writes: 'instead of working, people trade and extract financial profit from all sorts of things [...] Only labour [*dělnictví*] and the work of labouring men are outside the terrible state of degeneration and death [...] modern artists create like craftsmen, they are labouring men, they are a branch of the labouring class and in this sense above all are communists.'[36] For Vančura, the writer, like the craftsman, 'organizes' – gives form – to the reality emerging in his hands. Here already we see his understanding of communism not as an economic method or a political dogma, but an intuitive, holistic approach

arms folded under his apron and listened to the voices of his house. Upstairs his wife was singing, the workshop resounded with laughter and in the yard someone swore, evidently not to curse someone [...] Marhoul stayed outside. People walked past and gave him the time of day [...]' (ibid., pp. 49–50).

35) 'Ere the cock crows a second time, Jan Marhoul has forgotten about everything. Now he is mixing bread and his five senses are working like five-armed god. Here he reigns with his wooden paddle, like an oarsman trying to tame a wild sea. His money worries are gone, he is young like all children and does not think, just as children do not think about anything other than what is at that moment moving in their hands. His skilfulness became miraculous doing work that was more a game than hard labour; all the better that in this way he earned his daily bread' (ibid., p. 56).

36) V. Vančura, *Řád nové tvorby*, Prague, 1972, p. 55.

to life that his misfits tend to retain but his proletarian characters seem to have lost.

Götz equates Marhoul's character with proletarianism, 'the fresh spring of a new life force',[37] while Kundera describes him as a 'lousy petty bourgeois [...] [who] is in his internal character a proletarian and gravitates towards proletarianism'.[38] The narrator, however, declares: 'Býti dělníkem. Jan Marhoul jím nebude, nemá tvrdosti tohoto stavu. Jan si hraje a jeho ustavičná rozjitřenost je daleka kázně.'[39] It is his wife, Josefina, of whom the narrator says: 'Jestliže Jan byl blázen, ani ne zuřivý, Josefina zůstávala dělnicí; její inteligence byla přímá a úzká jako cesta, po níž jí bylo souzeno jíti.'[40] These remarks encapsulate the ambiguity of the novel; somehow, though the narrator praises proletarian discipline and directness, these qualities, while echoing the attitude expressed in 'Samotný chlapec' and 'Vzpomeň si na něco veselého', are secondary to those of Marhoul, the qualities of secondary characters, indicators of a restricted, adaptable humanity.

At one point, as their lives worsen, the narrator comments: 'Josefina se vzdalovala od manžela, měníc se, zatímco on zůstával, čím byl.'[41] This remark might suggest that Josefina is a more positive character than her husband, but in Vančura's writing, changes of character suggest deterioration, adaptation to circumstances, self-limitation and subordination to a hostile external world. He favours those who, by contrast, in the face of experience remain true to themselves or who come to a greater knowledge of their natures, like the Jans in 'Cesta do světa' and *Tři řeky*, or Markéta Lazarová, who is freed from religious dogma into a fuller understanding of herself as a human being. Faced with an increasingly straitening reality, practical Josefina moves from self-deluding trust in her husband to the misery of the daily struggle for survival. To an extent one can see in her the beginnings of a revolution-

37) F. Götz, *Literatura mezi dvěma válkami*, Prague, 1984, p. 7.

38) Kundera, *Umění románu*, p. 28.

39) 'To be a worker. Jan Marhoul will not be, he does not have the toughness of this estate. Jan plays and his constant agitation is far away from discipline' (Vančura, *Amazonský proud etc.*, p. 87).

40) 'If Jan was a madman, and not even ferocious, Josefina remained a worker; her intelligence was straight and narrow like the road along which she was fated to walk' (ibid., p. 59).

41) 'Josefina was growing distant from her husband, changing, while he remained what he had always been' (ibid., p. 100).

ary consciousness; she recognizes their isolation and the need for the poor to unite – 'Kdyby celé náměstí stálo kolem našeho hladu, volali bychom marně, ledaže by všichni chudí řvali s námi'[42] – and asks why Marhoul did not strike the miller when he confronted him. However, her growing realization of their situation prompts only increasing despair about their own prospects and the prospects of their son. Though she turns on her husband for continuing to harbour foolish hopes, at the end of the novel, she starts trying to reassure him, knowing all hope is gone.

The other 'proletarian' characters, Durdil, Rudda and Deyl similarly differ from Marhoul in their defeatism, their willingness to find an accommodation with a loathsome world and their efforts to persuade him to do the same. The novel thus does not seek, as it might have, to contrast one proletarian's journey towards revolutionary consciousness with another's failure to make that journey, but depicts the discrepancy between the ideal of human existence, what Lukács, quoting Marx, describes as the "'realm of freedom', the end of the 'pre-history of mankind'," and the present reality which deforms both rich and poor, in which that ideal cannot survive and in which the prospects of a strong revolutionary collective look distant.

Vančura does not, however, leave the reader without hope that a society based on 'pure humanity' might be realized. Late in the novel, the narrator refers to Marhoul's son, Jan Josef as 'the only certainty of my game'.[43] In the context, it may mean that his fate is sealed, his drift away from a pointless education into delinquency will continue, and at best he will become a hired hand, as his mother predicts. However, in a novel that emphasizes nature, his name suggests that he is a combination of his father and mother, the combination of the dreamer-optimist and the practical worker that defines for Vančura the Avant-garde writer. Whereas, at the beginning of the novel, Marhoul, the petty bourgeois, is concerned about his son's material inheritance – 'Bude pekařem [...] a tento dům bude jeho'[44] – at the end, when that has long since been lost, Vančura turns attention to Jan Josef's genetic inheritance, which can never be taken from him.

---

42) 'If the whole square stood around our hunger, we would call out in vain unless all the poor roared with us' (ibid., p. 102).
43) Ibid., p. 142.
44) 'He will be a baker [...] and this house will be his' (ibid., p. 50).

The fact that, according to Karel Nový, the novel was based on the experiences of Nový's father, a baker in Benešov, lends this interpretation the possibility of the author's subtle homage to his writer-friend.[45] However, Jan Josef may also be identified with Vančura himself. Blahynka gives the biographical reasons for making this connection: Vančura, who apparently had something of a problematic adolescence, had met Nový at the Benešov grammar school so excoriated in the novel.[46] The description of the different ways in which Marhoul and his wife care for the dying worker, Durdil – 'Jan byl knězem Františkovým a Josefina byla jeho lékařem'[47] – may be seen not only as a symbolic expression of the combined spiritual and practical role of the Avant-garde writer in ailing contemporary society, but also as an allusion to Vančura, the doctor-writer.

At the same time, however, the hope that Jan Josef might prove to be a combination of his parents may also reflect Vančura's interest in his own 'genetic inheritance'. In Ludmila Vančurová's account, Vančura's family are frequently shown to have influenced his novels. Most obviously, *Markéta Lazarová* draws on stories about his line, the medieval Vančuras of Řehnice, and is dedicated to his cousin, Jiří Mahen. The plot of *Útěk do Budína* apparently draws on the unsuccessful elopement of Vančura's sister, aged sixteen, and his mother's unfeeling response, and his family forms the basis for the Horvat family in *Rodina Horvatova*.[48] In *Pekař Jan Marhoul*, however, Vančura may be seen to mythicize the characters of his parents as aspects of his own personality. Early in her memoirs, Ludmila Vančurová describes how, soon after they met, Vančura characterised his parents to her:

> his great love was his father [...] he was like his father in that he liked to
> be surrounded by a happy atmosphere and good cheer, he was merry and
> warm-hearted, generous to a fault and at the same time a bit of a rogue
> and a fixer [...] [his mother] was the total opposite of his father. She was

---

45) Nový wrote his own, much more conventionally social realist novel based on his childhood in *Městečko Raňkov* (The little town of Raňkov, 1927), dedicated to Vančura.
46) See Blahynka, *Vančura*, p. 28.
47) 'Jan was František's priest and Josefina was his doctor' (Vančura, *Amazonský proud etc.*, p. 114.)
48) L. Vančurová, *Dvacet šest krásných let*, Prague, 1974, hereafter Vančurová, *Dvacet šest krásných let*, p. 134.

business-like, made plans on behalf of everyone, organised and ran the household with a firm hand.[49]

Particularly in the context of *Pekař Jan Marhoul*, this passage allows us to see the conflict in Vančura's fiction between artistic imagination and practical action, and the striving to balance or reconcile in his fiction the strict, sober tendency toward order and system and the insouciant, poetic tendency to live for the present as a response not only to contradictions within the left-wing Avant-garde, but also within the author's own identity. Vančura's contrasting attitudes to each of his parents seems mirrored in the implied author's love of Marhoul as a model not of flawed humanity, but of a humanity that is naturally and joyfully foolish and imperfect, and his more distanced, solemn sympathy with Josefina. This sympathy is later expressed very differently in *Útěk do Budína* in the narrator's efforts to understand the nature of the bourgeois mother's love for her wilful daughter, which manifests itself as cruelty.

Throughout his fiction, Vančura expresses affection for those who err. In *Konec starých časů*, his squalid librarian-narrator, Spera, who is frequently the mouthpiece of the implied author, suggests that the apparently perfect human being is actually less human:

Dokonalý člověk, na němž nenajdete chybičky a který si zaslouží úcty a lásky, bývá obyčejně pranezábavný. Počestnost, spravedlivá mysl a čistota vyhladí na svých soustruzích kdejaký vrub, kdejakou vyvýšeninu ducha a jejich dílo je nakonec hladké, pravidelné a souměrné, takže nad ním krčíte rameny.[50]

In *Pole orná a válečná*, the implied author's scorn for the priest Josef Danowitz is somehow compounded by the fact that 'half his sins were made up'.[51] Alongside the depiction of a 'prodigal father' in *Pekař Jan Marhoul*, allusions to the prodigal son recur in his work, for example

49) Ibid., p. 11.
50) 'The perfect human being, with whom you cannot find the slightest fault and who deserves respect and love, is most often utterly unentertaining. Honesty, right-mindedness and cleanliness plane away every indentation, any elevation of the spirit on their lathes and their finished product is ultimately smooth, regular and symmetrical, leaving you nothing to do but shrug your shoulders at it' (V. Vančura, *Konec starých časů*, Prague, 1947, p. 256).
51) Vančura, *Amazonský proud etc.*, p. 292.

in *Hrdelní pře*, when they are directed at Půlpytel, the character closest to the implied author's position. In a tale recounted in *Rozmarné léto*, a certain Blažej Okurka has an affair with a widow, much to the fury of his wife, who calls him 'marnotratník' (a profligate man). She is, however, ultimately persuaded to forgive him and he agrees to mend his ways.[52] Vančurová perhaps surprisingly suggests that in *Útěk do Budína* Vančura wrote 'a little of his fears for himself and his own possible fate' into arguably his most prodigal son-character, Tomáš.[53] The promising son of a well-known Slovak landowning family studying in Prague, he elopes with a rebellious bourgeois fellow-student, Jana, but proves unable to live up to her love, is unfaithful, falls into a decadent world of carousing and prostitution and ultimately commits suicide. His self-destructive hedonistic individualism contrasts with the unthinking collectivism embodied by Jana and his father, who are brought together in an ostensibly platonic unity at the end of the novel.[54]

Vančura's 'praise of folly' is also evident in the recurring motif in his work of Don Quixote, the ultimate knight errant in both senses. Urx was the first to draw attention to this motif in Vančura's writing in his review of *Pekař Jan Marhoul*, where he links Marhoul and Cervantes's hero through 'their simplicity and naive faith and the discrepancy between their kingdom of the pure heart and the conventionality of the world'.[55] Vančura seems to conceive of himself, and perhaps the Avant-garde writer in general as a quixotic figure, tilting at windmills in stubborn pursuit of his ideals. This identification is made explicit in the 1937 story 'Občan don Quijote', discussed in Chapter Seven.

The other Vančura character who most invites comparison with Quixote is the comic and sad Pilipaninec, the giant Ruthenian in *Poslední soud* who comes to Prague in the late 1920s with other members of his village to await clearance to travel to America and start a new life. Like Marhoul, Pilipaninec is larger than life compared to the other characters in the novel. Together with the beggar Ramus and the eccentric academic Weil, the reader watches him arrive in the novel: 'Snažil se býti

52) See V. Vančura, K. Konrád, J. J. Paulík, *Poetistická próza*, Prague, 2002, hereafter Vančura et al., *Poetistická próza*, p. 144.
53) Vančurová, *Dvacet šest krásných let*, p. 134.
54) The two settle in rural Slovakia, which, through the contrast between decadent, exotic Budapest and materialistic bourgeois Prague, emerges in the novel as an ideal, harmonious place that is being destroyed by First Republic capitalist interference.
55) Urx, 'Moderná próza', p. 119.

dopodrobna neviditelným v jakémsi mimikry, pro něž se rozhodl, když odložil barvy lesa a přijal městskou šeď a zmírnil ruměnec venkovské národnosti, jenž ho prozrazoval. Ale i tak byl patrný na dvě míle a jeho úsilí vycházelo naprázdno. Zaražené obličeje v kloboucích ustupovaly jako voda, do níž vniká lodní kýl.'[56] His size renders him at once comical and threatening in his new environment, and serves as a metaphor for the impression he gives of possessing incredible hidden strength for which he can find no outlet. Coming from the east to a dreary, unfriendly Prague, he might be compared, as Píša suggests, to an heroic knight or *bogatyr* from a Russian folk tale, looking in vain for a deed to do.[57] Weil finds him work with a crew of sandmen who dredge the Vltava, but Pilipaninec is not impressed: 'tento počátek věru nebyl ani hrdinský, ani krásný.'[58] Later, one of the sandmen, Dejm, who is jealous of him, goads him, saying: 'Vykonej jeden ze svých hrdinských skutků! Ukaž proslulou odvahu, o níž jsi tak dlouho mluvil!'[59] Pilipaninec responds not by tilting at, but by setting fire to a disused mill. Suddenly realizing that there are two old men inside, he rushes in to rescue them, carrying one out on his back.

Bedřich Fučík recalls a conversation between Vančura and Olbracht during the filming in Ruthenia in 1933 of *Marijka nevěrnice*, in which Vančura, asked which was his favourite of his own works, chose *Poslední soud* 'because every mother loves her crippled child the most'.[60] Though he won a state prize for the novel (which he accepted, to the infuriation of Teige and others on the left), the novel received mixed reviews, mostly, like Peroutka's, mentioned earlier, questioning the style. Karel Sezima, who admired *Pekař Jan Marhoul* and had defended *Pole orná a válečná*, considered *Poslední soud* an 'honourable defeat' and commented of the style: 'It does not betray a painful creative block or uncertainty so much as the

56) 'He was trying to be to the minutest detail invisible using some kind of mimic colouring which he had chosen when he put aside the colours of the forest and accepted the urban grey and moderated the ruddy cheeks of rural nationhood that gave him away. But even so he was perceptible from two leagues away and his efforts came to naught. Startled faces in hats drew back like water parted by the keel of a boat' (Vančura, *Amazonský proud etc.,* p. 315).
57) Píša, *Dvacátá léta*, p. 326.
58) 'this beginning was truly neither heroic nor beautiful' (Vančura, *Amazonský proud etc.,* p. 322).
59) 'Do one of your heroic deeds! Show us the famous courage about which you have talked for so long!' (ibid., p. 400).
60) B. Fučík, *Čtrnáctero zastavení*, Prague, 1992, p. 129.

affectation and caprices of a genius, because of which you would almost be inclined to ascribe to the author a deliberate muddying of the waters to make them appear deeper.'[61]

Though Vančura published a reply rejecting Peroutka's right to pass judgement on literature, perhaps in indication of the importance of the novel for him, he published a revised version in 1935, intended, according to Mukařovský, to 'bring the work closer to the reader by softening the excessive stylistic pecularities'.[62] In his comparative analysis of the two versions of the novel, Oldřich Králík, noting that none of the revisions dealt with problems highlighted by Peroutka, concluded that changes in punctuation and a shift to events happening in sequence rather than simultaneously produce a more concrete and sharply delineated world in the second version, making the work easier to follow without necessarily improving it or really having a impact on its complexity.[63] The 1929 original version of the novel was not re-published until the Česká knižnice edition in 2000. In this original version, which I use for this discussion, far from being a superficial novel masked by linguistic virtuosity, *Poslední soud* might best be described as an outpouring of Vančura's preoccupations and aspirations: the sense of transition, the yearning for strength, the discrepancy between east and west, the inherent collectivity of human existence, intimated by language while it cannot exist more fully, modern civilization's capacity only to perpetuate alienation and injustice, and the possibility – still distant – of a new order that might bring them to an end.

The novel is permeated by a mood of waiting, suggested by the title itself. Prague is merely a place of transit for the Ruthenian immigrants as they wait for clearance to move on. One, Mejgeš, is tormented by guilt and by the fear that his guilt may be discovered. He and Pilipaninec appear to have been motivated to leave their village, Ljuta, after their involvement in the murder of a gamekeeper, whom Mejgeš shot. He is therefore waiting to be judged, not only or so much by the authorities as by God. The reader also waits for Mejgeš to be caught, but above all waits for the moment when Pilipaninec's patience is exhausted. While the Ruthenians wait, the Czech characters appear merely to be drifting,

61) K. Sezima, 'Z nové tvorby románové III: Surrealisté', *Lumír*, LVI (1930), p. 198.
62) J. Mukařovský, 'Doslov' in V. Vančura, *Poslední soud*, Prague, 1958, p. 168.
63) See Králík, O., 'Příspěvek ke studiu Vančurova stylu', *Slovo a slovesnost*, 5 (1939), 1, pp. 65–78.

their lives bereft of meaning beyond the daily grind. As in *Pekař Jan Marhoul*, in *Poslední soud* Vančura focuses on characters who find themselves, or have chosen to be, on the margins of contemporary society. The beggar Ramus used to be a carpenter, but his village and his trade were swallowed up in the expansion of Prague. Weil, a philosopher and astronomer, has rejected a career in dusty academia and feels more at home among the marginalized on the streets. He may be linked to his namesake, Ervín Weil from 'Cesta do světa' and to Dr Mann in *Tři řeky*, who are similarly well-intentioned, essentially positive characters who are nevertheless limited in what they can achieve by their bourgeois natures and perhaps by the times in which they live. The sandmen make up a peculiar community of their own, which includes the hatchet-man and watchman from the mill.

The arrival of the Ruthenians might be counted on to provide an injection of inspiring eastern unity and strength, but instead the Prague environment renders them timid, homesick, superstitious and uncertain. Their encounter with the people of Prague is fraught with mutual misunderstanding, creating a collective apparently united only in their alienation and powerlessness, the exact opposite of the synthesis for which Vančura yearns. Eventually Weil, frustrated in his efforts to help them, demands that they give up their dreams, memories and fears and 'act like people in the West'.[64] The novel reiterates the encounter of the mountain and the river in *Pole orná a válečná*. The opening chapters of that novel describe how the intertwining of the fates of two incongruously named characters, the elderly Hora (Mountain) and the backward Řeka (River), ends in the pointless murder of Hora by Řeka. In *Poslední soud*, the meeting of the Carpathians with the Vltava, embodied by the two sets of characters, likewise produces the opposite of the fairy tale promised by these mighty phenomena. The mountains do not symbolize timelessness, the cohesion of ancient tradition, but the Ruthenians' stubborn retreat into themselves, and the river does not symbolize dynamism and vigour, but the shallow insipidness of the silted-up Vltava in Prague: 'Ptáci všech barev vody a ledu stali se šedými a jiní zčernali ve špatném přírodopisu města. Proud se opožďoval.'[65] The outcome of this coming together is captured in the narrator's description of Pilipaninec, staring at the

64) Vančura, *Amazonský proud etc.*, p. 393.
65) 'Birds of all the colours of water and icy became grey and others went black in the bad natural history of the city. The current was falling behind' (ibid., p. 371).

sandmen's work: 'Karpaty, ve kterých hladověl, nížily se v hromady písku a ubohá smítka, uvíznuvši v deštění naběráku, zbyla z lesů.'[66]

The novel does not straightforwardly assert the superiority of the east over the west, as in Vančura's earlier essay, but expresses the degeneration of the eastern, at least partly through the influence of the western, and genuinely attempts to explore the emotional experience of the migrants. Ruthenia is depicted entirely through the memories of the characters who have left it, and therefore has a misty, unreal quality that increases as memories become blurred: 'Čas zvolna míjel, Ljuta a město se směšovaly jako dvé řek.'[67] Prefiguring the portrayal of the Slav tribes' Carpathian homeland in the first chapter of the *Obrazy z dějin národa českého*, Ruthenia appears as a mythical, pre-historical place, where human beings live in a savage, unmediated relationship with nature, where gesture dominates language and intuition reason. Describing Pilipaninec's arrival in Prague's busy station, the narrator writes: 'Vteřiny probíhaly hlučně jeho tepnou a ticho, koruna kadeřavé hory, bylo ztraceno.'[68] The silence of the Carpathians is replaced not only by the noise of the city, but also by a silence that expresses not peace, but the fear and uncertainty of waiting: 'ticho připomínalo příliš pochybovačnost.'[69] In this context, the killing of the gamekeeper has the quality of original sin, casting Mejgeš and Pilipaninec from their wild paradise.

At the same time, however, Vančura often alludes to the Czechoslovak colonization of the desperately poor region after the First World War, the baleful intrusion of the West on the East. Mejgeš describes how: 'Republikanští úředníci [...] přicházejí do chalup se zjevným přáním rušiti vesnický řád, způsob orby, trestů a sklizně. Nic se jim nelíbí a proti úmluvě přeměňují i domácí věci, jakkoliv mají moc jen nad veřejnými skutky.'[70] Later, the narrator comments of the authorities' decision to

66) 'The Carpathians, in which he had starved, shrank into piles of sand and a wretched cinder, stuck in the sides of a shovel, was all that was left of the forests' (ibid., p. 320).
67) 'Time passed slowly, Ljuta and the city merged like two rivers' (ibid., p. 394).
68) 'The seconds coursed noisily through his arteries and silence, the crown of the curly-headed mountain, was lost' (ibid., p. 323).
69) 'The silence too much recalled doubting' (ibid., p. 375).
70) 'The Republic's bureaucrats [...] come to cottages with the obvious desire to disrupt village order, the method of ploughing, punishing and harvesting. They do not like anything and in contravention of our arrangement they also transform household matters, even though they only have power over public affairs' (ibid., p. 359). Vančura associates this attitude with the didactic understanding of culture, typified by the puppet theatre organized for the immigrants, which puts on plays about the dangers of alcohol.

quarantine all the Ruthenians after a girl is found to be dying of typhus: 'Vracela se léta převratu, léta překotných nařízení a zdravotnického šílenství, jež mělo zorati Poloniny a vymýtit nákazu listinou, jediným lékařem (jenž, žel!, byl téměř voják), jedinou škaredou ošetřovatelkou ze Spojených států.'[71] The impact of the western, both in Ruthenia and on the Ruthenians who travel west, is entirely negative.

The contrast between the western and eastern is encapsulated in the two women who love Pilipaninec. The seamstress Odeta is the superficial, coquettish embodiment of western modernity, the cause of conflict between Dejm and Pilipaninec: 'Odeta po způsobu stavů, které žijí z proměn vkusu, považovala vše, co je v krejčovství nenadalé a překvapující, za známku osvícení a pokroku, proto byla její sukně a její sluneční tak krátké, proto měla šátek na rameni a několik závěrečných úsměvů, když vystupovala.'[72] Far from condemning her, however, Vančura's treatment of her is sentimental; her exotic name, perhaps an allusion to the ballet *Swan Lake*, masks her more ordinary real name, Štěpánka, just as her fashionable clothes mask her poverty. She tells Pilipaninec: 'Přivlastnila jsem si to jméno, protože zní lépe, ale nedomnívejte se, že jsem příliš rozmarná.'[73] Mejgeš's daughter, Iliadora, by contrast, is described as 'tvář vášnivé vážnosti',[74] the embodiment of eastern depth, strong, standing up for Pilipaninec to her father and quietly bearing the burden of the alien city and her unrequited love, vaguely reminiscent of Josefina Marhoulová in her stoicism. The Ruthenians, however compromised by their contact with the western, nevertheless live with more intensity and sincerity than their Bohemian counterparts. When Mejgeš goes into a church and confesses his crime aloud, desperate for forgiveness, he is thrown out by the congregation, who think he is drunk.

71) 'The years of the takeover [Czechoslovak independence] returned, years of hasty decrees and health service madness, which was supposed to plough up the Polaniny plateau and clear away infection with an official document, one doctor (who was, alas, virtually a soldier) and a single ugly nurse from the United States' (ibid., p. 390). Vančura sarcastically notes that the doctor believes that illnesses are punishments from God.
72) 'Odeta, in the manner of those estates that live on changes of taste, considered everything that is sudden and surprising in tailoring as a sign of enlightenment and progress. This is why her skirt and her parasol were so short and that is why she had a scarf on her shoulders and gave a few final smiles as she was getting off [the tram]' (ibid., pp. 356–7).
73) 'I took that name because it sounds better, but do not suppose that I am very vain' (ibid., p. 403).
74) 'the face of passionate seriousness' (ibid., p. 353).

In the context of the two women, Pilipaninec emerges as a linking figure, yearning to return to Ruthenia, but also yearning to be accepted and to find his place in Prague. His frustration at his inability to bridge this contradiction culminates in his senseless act of destruction. The fire, however, paradoxically acts to create a sense of collectivity and unity. Realizing that Pilipaninec started the fire, Weil and Dejm both take ultimate responsibility. Weil thinks: 'Je pouhý chlapec, prokázal mi nespočetné služby, je mírný, a my jsme rozdmýchali oheň.'[75] In a scene somewhat reminiscent of the Indians in 'Proud amazonský', when the seriously injured Pilipaninec regains consciousness, lying in the sandmen's boat, the narrator describes the moment of reconciliation and unthinking comradeship for which Pilipaninec has always longed: 'Dejm přiklekl a opřel mu hlavu o svá kolena. Tu se raněný usmál.'[76] With Pilipaninec facing charges of arson, the dying hatchet-man from the mill tells the authorities the 'beautiful lie' that he caused the fire by lighting a cigarette carelessly.

These acts of solidarity reflect a collectivity that has always been there, unrealized, not only in their shared 'misfit' status, but also contained in the common language spoken between Weil, Ramus and Pilipaninec at the beginning of the novel:

Nikdo nebyl v nebezpečí, že by se nedorozuměl mluvě češtinou, jež propůjčuje vodopád časování bez námitek a dovoluje, aby kmeny jejího lesa obrostly chybami a zvuky právoznalců, již přikvapili bez slovníku u vážné snaze mluviti slovensky a rusínsky. Na této jemnosti (jež není krupobitím, abyste se pohoršovali) málo sejde. Proti zvonům latiny, francouzskému fagotu a pilníkům jazyka německého, jež zaplavují vesmír, jsou tyto hlasy tiché a komolé; a přece se berním správám nepodařilo zmrhati a zamlčeti vše, co je v této řeči čisté a krásné.[77]

75) 'He is a mere boy, he has performed countless services for me, he is peaceable and we fanned the flames' (ibid., p. 412).
76) 'Dejm knelt down beside Pilipaninec and rested his head on his knees. At this the injured man smiled' (ibid., p. 415).
77) 'No one was in danger of not making himself understood by speaking Czech, which confers a waterfall of conjugations without demurring and permits the trunks of its forest to be covered in the mistakes and noises of lawmakers, who trotted up without a dictionary in a serious attempt to speak Slovak and Ruthenian. This subtlety (which is not a hailstorm that would appal you) does not matter much. In contrast to the bells of Latin, the French bassoon and the metal files of the German language that flood the universe, these voices are quiet and truncated; and yet the tax authorities have not managed to ruin

This passage is Vančura's most explicit expression of affection for Czech in his fiction, which he admires because of its ability to tolerate and even rejoice in diversity and aberration. In contrasting this understanding of language with a notion of language that is 'administered', broken down and restricted by rules, he conveys both his view that Czechness has become corrupted through contact with capitalist western ways, and his advocacy in the novel of a collectivity based not on judgement, on proscription and prescription, but on forgiveness.

This notion of collectivity finds full expression in the final chapter, which is told from the perspective of Ramus. Taken ill on his way to watch the court hearings of Pilipaninec and of Mejgeš, Ramus sees the events in court simultaneously with the judgement of his own soul, as he lies dying in the sandmen's boat. Several of Vančura's works end with a dream or vision of the coming of a new, just world, seen either by the Avant-garde narrator (for example in 'Býti dělníkem' or *Pole orná a válečná*) or by elderly, outsider, story-teller characters like the watchman Damian Kůrka in *Rodina Horvatova*, as they die. In *Poslední soud*, Ramus serves as the guardian of the hidden collectivity of human existence. He is described as the 'gardener of the story' and, rather like the Avant-garde artist embodying privileged knowledge of not only the past, but also the future: 'Byl příliš stár a se snadností, s níž se vracel do starých časů, uhadoval i věci budoucí.'[78] His intuition or higher vision is reflected in the fact that he is almost blind. As Blahynka points out, his name is the Latin for 'tree-branch'.[79] It recalls a metaphor from 'Cesta do světa' articulating the interconnection between the individual human being and the surrounding world: 'Veliké moře dotknulo se ramenem řeky dětských myslí, jako les se dotýká větví okna samotařova domu.'[80] His vision of the last judgement is a vision not just for himself, but for all humanity.

or silence everything that is pure and beautiful in this language' (ibid., p. 315). Vančura alludes sarcastically here to the attempt of Czech First Republic establishment figures to speak the other languages of the new republic, which he implicitly presents as a hypocritical effort by the colonizer to reach out to the colonized that merely intensifies division. In *Pole orná a válečná*, the narrator describes the language spoken by the aristocratic Josef Danowitz to a peasant he meets on his way to his family's Polish estate as 'Polish disfigured in the style of the Slovak of later politicians' (ibid., p. 218).

78) 'He was too old and with the same ease with which he returned to old times he also predicted the things of the future' (ibid., p. 398).

79) See Blahynka, *Vančura*, p. 155.

80) 'A great sea touched the child's thoughts with the arm of a river, just as a forest touches the window of a loner's house with a branch' (Vančura et al., *Poetistická próza*, p. 16).

Blahynka compares Vančura's *Poslední soud* with Karel Čapek's story of the same name, dating from 1919 and included in his *Povídky z jedné kapsy* ten years later.[81] Čapek's story fits with his concern about the refusal to take responsibility that arises in human behaviour through belief in the last judgement of God. In the story, God declines to judge a multiple murderer, passing the responsibility to former judges in heaven, who cast the man into hell. Vančura also criticizes the restrictive effect of what he characterizes as a blind, superstitious belief in God on the ability of human beings to live life, most obviously in *Markéta Lazarová*. However, in Vančura's *Poslední soud*, the judge does not relinquish the right to judge, but judges with understanding for the nature of the human being, reflecting the narrator's earlier assertion, an echo of Kolovrat at the end of *Nemocná dívka*, that 'každá odvaha má chviličku váhání, každý smích špetku smutku, každý zločin stopu ušlechtilosti a oslnění stín'.[82] Blahynka writes: 'Karel Čapek's God with a kindly sigh *observes* the world, but does not intervene in its course, taking the role of *witness*. Vančura's judge *judges* with understanding for the human being with a pure heart; *he creates a new order*.'[83]

Having heard the cases of Ramus, Pilipaninec and Mejgeš, the judge, smiling, leaves the court-room, returning with a little child, who is playing with an apple. The child's identity is blurred between that of Ramus's son, who died in infancy and is now returned to him as his reward, and the image of the Christ-child in Renaissance painting, who often holds an apple symbolizing the redemption of sin. Catholic critics like Bedřich Fučík and Čep saw the stirrings of religious faith in this conclusion. However, Vančura's image does not reflect the eradication of original sin, but the embrace of an innately aberrant humanity. Just before he sets fire to the mill, Pilipaninec sees floating on the river 'jablíčko nesoucí otisky dětských zoubků', which are described as 'sotva znatelné stopy štěstí'.[84] At the end of the novel, the narrator says of the child: 'Dítě, hrajíc si s jablkem, potlačovalo úsměv, ale nakonec obnažilo mléčné

81) See Blahynka, *Vančura*, p. 151.
82) 'every courage has a tiny moment of hesitation, every laughter a pinch of sadness, every crime a trace of nobility and the shadow of being dazzled by the sun' (Vančura, *Amazonský proud etc.*, p. 333).
83) Blahynka, *Vančura*, p. 151.
84) 'an apple bearing the tooth-marks of a child [...] the barely perceptible traces of happiness' (Vančura, *Amazonský proud etc.*, p. 404.)

zoubky a všichni, kdo byli přítomni, opětovali tento milostný vzkaz.'[85] The teeth that bite and smile are as important to Vančura's image as the apple, expressing the willingness to taste life to the full, like the virgin tempted in 'Ráj', and the readiness to forgive. The child's smile, like the quixotic motif in Vančura's writing, signifies a noble, complete humanity, good-natured, playful, intuitive, free and imperfect.[86]

---

85) 'The child playing with the apple suppressed a smile, but finally bared its milk teeth and all who were present returned this message of love' (ibid., p. 430).

86) Mukařovský writes, somewhat incoherently in his notes towards a study of Vančura's narrator: 'The child's smile, the most fleeting of phenomena, is for the poet a symptom of the meeting of all times and spaces. The smile of a child, a being not yet socially determined, unburdened with the temporality of human society and resting essentially in sheer humanity as a natural phenomenon, gains in importance for him. It is therefore for Vančura, in humanity as a natural phenomenon, an ontological constant. In this humanity, however, resides not only the child about whom we are speaking, but also Vančura's narrator himself.' (J. Mukařovský, *Vančurův vypravěč,* Prague, 2006, p. 30.)

POLE ORNÁ A VÁLEČNÁ AND ROZMARNÉ LÉTO:
THE JUDGEMENTAL PHILANTHROPIST

The smile that ends *Poslední soud* epitomizes Vančura's advocacy of love, which increasingly dominates his subsequent work. One cannot argue, however, that Vančura shifts from an Old Testament 'judgemental love' to a New Testament 'forgiving love', rather that he strives to balance these two perspectives throughout his writing, perhaps as he strives to reconcile the contrasting attitudes to life that he identifies in his mother and father, always leaning in the end towards the latter. These shifts may be associated with two distinct attitudes that the narrator adopts towards to the characters whose lives he describes, either sympathetic and empathetic, as in his first and fourth novels, *Pekař Jan Marhoul* and *Poslední soud*, or in very different ways superior and even mocking, as in his second and third novels, *Pole orná a válečná* and *Rozmarné léto*.

Pole orná a válečná undoubtedly constitutes the strongest expression of 'judgemental love' in his writing, for here he implicitly presents the decaying imperial Europe of the First World War as the world just before the Flood. In Genesis we read: 'The earth also was corrupt before God, and the earth was filled with violence. And God looked upon the earth, and, behold, it was corrupt; for all flesh had corrupted his way upon the earth.'[1] In his other work, Vančura foregrounds the discrepancy between his conception of humanity and its contemporary, straitened form, for example through the contrast between Marhoul and the other characters, or through the contrast between the real and what can be imagined in *Amazonský proud* and *Dlouhý, Široký, Bystrozraký*. In *Pole orná a válečná*, however, which depicts the impact of the outbreak of the First World War on the peasantry and nobility of Ouhrov, a fictional estate on the middle Vltava, Vančura, in Václavek's description, expresses 'idealism through its negation',[2] portraying a fatally imbalanced world of deformed human beings

---

1) Genesis 6: 11–12.
2) B. Václavek, *Od umění k tvorbě*, Prague, 1928, hereafter Václavek, *Od umění*, p. 137.

whose human qualities have been erased or distorted, and leaving the reader to recognize the discrepancy.

Vančura plays with the expectation of contrast in the title, which perhaps alludes to Isaiah: 'And he shall judge among the nations and shall rebuke many people: and they shall beat their swords into plowshares, and their spears into pruninghooks: nation shall not lift up sword against nation, neither shall they learn war any more.'[3] If this passage encapsulates the transformation for which the implied author yearns, then the world he describes is its reverse, turning its plowshares into swords. Where the reader might anticipate a distinction between the portrayal of farming and of battlefields, however, Vančura strives to evoke the misery of the peasants' labour on the land, for example at harvest time at the beginning of the fourth chapter: 'dělníci běželi k proudu ponořiti v něj ruce plné ran. Polní nádeníci jsou příliš bolestní, než by mluvili, a ranění mlčením tak dlouhým, podobají se hrobu, v jehož hlubinách doposud se hýbe krvavé srdce. Mlčí dávajíce růsti svým plodinám a řev, jímž čas od času se otvírají, není než naříkání.'[4] In this context, the war is not a sudden, anomalous interruption, but the logical culmination of a system founded on what is presented as the absurd, brutal waste of human effort and life.

Similarly, the expected contrast between the terrible lot of the peasantry and the grand existence of the aristocracy does not materialize, as Emil Lukeš points out in his study of the novel: '[the manor house] is as vile and ugly as the lives of its inhabitants [Baron Danowitz and his two sons], who are not men worthy of the name, are empty.'[5]

---

3) Isaiah 2:4 (repeated in Micah 4:3). Vančura is perhaps also alluding to this passage in *Pekař Jan Marhoul*, where the narrator comments: 'Kdyby Marhoul měl v ruce nůž, byla by to sadařská žabka. Až by ji sevřel tváří v tvář chlapovi, jenž mu odvádí Josefinu, zatřpytila by se jako znamení míru' (If Marhoul were to have a knife in his hand, it would be a pruning-knife. And when he clenched it face to face with a man who was taking Josefina from him, it would glint as a sign of peace; V. Vančura, *Amazonský proud – Pekař Jan Marhoul – Pole orná a válečná – Poslední soud*, Prague, 2000, hereafter Vančura, *Amazonský proud etc.*, pp. 57–8).

4) 'the workers ran to the current to plunge into it their hands full of wounds. The field labourers are too afflicted to talk and, wounded by such a long silence, they resemble a grave, in the depths of which a bloody heart still moves. They are silent, letting their produce grow and the roar with which from time to time they open themselves is nothing but moaning' (Ibid., p. 196).

5) E. Lukeš, 'Vančurova Pole *orná a válečná*: K otázce kompozice, syžetu a ideového smyslu', Acta Universitatis Carolinae 1973: Philologica 3–4, *Slavica Pragensia XVI*, 1975, hereafter Lukeš, 'Vančurova Pole *orná a válečná*', p. 76.

Lukeš sees the novel as a sarcastic reversal of *V zámku a podzámčí* (In the manor house and in the peasant cottages, 1856) by Božena Němcová (1820-62), in which a representative of the selfish nobility discovers within herself the generosity of spirit of the peasantry: 'Against the prevailing Revival image of the peasantry and our native fields, against the false illusion and idealization of rural life, [Vančura] sets the naked bitter truth of the Ouhrov manor: misery and hunger, lawlessness, hard grind and the passion and madness of drink.'[6] What is essentially feudal capitalism has caused the equal degeneration of both those who own labour and those whose labour is owned. Marx writes of industrial capitalism:

> The property-owning class and the class of the proletariat represent the same human self-alienation. But the former feels at home in this self-alienation and feels itself confirmed by it; it recognises alienation as its own instrument and in it it possesses the semblance of a human existence. The latter feels itself destroyed by this alienation and sees in it its own impotence and the reality of an inhuman existence.[7]

In *Pole orná a válečná*, the reader can see this alienation, but the characters do not seem aware of it. The lack of difference between peasantry and nobility is intensified in the structure of the novel, which is composed of numerous plot threads tracing the fates of different peasant and aristocratic characters, particularly the two Danowitz sons and the 'village idiot', Řeka. Hodrová notes that the novel works on the principle of 'zones' running in parallel, not linked by causality, a fragmentariness which in her view corresponds to the character of war-time.[8] The fragmentariness and paralleling technique may, however, be more associated with Vančura's efforts to characterize human relations in the world he portrays. While the reader notices numerous parallels between the 'lives' described, often sustained by parallel motifs, the characters themselves are oblivious to them. Their lack of awareness reflects the isolation of individuals in this society, whereas the reader, by seeing them, is reminded of the unrealized collectivity of human existence.

6) Ibid., p. 72.
7) Quoted in G. Lukács, *History and Class Consciousness*, translated by Rodney Livingstone, London, 1971, p. 149.
8) See D. Hodrová, *...na okraji chaosu...*, Prague, 2001, p. 412.

The plot threads in the novel repeatedly confound the reader's expectations, petering out, ending bathetically or remaining unresolved, reflecting how, on contact with this distorted world, all attempts at action founder and end in wretched absurdity. A central example is Řeka's plan to murder the Jewish shop-keeper and pub owner, Lei, who profits from the peasants' misery. Řeka is drawn to shiny things like a child or a bird, and believes that by taking the Jew's money he will force the other peasants to respect him more. Despite this wrong-headed motivation, the implied author seems initially to approve of his plan as a vague sign of anti-bourgeois rebellion. The gap between his plan as he imagines it and its actual outcome is signalled when, instead of an axe, all Řeka can find is an adze, a clumsier, less heroic and dramatic implement. Having failed to murder Lei, Řeka breaks into the manor house. He enters the baron's chamber, leading the reader to believe that he might actually kill the baron, who, his head plunged into a basin of water, at that moment resembles a 'bull bowing its neck to be slaughtered'.[9] Řeka, however, again falters and only steals some papers because of the pretty watermark on them. The papers turn out to be valuable property deeds, and, though neither character realizes, they form a link between Řeka and Josef Danowitz, who is later accused by his father of stealing them. Typically of the novel, however, the baron never resolves the mystery of their disappearance.

On leaving the manor house, Řeka finds a rope and, climbing a beam in the stables, slips the rope over the sleeping head of a decrepit former stable-hand, Hora. The narrative focus on Hora in the opening chapter perhaps suggests to the reader that he will be a significant character, but his death in Chapter Four indicates that his significance lies in foreshadowing the fate of all the characters in the novel. A counterpart to Durdil in *Pekař Jan Marhoul*, Hora, whose face is described as a 'treasury of calamities', has been unable to work properly since a horse kicked him, and is trapped in a living death, lost in his memories as he waits for the end. In an example of parallel motifs, the description of the old baron cited above is foreshadowed earlier in the description of Hora: 'vlekl svou nohu těžší prase, jež cestou k jatkám cloumá provazem řezníkovým.'[10] His useless leg emerges from this metaphor apparently livelier than its

---

9) Vančura, *Amazonský proud etc.*, p. 206.
10) '[...] he dragged his leg, which was heavier than a pig jerking the butcher's rope on the way to the slaughterhouse' (ibid., p. 198).

owner. In a reflection of the lack of the intuitively empathetic collectivity to which Vančura aspires, the other peasants avoid Hora as the herd avoids a sick animal, unable or unwilling to recognize their fate in his.

The moment of the murder, when the river (Řeka) finds itself above the mountain (Hora), completes an internal game played with the two characters' names that reflects the upside-down world of the novel. Hora, after all, is the complete opposite of the common Czech epithet 'a man-mountain' (*chlap jako hora*), while, given that the river in Vančura embodies the harmonious co-existence of freedom and order and playfulness and intuition, the foundling Řeka's surname, 'a bureaucrat's poem' invented to differentiate him from his foster-father's true son, similarly reflects the man he ought to be, not the man he is. Their shared Christian name, František, suggests their forgotten common humanity, as embodied by St Francis of Assisi.

Řeka's killing of Hora is equated in the novel with Gavrilo Princip's assassination of the Archduke Ferdinand, news of which reaches Ouhrov at the same time, entirely eclipsing Hora's death. The news means little to the peasants and less to Řeka, who in his confusion thinks his action has caused the war.[11] For the narrator, the deaths of the Archduke and Princip are a senseless waste of life and strength, since no good comes from them. In this world of isolated, alienated individuals, revolt can only be destructive, achieving nothing but the ruin of that world. Despite the calls in his writing from 'Býti dělníkem' onwards for the oppressed to rise up, and the allusions to misplaced or absent aggression, in *Pole orná a válečná* Vančura suggests that violence belongs to the world that is wiped out by the ultimate manifestation of that violence, the world war. Implicitly, out of that devastation, however, will be born a collective, united in its belief in communism, which will march in triumph into the new world, meeting no resistance as the old world crumbles around it.

All other human actions in the novel are similarly stripped of the courage or nobility with which, in another world, they might have been endowed. Ervín Danowitz, a military officer and man of action, might in a different world have been, for the implied author, the most positive character in the novel. Until the war breaks out he maintains the

---

11) Vančura repeats this device of self-confusion or self-delusion, a symptom of the disconnectedness of contemporary existence, in *Učitel a žák*, in which the student, Jan, crazed by the desire to recreate the adventure and drama of literature in his staid bourgeois life, believes he is responsible for the death of his uncle, who has had a heart attack.

fashionable pose of the bored, arrogant aristocrat. Once at the front, however, he shows himself to be a better strategist, soldier and man that his senior officers, fighting bravely and standing by his men, whom he treats as equals on the battlefield: 'Jeho divoká obraznost, jíž se dostalo válečných ostruh, projevila se nejen statečností, vystavovanou poněkud na odiv, ale i bláznivým soucitem.'[12] However, the fact that he only realizes himself as a human being in war indicates that he is a perfect product of the society which has shaped him and distorted these human qualities for its own needs. He is the character most comfortable in the environment described in the novel; the narrator remarks early on of him: 'věřil v šlechtictví, a tato víra propůjčoval mu něco klidu.'[13] Ervín does not die the heroic death in battle that he and the reader might feel he deserves, but a slow, humiliating death from dysentery. At his death, the narrator says: 'Spi, Danowitzi, byl jsi příliš oslněn světem, jehož zkáza nadchází.'[14] The vague hints of implied authorial sympathy for him possibly reflect that, in Vančura's conception, the new human being will possess an aristocratic self-confidence and sense of freedom.

By contrast, the implied author reserves his greatest scorn for Josef Danowitz, the second son of the family, whose father forces him to enter the priesthood to reduce the demands on his finances. In *Pole orná a válečná*, Vančura is at once Decadent in presenting religion as a spent force in a world that has lost all sense of the sacred and Marxist in implying that communism is the new truth, supplanting Christianity and seizing its metaphors. A priest predicting to Baron Danowitz the passing of the aristocracy and the priesthood comments: 'Snad, když slovo boží je němé a císařové platí za otrapy, když otcové jsou katany a odbojní synové se vzpouzejí a kradou, snad v tomto zmatku nad hrůzami bitev a hladu bude platiti slovo, jež slabikuje nová víra. K ďasu, bude nám nakonec zoufati, nebo se radovati? Království chudých nebylo z tohoto světa.'[15]

---

12) 'His wild imagination, having gained the spurs of war, manifested itself not only in courage, which was rather put on display to be admired, but also in insane compassion' (Vančura, *Amazonský proud etc.*, p. 253).
13) 'he believed in the nobility, and this belief afforded him a little calm' (ibid., p. 177).
14) 'Sleep, Danowitz, you were too dazzled by a world whose destruction is approaching' (ibid., p. 294).
15) 'Perhaps, when the word of God is mute and emperors are considered vagabonds, when fathers are killers and rebellious sons rise up and steal, perhaps in this confusion above the horrors of battles and hunger, a word pronounced by a new faith will take

Christianity is portrayed as distanced from the lives of ordinary people. When Hora, as a young man, makes a peasant girl pregnant, the parish priest agrees to marry them, while recognizing that the Church's teachings have little meaning or power for the couple. He proceeds with the marriage instruction, though the couple can barely make sense of it: 'Pětkráte slyšeli kněze mluviti jazykem knih, aniž rozuměli jinému než podobenství o zrnu hořčičném, vypravování příhod marnotratného syna, jehož litovali, a řečení o zázracích, žel, příliš božských. Kněz sám nemohl tvrditi, že tyto věci souvisejí s potřebou sňatku.'[16] Just as he is about to kill the baron, Řeka is distracted by a picture of the parable of the Good Samaritan above the baron's bed. The double implication is that the story – and by extension religious teaching – has no impact on the baron's hypocritical, Pharisee-like attitude to those in need, but prevents an act that might at least be construed as a blow against injustice.

For the implied author, however, Josef's central failing is not his slavish but empty Catholicism, but his self-centred weakness in the face of the realities of life, his solitariness and his readiness to flee into the comfort of his own thoughts: 'Josef byl z mužů, již nemají sdostatek ducha ani sil, aby pracovali o současných věcech.'[17] In an inverted version of the prodigal son story, Josef asks his father for his share of the inheritance not so that he can live life to the full, but so that he can abandon the real world and make a pilgrimage to the Holy Land. By describing Josef as 'slaboduchý muž, příliš pozdě narozený, aby se mohl státi svatým',[18] the narrator vaguely acknowledges that his intention might once have been noble. The beginning of Josef's journey coincides in the novel with Řeka's preparations to commit murder, and like Řeka, Josef abandons his original grand plan for a far less demanding and meaningful venture. The account of his journey, which contains most of the rare moments of comedy in the novel, describes how he is confronted with the 'proper

effect. By the devil, will we in the end despair or rejoice? The kingdom of the poor was not of this world' (ibid., p. 295).

16) 'Fivefold did they hear the priest speak in the language of books, without understanding anything except the parable of the mustard seed, the tale of the adventures of the prodigal son, whom they pitied, and the talk of miracles, alas, all too divine. The priest himself could not say that these things were connected with the need to marry' (ibid., p. 162).

17) 'Josef was one of those men who no longer have enough spirit or strength to work for the things of the present' (ibid., p. 184).

18) 'a weak-willed man, born too late to become a saint' (ibid.).

and merry roughness' of real life, from which he has been sheltered, and with typically Vančurean men – a tramp, a road-mender and a peasant – who live in harmony with life. The episode is a fleeting glimpse in the novel of a hearty, feral existence, intensified by the underlying humour which Vančura considers a central element of this way of living. The road-mender finds Josef alone by the roadside, cursing his misfortune, so absorbed in his self-pity that he mistakes the appearance of the road-mender for a vision. The road-mender tells him: 'svou věc můžete vyhrát, jen pokud budeme mluvit!'[19] Josef's fundamental failing is his inability to commune with other human beings, to form relationships and become part of a collective life. Realizing that he is hopelessly ill-equipped not only for this world, but also for the journey he hoped to undertake, he retreats to the family's Polish estate.

In the world of *Pole orná a válečná*, the 'Amazonian current' – the positive influence of women – is absent. The very few, minor, female characters, mostly nameless peasant women, prostitutes and abandoned wives, are mere victims of the aggression pent up in men who lack a meaningful outlet for their physical and creative energy, the only exception being the nuns who have withdrawn from this catastrophic world. Sexual intercourse in the novel expresses neither love nor the desire to procreate. Whether through the whoring of the fired-up hussars about to go to the front or the savage mating of the peasants among the livestock, it is presented as a futile waste of aggression that might be better used in some violent uprising against injustice, the desperate, animal-like attempt of those condemned to extinction to feel momentarily alive:

Zatím ve stodolách a ve stozích dvorské děvečky očekávaly své truchlivé milence. Vcházeli k nim hrubí a divocí aspoň v této chvíli. Hrome, mohli zlomiti hnáty těmto klisnám, stejně nedočkavým a stejně obžerným maličkou vášní. Vyrážejíce jek rozkoše a blázníce muž a žena sbydleli v křečích, nerozpoutávajíce páchnoucího objetí, dokud zbylo něco krve v pahýlu vášně.[20]

19) 'You can only win your cause if we talk' (ibid., p. 217).
20) 'Meanwhile in the barns and haystacks the girls of the estate waited for their melancholy lovers. They came to them coarse and wild, at least at this moment. By thunder, they could break the limbs of these fillies, just as impatient and just as gluttonous in their tiny passion. Crazed, emitting shrieks of lust, man and woman came together in spasms, not loosening their stinking embrace while there was still some blood left in the stump of passion' (ibid., p. 202).

What is left of sexual desire, where aroused by more than opportunity or instinct, derives from a faint, unarticulated final yearning to experience momentarily the humanity that has been lost. The narrator comments of the married woman who, with her husband sent to the front, offers herself to the ostensibly repulsive Řeka: 'Bylo jí třeba hříchu a trýzně, aby nalezla pláč, který již pustl.'[21] Similarly the old peasant, Ber, takes up with a loose woman in the ruins of the Danowitzes' Polish estate: 'Převraceli se v pelechu, odporní jako potkani a jako mršina. Zakoušeli sprostot, jejichž hloubka hraničí s bolestí.'[22]

In the first chapter, the narrator describes how Hora conceives a child with an unattractive peasant girl during a loveless, mechanical sexual encounter in a stable amid the neighing of the horses. Their marriage of necessity, conducted out of unthinking obedience to convention rather than active faith, is rendered doubly meaningless when the girl and child die during the botched delivery. In an example of how Vančura uses his medical experience in his fiction, the narrator describes the findings of the autopsy in detail:

Při otevření břicha od dělohy až k játrům prosvítala sraženina krevní, krytá podbřišnicí. Po zdvižení těchto hmot objevila se ručička plodu, ovinutá pupečníkem. Ze zevních rodidel vytékalo něco krve. Děloha zela hrozným otvorem a odtud vystupovalo lůžko s blanami. Tělo dělohy bylo prázdné. Plod vězel z největší části v hrdle v jednoduché prvé řitní poloze, asi tak, že hlava plodu ležela mezi oběma nožkami a levou ručičkou. Pravice, vtlačená nazad ke křižové kosti, byla červená a zpuchlá.[23]

Píša is no doubt right to reject the association of the novel with Naturalism's pursuit of realism through physiological description and

---

21) 'She needed sin and torment to find the tears that had dried up' (ibid., p. 243).
22) 'They rolled over and over in the straw, as disgusting as rats or carrion. They tasted filth, the depth of which bordered on pain' (ibid., p. 261).
23) 'On opening the stomach from the womb to the liver, a blood clot showed through, covered by the lower abdomen. After lifting this mass, the little hand of the foetus appeared, with the umbilical cord wound round it. A little blood flowed out from the progenitals. A terrible opening gaped in the womb and from there protruded the placenta with membranes. The body of the womb was empty. The foetus was trapped for the most part at the cervix in a simple posterior anterior position, approximately in such a way that the head of the foetus was lying between both its legs and its left arm. The right arm, pushed back towards the sacrum, was red and swollen' (ibid., p. 165).

to link it more with Decadence's search for symbols.[24] The image of the dead child, the culmination of a process lacking any sense of love, beauty or sacredness, seems to function more as a key, defining symbol of the world that is born before the reader's eyes in the novel and dies in hideous, hyperbolically described torment.

Writing in 1978, Blahynka argued that Czech criticism had yet to come to terms with *Pole orná a válečná*. In his view, more could be gained by comparing the novel not with Vančura's preceding fiction, but with an early review he wrote of an exhibition of battlefield paintings in which, as later in *Pole orná a válečná*, he compares the battlefield to Golgotha.[25] As a young man, Vančura had wanted to be a painter, and for Blahynka, the novel is best understood as a 'cycle of images, the motifs of which correspond, interlink and graduate'.[26] The novel does not so much present ideas that demand an intellectual response from the reader as vivid, textured pictures of tormented humanity that demand an intuitive, non-verbal, emotional response, echoing the visceral outrage of the narrator. Indeed, on the basis of this novel, Götz argues that 'one may learn more about Vančura and his art from an analysis of his poetic images than from an analysis of his motifs and ideas, since the whole intensity of what interests him creatively is focused on them'.[27]

The paradoxical nature of *Pole orná a válečná* is epitomized by the fact that a novel which seeks to leave the reader beyond words or lost for words simultaneously, as Blahynka notes in his second useful contribution to its interpretation, describes how those long silenced might find their voice. The novel opens with a description of Ouhrov, perhaps, like all Vančura's settings, a metaphor for Bohemia: 'hluboká ornice a špetka jílu na zapadních svazích pahorkatiny nepojmenované, dno všednosti, podlaha bídy, daleko není tak nicotná, aby z ní nevzešly lesy. Vzejdou právě tak, jako řeč, než konečně zazní hlasem, vzchází za dlouhého mlčení.'[28] The passage encapsulates both the bleakness of the novel and

---

24) A. M. Píša, *Dvacátá léta*, Prague, 1969, hereafter Píša, *Dvacátá léta*, p. 151.

25) M. Blahynka, *Vladislav Vančura*, Prague, 1978, hereafter Blahynka, *Vančura*, p. 123–24.

26) Ibid., p. 130.

27) F. Götz, *Jasnící se horizont*, Prague, 1926, hereafter Götz, *Jasnící se horizont*, p. 225.

28) 'A deep arable land and a pinch of loam on the western slopes of an unnamed upland, the pit of ordinariness, the floor of misery, is in no way so worthless that forests could not rise up from it. They will rise up just as language rises during a long silence before it finally rings out in a voice' (Vančura, *Amazonský proud etc.*, p. 155).

the promise it contains of an end to that bleakness, the forests alluding perhaps to forests of human beings, a collective rising up and speaking out. The connection is made clear when the lines are repeated in the last chapter as the narrator imagines oppressed workers rising from the ashes of the war to establish a new, just order: 'Staré pokolení dělníků a noví příchozí vzbouří se pod ranami a šviháním, měděné mračno klidu se otevře bleskem. Závora chudáctví je zlomena a těsné místo se šíří v prostor.'[29] Through the repetition, Vančura seeks to show how Ouhrov, isolated and enclosed at the beginning of the novel, has been opened up by the war to the world and to the possibility of a new beginning.

Tracing the references to silence and speech in the novel, Blahynka associates the silence with the silence of Marhoul's death-bed at the beginning of *Pekař Jan Marhoul*, a symbol of isolation, of the absence of collectivity. In the world of the novel, language has lost its meaning, whether the language of the scriptures or the mindless babbling of Řeka, which appears to be little more than a chaos of things he has heard others say (including the language of the scriptures): 'Chudoba ducha nutila příjimati řeč, jíž se mluvilo i tehdy, nebyla-li jeho řečí.'[30] Blahynka suggests that Vančura implicitly evokes an imagined etymology between Řeka and *řeč* (speech), creating an additional discrepancy between his name and his nature. At the end of the novel, Řeka, who has been charged with the task once done by Hora of taking horses from Ouhrov to the front, is fatally injured in an explosion on the battlefield, in which his tongue and lips are blown off. Left by the centuries with so little of his original humanity, the war takes its last vestiges, not only his ability to speak, but also the identity once invented for him, which he cannot communicate to anyone, before taking his life.

Where Marhoul represents a man whose humanity remains miraculously untouched by the world around him, Řeka symbolizes the total deformation and eradication of that humanity. Blahynka rather hastily rejects Götz's association of Řeka with Marhoul: 'Řeka is a completely different person mentally and socially, Marhoul's opposite. Marhoul was

29) 'The old generation of workers and new arrivals revolt under the blows and whipping, the coppery storm-cloud of calm opens with a flash of lightning. The barrier of poverty is broken and a confined spot expands into the space' (ibid., p. 305).
30) 'Poverty of spirit necessitated the acceptance of speech which was uttered even if the words were not his language' (ibid., p. 281). Mukařovský notes that Řeka's thoughts are permeated with quotations from popular songs (see J. Mukařovský, *Vančurův vypravěč*, Prague, 2006, p. 62.)

a poetic misfit, a cordial friend, a self-sacrificing man who never thought of money as long as he lived; Řeka, who does not think of anything else, is a total idiot, an egoist who has none of Marhoul's misguided greatness.'[31] Though he is the direct opposite of Marhoul, his character serves the same function in the novel. Just as the narrator of *Pekař Jan Marhoul* repeatedly refers to his madness and folly, so the narrator of *Pole orná a válečná*, more harshly, repeatedly describes Řeka as an idiot, ridiculed and ignored by the other peasants. In both cases, through this technique Vančura encourages the reader to judge the characters, while hoping that instead he will judge the vileness of the world which they expose in completely opposing ways. Unlike in *Pekař Jan Marhoul*, where Vančura resists the identification of Marhoul with Christ, in the final chapter of *Pole orná a válečná*, in which the narration moves decisively to a visionary plane, the narrator encourages the interpretation of Řeka's death, on a Friday, at the battle at Görlitz, explicitly described as Golgotha, at the age of thirty three, as a metaphor for Christ's crucifixion. In an allusion to Matthew's description of Christ's death, the narrator declares: 'Opona chrámová je vedví a končí období Starého zákona.'[32] With Řeka's death, the narrator imagines, the old, judgemental, divided and distorted world and its 'law' is destroyed and a new, balanced, harmonious world will arise, implicitly based on Christ's words to his apostles that distinguish the New Testament from the Old: 'A new commandment I give unto you. That ye love one another; as I have loved you, that ye also love one another.'[33]

In *Pole orná a válečná*, Vančura expands on the central implication of 'Býti dělníkem', which the final chapter of *Pole orná a válečná* resembles in style and tone, that in the very darkest time the very brightest hope might be glimpsed and that the terrible collectivity founded on hate, forced on people by the recent war, contains an inverted intimation of a future, freely formed collective founded on love. This perspective, and the thematicization of the oppressed recovering their voice, links *Pole orná a válečná* to Expressionism. The influence of Expressionism is apparent in the other great Czech prose work about the war, the cycle of short stories *Lítice* (The furies, 1916) by Richard Weiner (1884-1937). In early 1922,

31) Blahynka, *Vančura*, p. 122.
32) 'And the veil of the temple is rent in twain and the age of the Old Testament [literally Law in Czech] comes to an end' (Vančura, *Amazonský proud etc.*, p. 306.)
33) John 13:34.

Götz associated the Literární skupina with Expressionism's 'love of the human being as an absolute and ultimate value'.[34] This claim provoked hostile attacks from Teige, who saw the Brno grouping as a 'product of compromise, uniting bourgeois and passé with more or less revolutionary artists',[35] and Jaroslav Čecháček, who made an implicitly nationalist point, linking Götz with Spengler and the 'empty, sterile, petty-bourgeois', pseudo-revolutionary literature prominent in contemporaneous Germany.[36] These attitudes preface Lukács's late 1930s attacks associating Expressionism with Fascism, which were rejected by Bertold Brecht.

The definitive collection of German Expressionist verse, compiled by Kurt Pinthus in 1919, is entitled *Menschheitsdämmerung*, a consciously ambiguous title that, as Pinthus's translators point out, reflects that the 'destructive and utopian elements of the movement' could not be separated.[37] Pinthus writes: 'These poets sensed early how the human being was sinking into the twilight..., sinking into the night of decline..., in order, however, to emerge again into the brightening dawn of a new day.'[38] Vančura's surprising, radical return to the theme of the war and the Expressionist aesthetic may have been motivated by a desire to remind his contemporaries of this double-faced, quintessentially Avant-garde position. In his study of Expressionism, Walter Sokel argues that the goal of the Expressionist artist is, in contrast to the Marxist, not the material, but the 'inner spiritual regeneration' of the human being.[39] Pinthus writes: 'the best and most passionate of these poets taught not against the external conditions of humanity but against the condition of the mutilated, tormented human being himself.'[40] This spiritual regeneration is for Vančura, as an artist, the unequivocal priority of his work, and is mirrored in what Václavek describes, in a comment cited earlier and inspired above all by the language of *Pole orná a válečná*, as 'the

34) F. Götz, 'O Hosta a o ty, kteří stojí za ním' in Š. Vlašín (ed.), *Avantgarda známá a neznámá*, Vol. 1, Prague, 1970, p. 197.
35) K. Teige, 'O expresionismu' in ibid., p. 203.
36) J. Čecháček, 'Politický expresionismus' in ibid., p. 236.
37) K. Pinthus, *Menschheitsdämmerung: The Dawn of Humanity*, translated by Joanna M. Ratych, Ralph Ley and Robert L. Lonard, New York, 1994, hereafter Pinthus, *Menschheitsdämmerung*, p. 2.
38) Ibid., p. 30.
39) W. H. Sokel, *The Writer in Extremis: Expressionism in Twentieth Century German Literature*, Stanford, 1959, p. 146.
40) Pinthus, *Menschheitsdämmerung*, p. 34.

regeneration of the degenerated language of poetic prose'. Humanity is destroyed and reborn in the Flood of language.

Describing the structure of the novel, Lukeš identifies two apparently opposed methods:

> [There is] a firm, calculated, rational intention that has its own logic and develops causally as in the 'classic novel'. In contrast to this, within the individual chapters, the spontaneity of Vančura's narrator often asserts itself, a causal motivation is lacking, episodes and motifs are arranged and developed freely, polythematically, and we may therefore speak of a free, lyrical compositional connection.[41]

The importance of organization is evident in the complex web of parallels that underpin the structure of the novel and that, as Lukeš argues, undermines descriptions of the novel as a straightforward expression of chaotic disintegration or an 'associative stream of consciousness'.[42] Rather, the appearance of chaos contains intimations of the order to come. The two methods, harmonized in the novel, may be seen to correspond to the combination of grim discipline and intuitive freedom that Marhoul's son, Jan Josef, as a metaphor for the Avant-garde writer, may come to embody. The part-apocalyptic, part-evangelical narrating voice of *Pole orná a válečná* alone in the novel represents the dynamic human wholeness and potency for which it yearns, the promise of the restoration of an epic vision, absorbing the scattered voices and registers of the novel into itself and becoming in effect the unified voice of collective humanity in its torment and its hope of resurrection.

Vančura's exploitation of Expressionist aesthetics in *Pole orná a válečná* merits comparison with the major Slovak Avant-garde novel about the First World War, *Živý bič* (A living scourge) by Milo Urban (1904-1977), which was published two years later in 1927. The proximity between the two novels is explored by Miloš Tomčík, who notes that Urban admitted in a 1931 article reading *Pole orná a válečná* while writing his novel.[43] *Živý bič* describes the impact of the war on the inhabitants of a fictional village, Ráztoky, in the remote Orava region where Urban grew up. The name

41) Lukeš, 'Vančurova Pole *orná a válečná*', p. 79.
42) Ibid.
43) See M. Tomčík, 'Dva romány na jednu tému' in his *Literárne dvojobrazy*, Bratislava, 1976, hereafter Tomčík, 'Dva romány', p. 223.

of the village, meaning 'watershed', reflects the structure of the novel, in which the collective fate of the village is traced and reflected, as in *Pole orná a válečná*, through the individual fates of different characters drawn from that setting. Urban, like Vančura, asserts the collectivity of human existence that is recognized by the reader but not by the characters, but where the fates of Vančura's characters run in alienated parallel, the fates of Urban's are interwoven in the narrative like the scourge of the title. The narrator describes a crowd of villagers burying their children, who have died of dysentery: 'Odnášali ich v drevených truhličkách: budúcnosť svoju niesli, svoje nádeje. Pred nimi hrk, hrk a za nimi zhrbené chrbty, sklonené hlavy, splietajúce sa v ťažký bič ničoty.'[44] Urban's text embodies the notional unity of the Avant-garde perspective perhaps even more than Vančura's, with its obvious allusions to Communism, since the implied authorial position cannot easily be identified with a particular ideological direction. Indeed, the image of the woven whip most obviously recalls the origins of the term Fascism in the metaphor of the Roman *fasces*, or bundle of rods that together cannot be broken.

In *Živý bič*, the motif of the 'living whip' is initially associated with the war and the motherland that has visited the war on its people but comes to be associated with the villagers who eventually lash back against the motherland. At the beginning of the novel, the son of one family in the village, Ondrej Koreň, returns from the front having lost an arm and with a scar that is compared to a wound inflicted with a whip. Somewhat like Řeka, he has also been struck dumb, but his dumbness symbolizes only the initial effect of the war on the villagers, who are unable to respond to the enormity of what has happened. Throughout the novel the use of certain words is compared to the effect of a whip; for example, when the army doctor monotonously repeats the word 'schopný' (fit [for action]) to the newly called-up recruits, or when the repulsively portrayed local notary, Okolický, reminds the village magistrate of his responsibilities to the motherland (*vlasť*): 'Notár Okolický pritlačil to zázračné slovo; richtár pri jeho počutí sa schúlil, zamihal očami ako pes, keď bičom švihnú ponad neho.'[45]

44) 'They took them away in tiny coffins: they were carrying their future, their hopes. Before them rattle rattle and behind them hunched spines and bowed heads, weaving themselves together in a heavy whip of nothingness' (M. Urban, *Živý bič*, Bratislava, hereafter Urban, *Živý bič*, p. 224).

45) 'Okolický emphasized the magic word; on hearing it, the magistrate cowered and blinked his eyes like a dog when a whip is cracked over him' (ibid., p. 83).

In the first part of the novel, Urban suggests that the villagers occasionally imagine, appearing on the horizon, a 'bold, unfettered man, calling for the freedom of hands, for the freedom of the spirit'.[46] Whereas Vančura, throughout his fiction, never moves beyond a much more elliptically expressed version of this vision to its incarnation in the text, in the second part of Urban's novel this man appears in the form of Adam Hlavaj. His first name signals that he is the 'new man' of the future, a deserter from the army, who comes secretly back to the village speaking of revenge for the injustices that have been done. Soon after his return, Urban describes how he inspires one of the less easily cowed villagers, using the motif of the whip in a new way: 'Hlavajove slová pôsobili naň ako bič: vyvolávali zvláštny druh bolesti, ktorá príjemne šteklila a rozčuľovala človeka. Opájali. Zdalo sa, že za každým jeho slovom sú bodky, vyplnené krajšou budúcnosťou, nový svet, do ktorého len on môže voviesť.'[47] Hlavaj gradually awakens the villagers from their passivity to violent, destructive action against state representatives and property: 'Ráztočania, mäkký, poddajný ľud, čo toľké roky dal sa hniesť príkorím, zmenil sa na živý, mocný bič, vystrel sa vo vzduchu, zapraskal a po dlhom váhaní, okolkoch zaťal do živého.'[48]

Urban views their reaction as the shedding of centuries of 'civilization', of education and religion that 'tlmilo pudové prejavy človeka a nútilo ho podrobiť sa vládnúcej moci s odovzdaním sa do vôle Božej'.[49] Urban celebrates the fact that, in revolt, people become once again creatures of instinct; from this act of catharsis will emerge a 'new man', comparable to Vančura's own conception of the complete human being in Jan Marhoul:

človek, ktorý nepotreboval pre svoj život zvláštne účely, ktorý žil len preto, aby žil a žil radostne. Bol to človek, ktorý sa tešil zo slnca i z povíchrice,

46) Ibid., p. 68.
47) 'Hlavaj's words had the effect of a whip on him; they provoked a strange kind of pain which pleasantly tickled and excited a person. They intoxicated. It seemed that behind each word were points filled with a more beautiful future, a new world into which only he could lead you' (ibid., p. 169).
48) 'The people of Ráztoky, soft, submissive folk, who for so many years had let themselves be moulded by injustice, changed into a living, powerful whip, stretched out in the air, cracked and, after long hesitation, cut to the quick' (ibid., p. 283).
49) 'suppressed the human being's instinct and forced him to subjugate himself to the governing power by submitting to the will of God' (ibid., p. 29).

ktorému každý deň bol krásnym ohnivom, ktorý zo všetkého vychodil víťazne: ak bol porazený, nezostával s Jeremiášom v priekope, ale vstával, otriasol sa ako pes a šiel ďalej, lámuc pred sebou prekážky.[50]

This new man emerges from violence, but he is not defined by it; the novel ends not with the terrible violence that it seems to promise, but with Hlavaj's laughter, as for Vančura, the essence of his freedom.

In its account of a collective finding its voice and turning on its erstwhile masters, Urban's novel is more realist in style and more didactic and populist than Vančura's. Tomčík remarks: 'Vančura is more unambiguous in artistic interpretation of reality. He stands above it, ruling over its disintegrating processes like a biblical prophet or judge, or like stern Jehovah'.[51] Where Vančura's narration is marked by shifts of high-flown rhetorical style that distance narrator and reader, Urban's employs satire, sarcasm, slapstick comedy, sentimental and adventure episodes, journalistic passages, and straightforward invective in an effort to engage the reader as far as possible. The contrast in style, however, also reveals the greater uncertainty and scepticism of Vančura's novel. Urban essentially celebrates liberation, the overthrowing of Hungarian dominance, implicitly as the first step towards a better world for the Orava peasants and a better human being. Vančura's novel ends, by contrast, with a macabre image of degeneration, of a dead face waiting for resurrection: 'Poslední voják světové války, vrah, jenž nebyl souzen, naslouchá. Jeho tvář tygrovaná červy a plačící rána hledí vzhůru, čekajíc, kdy bude rozmetáno slavné návrší nad jeho hrobem.'[52] By returning in 1925 to the theme of the war, Vančura seems to assert the failure of the liberation that Urban celebrates, and the failure as yet of those who hoped, in the immediate post-war years,

---

50) 'a human being who did not need special purposes for his life, who lived only to live and to live joyfully. He was a human being who rejoiced at the sunshine and at the blizzard, for whom every day was a beautiful furnace, who emerged from everything victorious. If he was defeated, he did not remain with Jeremiah in the ditch, but got up, shook himself off like a dog and went on, smashing all hurdles before him' (ibid., p. 160).
51) Tomčík, 'Dva romány', p. 236.
52) 'The last soldier of the world war, the murderer who did not stand trial, hearkens. His face, tiger-striped with maggots, and his weeping wounds gaze upwards, waiting for the time when the glorious mound above his grave will be swept away' (Vančura, *Amazonský proud etc.*, p. 306).

that the war would mark the coming of a new, just world to realize their aspirations.

Pole orná a válečná, which Šalda described as the 'mightiest of war novels', seems somewhat under-rated in the context both of Czech literary history and Vančura's own work, not to mention the history of Modernist fiction. Vančura bears some responsibility for this. According to Vančurová, he was disappointed that, after the novel, critics tended to characterize him as a 'poet of destruction and terror'.[53] Píša commented that, in the context of contemporary 'salon sentimentality' and jolly, light lyricism and novel-writing, Vančura appeared as a 'tenacious outsider smelling of blood and manure'.[54] Writing in 1926, Götz, who considered *Pole orná a válečná* 'the first great, strong novel of the young generation of which one can be proud', described him as a 'strangely gloomy poet', marked by 'moral nihilism' and a 'hateful disgust for the world'.[55] In this context, his next work, the short novel, *Rozmarné léto*, pointedly subtitled 'Humoristický román' (A humorous romance), might be seen as a light, lightweight riposte to those critics. At the time of its first publication, *Rozmarné léto* was seen by such critics as Fraenkl as a 'digression and a pause for breath',[56] a transparent in-joke for his Poetist friends and perhaps the residents of Zbraslav, and was not re-published in Vančura's lifetime. Thanks to Menzel's film version, however, *Rozmarné léto* now competes with *Markéta Lazarová* to be Vančura's most widely known and most frequently re-issued novel.

In *Rozmarné léto*, the somnolence of a provincial Bohemian spa town is disturbed by the arrival of Arnoštek, a travelling showman, who has come from Holland via Paris, and his assistant, Anna, of whom the narrator says: 'ta se jmenovala za svobodna Nezválková a její otec, jenž byl veliký hříšník, všechno uměl a skládal krásné básně.'[57] As Vančurová asserts in her memoir, the town is a fictionalized Zbraslav, which lies at the confluence of the Vltava and the Berounka south of Prague, with Vančura drawing on local friends for burgher characters like the spa

---

53) L. Vančurová, *Dvacet šest krásných let*, Prague, 1974, hereafter Vančurová, *Dvacet šest krásných let*, p. 85.
54) Píša, *Dvacátá léta*, p. 147.
55) Götz, *Jasnící se horizont*, p. 219.
56) P. Fraenkl, 'Rozmarné léto', *Rozprávy Aventina* II (1926–27), p. 143.
57) 'Her maiden name was Nezválková and her father, who was a great sinner, could do anything and composed beautiful poems' (V. Vančura, K.Konrád, J. J.Paulík, *Poetistická próza*, Prague, 2002, hereafter Vančura et al., *Poetistická próza*, p. 134).

supervisor Antonín Důra.[58] However, the name of the town, Krokovy Vary, alluding to Krok, a fabled ancestor of all Czechs, indicates that it represents a microcosm of Bohemia. Given the obvious reference to Nezval in relation to Anna, and the Poetists' fascination for clowns, acrobats and street-performers, the arrival of Arnoštek and Anna may therefore be read as a satirical allegory of the mildly, briefly scandalous emergence of the Poetist Avant-garde in Bohemia.

As in *Pole orná a válečná*, Vančura uses an expansive, vigorous narrative style to expose the limited, unfulfilled lives of the characters he describes. For Píša, the humour in the novel derives from an essentially Bergsonian contrast between the 'stasis, immobility and indifferent certainty of the puppet and the pathos of the diction, the vehement gestures and the whole ceremonial ritualism of the fate of the characters'.[59] However, in *Rozmarné léto* the by turns raging, sarcastic, pontificating and lamenting narrative voice of *Pole orná a válečná* is replaced by a more jocular tone that draws attention to the highly stylized narration itself, exposing it as hyperbolic and parodic. The repetition of the narrative technique of *Pole orná a válečná* but in a miniature, self-conscious, banalized form reflects the shift in subject matter from pan-European conflict to provincial Bohemia, but perhaps also a shift in artistic aspiration. One wonders to what extent the work is a deliberate attempt to express the smallness and inconsequentiality of Bohemia and its Avant-garde, and to what extent Vančura has allowed his style to become domesticated by his Bohemian audience.

One might equally argue, however, that the tendencies towards 'judgemental' and 'forgiving' love, rather than combining to produce a force for change, cancel each other out in the novel, replacing the dynamism and militancy of *Pole orná a válečná* with an atmosphere of stasis, nostalgic regret and a questioning of the very possibility of change. Václavek comments that in the novel Vančura 'excludes [...] all ideology, all service to personal and suprapersonal problems and all serious treatment of story and permits only comic merriment to flow [...] We miss the sharp, pugnacious tempo [...] it is put together too masterfully, with too much certainty'.[60] Some critics have seen a corrective function in the humour of *Rozmarné léto*. Kundera argues:

58) The Zbraslav equivalent was called Antonín Šůra. Vančura unflatteringly corrupts his name into a Czech word for 'hussy' or 'shrew'.
59) Píša, *Dvacátá léta*, p. 156.
60) Václavek, *Od umění*, p. 140.

Vančura shows smallness for what it is by treating it as though it were magnificent. He retained its content, reeking of almost total mediocrity, but mystified it with a deadly serious lofty expression [...] Vančura's parody has a double edge: the magnificence of the style unmasks the reality as ridiculously worthless; the ridiculous worthlessness of the reality reveals a style that is inflated.[61]

Kožmín, however, more accurately captures the tone of the novel when noting that the world described is fundamentally 'charming, not degraded'.[62] Vančurová insists that Vančura 'was not trying to write a realistic chronicle, but to write about the attractiveness of the river and Zbraslav and about happy times and male camaraderie'.[63] Hájková sees in the friendship between the three burghers a similar pale intimation of the free collective to come to that contained in the forced collectivity of exploitation and war in 'Býti dělníkem' or *Pole orná a válečná*: 'The human being is illuminated here in the moment of its birth, comical in its smallness, but not deserving total condemnation because of its undeniable capacity for life, and therefore correctable in its worthless present by a potentially more developed future.'[64] However, unlike 'Býti dělníkem' or *Pole orná a válečná*, the novel contains no references to the future to which Hájková alludes; the characters, whether Arnoštek or the burghers, are more a reflection of a humanity in decline, and their defining feature seems to be their total incorrigibility.

The novel seems essentially to be about the elusiveness of poetry, in art as in life, and perhaps particularly in Czech art and life. Blahynka barely develops his attractive suggestion that, while the flawed, child-like Arnoštek represents the poet, the beautiful Anna represents poetry.[65] If so, then Vančura characterizes poetry as a capricious but ultimately harmless *femme fatale*; in the novel Anna is pursued by the three main male burgher characters, but appears at once far too innocent and far too clever for them, seemingly willing to go with each of them in turn yet somehow slipping their clutches. Following the logic of the passage

61) M. Kundera, *Umění románu: Cesta Vladislava Vančury za velkou epikou*, Prague, 1960, p. 64.
62) Z. Kožmín, *Styl Vančurovy prózy*, Brno, 1968, p. 147.
63) Vančurová, *Dvacet šest krásných let*, p. 86.
64) A. Hájková, *Humor v próze Vladislava Vančury*, Prague, p. 1972, p. 23.
65) See Blahynka, *Vančura*, p. 135.

quoted above, Nezval is thus the 'father of poetry', or at least of Poetism's understanding of it. There are frequent allusions to his first major poem, 'Podivuhodný kouzelník' (The remarkable magician, 1922), which Teige considered decisive in shaping Poetism: 'Where the rest were, with more or less fieriness, rhetoricians and apostles of the revolution, Vítězslav Nezval was a poet. He brought his magical fairy tale, full of miracles and miraculous imagination. Thanks to his magician's dazzle, poetry came to life and remembers itself'.[66] Arnoštek, indeed, is part-conjuror, part-acrobat, possibly an allusion to Nezval's poem 'Akrobat' (The acrobat), which was not published until 1927, but which Vančura may have known about and which Nezval dedicated to him.

Arnoštek does not represent Nezval himself, but rather what Poetism has, in Vančura's view, become. The reader is encouraged to share with characters in the novel the suspicion that Arnoštek is a charlatan. Like an Avant-garde artist, Arnoštek wears many masks: 'Podobal se postupně luciperovi, sirce, šaškovi, opici, hasanovi, jablíčku, cvočku, pedelovi, opilci, bláznovi a nakonec, stanuv pěkně při kraji, měl tvářnost kazatele, když křičel, že jsou vzadu lidé, jimž lezou oči z důlků a kteří neplatili.'[67] The implication, however, is that this last face is not feigned, casting doubt on the purity of Arnoštek's motives. Somewhat like Janek the circus-bear in 'Poslední medvěď na Šumavě', Arnoštek and his art have become the captive of the capricious and superficial bourgeois audience, the stuff of insubstantial, meaningless gimmicks and tricks.

Here, as later in *Hrdelní pře*, which shares with *Rozmarné léto* a convivial band of middle-aged bourgeois central characters and a preoccupation with First Republic literary culture, Vančura underlines the contrast between humour as an intuitive world-view, for Vančura implicitly inherent in Nezval's writing, and calculated cheap comedy for temporary popularity and financial reward. The narrator comments:

Někdy bývá čas na nesmysly. Někdy se stává, že důstojné kníže církevní se popadá za břicho a řičí smíchy opakujíc znovu a znovu jakýsi vtip či

66) V. Nezval and K. Teige, *Manifesty Poetismu*, Prague, 1928, p. 15.
67) 'He resembled one by one a devil, a match, a jester, a monkey, a fakir, an apple, a hobnail, a beadle, a drunkard, a fool and finally, having taken up a position close to the edge, he had the expression of a preacher when he shouted that there were people at the back whose eyes were standing out on stalks and who did not pay' (Vančura et al., *Poetistická próza*, p. 156).

říkánku z předměstí. Dobrá. Kdo se směje, nepozbývá proto vážnosti (leda by se smál příliš dlouho), avšak běda těm rukodílným šaškům, kteří robí své potivé šprýmy po tři dny, aby potom mohli nastavit klobouk, noty nebo talířek. Běda Arnoštkovi, jenž setrval v Krokových Varech příliš dlouho![68]

After initial reactions ranging from mild curiosity to mild hostility, Arnoštek's audience tire of him, and towards the end of the novel he is brought down from his tightrope by the persistent tugging of an old man with a stick who thinks he has tempted fate enough. Anna asks the distraught Důrová, the supervisor's wife, who is in love with Arnoštek, to take his place, but she refuses, interpreting the invitation as an admission that he is a fraud: 'Já, pravila paní Důrová, ustávajíc v štkání a povstavši, já, správná měštka dbalá cti, bych měla obléci tyto kalhoty a před tváří nebe a před tváří svého lidu bych měla bráti podíl na šalbě a klamu, neboť ať tak dím, vaše představení je založeno a záleží v ubohých a směšných podvodech.'[69] Anna therefore finishes the show alone, the embodiment of poetry, her performance apparently effortless in its grace, beauty and wit, prompting far greater wonder than Arnoštek's, though she never leaves the grubby carpet of the makeshift stage: 'Když se Anna sdostatek naprocházela, jala se zlehka otáčivými pohyby naznačovati mrtvičné, hulvátské a krkolomné cviky Arnoštkovy. Byla při tom ještě krásnější. Bubnovala si na bubínek, zhusta se uklánĕla, smála se, stříhala očima, měla všechny přítomné za blázny, vodila je za nos a šlo to jako po šňůře.'[70] Poetry, Vančura seems to say, does not need a tight-rope to enchant.

68) 'Sometimes there is a time for silliness. Sometimes it happens that a distinguished prince of the church grasps himself by the belly and whinnies with laughter repeating over and over some joke or saying from the suburbs. Fine. He who laughs does not forfeit seriousness as a result (unless he laughs too long), however woe betide those homemade jesters who do their sweaty tricks for three days so they can then hand round a hat, a sheet of music or a saucer. Woe betide Arnoštek who stayed too long in Krokovy Vary!' (ibid., p. 168).
69) 'I, said Mrs Důrová, desisting from her sobbing and getting to her feet, I, a good burgher of honest virtue, should don these trousers and before heaven and my own folk should take part in a sham and a fraud, for forgive me for saying so, but your performance is founded and depends on wretched and ridiculous deceits' (ibid., p. 175).
70) 'When Anna had promenaded sufficiently, she began with lightly rotating movements to hint at Arnoštek's apoplectic, loutish and breakneck exercises. At this moment she was even more beautiful. She beat her drum, kept bowing, laughing, peeled her eyes, played everyone present for a fool, led them by the nose and carried it off like a dream' (ibid., p. 184).

Anna's offer to Důrová may be seen as Poetism's offer to its public to cease being merely passive consumers of art and become participants, to end the bourgeois notion of art as a profession practised by some for the amusement of others and start seeing every human being as a creative artist in the way he or she lives – or could live – life. Arnoštek stirs in Důrová an unarticulated, all but forgotten desire, but ultimately she lacks the strength or imagination to go beyond or against centuries of embourgeoisement. Důrová, like the she-bear in 'Poslední medvěd na Šumavě', is left only with nostalgic regret: 'Jak je krásné býti kadeřovým.'[71] The novel may thus be interpreted as a criticism of the unreceptiveness of the Poetists' public. Malevich, however, reads the conclusion as a criticism of Poetism, which in its drift away from the hard realities of life actually fails those who continue to endure them. For him, the final lines express a 'sad irony addressed to art which carries the human being into the world of dreams, free fantasy and beauty and then – like an acrobat on a tight-rope – throws him down into actual daily life, condemning its readers to a bitter sobering-up'.[72] Like Důrová, Arnoštek seems to lack courage, allowing the aspirations of the Avant-garde to be compromised and in effect defeated in his art. Vančura's sympathies nevertheless lean slightly towards the Poetist poet. At the end of the novel, Arnoštek strikes the retired major with a cane for seducing Anna, but the major, despite his belligerent words earlier in the novel, does not respond. For this reason, Anna – poetry – chooses to leave with Arnoštek – the poet – who was at least prepared to fight for her.

The conclusion of *Rozmarné léto* may therefore be read as a very un-Avant-garde-like assertion of the unbridgeability of the gap between art and life. As I have described, in Vančura's previous novels, discrepant, contradictory elements exist in a dynamic relationship, embodying the Avant-garde effort to overcome discrepancy in a new reconciliation. *Rozmarné léto*, however, appears to dramatize the failure of this effort; the style lacks substance just as the substance – the world described in the novel – lacks style. This failure might be regarded as the failure of Poetism or its audience but, in the context of a thread in Vančura's writing first made explicit in 'Cesta do světa' and culminating in *Alchymista*, seems fundamentally the failure of contemporary Bohemia, of which Poetism is itself no more than a product.

71) 'How lovely to be curly-haired!' (ibid., p. 189).
72) O. Malevich, *Vladislav Vanchura*, Leningrad, 1973, p. 60.

In her study of the development in Czech literature of this plot type – in which a mysterious stranger with apparent magical powers arrives in a conformist burgher setting – Hodrová associates *Rozmarné léto* with the deromanticization in 1920s fiction of the magician.[73] In contrast to what might be expected, the implied author does not identify with Arnoštek in his conflict with the townspeople, but rather views both from a similar ironic distance, essentially suggesting that they deserve one another. The title of the novel refers ostensibly to the rather poor summer the town is enduring, but its wateriness reflects the wateriness of the notionally idyllic life, the wateriness of what should be the townspeople's best years, the wateriness of Arnoštek's notionally revolutionary art, the wateriness of the 'unadventurous land' of 'Cesta do světa' or the 'feeble Bohemia' of *Pole orná a válečná* that Vančura's Renaissance alchemist will abandon in disgust. At one point Důrová comments: 'Toto léto je málo podivuhodné';[74] later, her husband remarks of Arnoštek's act: 'Tato dovednost [...] je málo podivuhodná.'[75] By placing the reader in the same position as the townspeople, wondering whether Arnoštek is a fraud, Vančura also implicates the reader in this wateriness. Because, however, Vančura's patronizing fondness for his characters displaces any note of contempt for their way of life, the implied reader is neither challenged nor offended, ultimately rendering the effect of the novel, in comparison to Vančura's previous work, itself rather watery.

73) See D. Hodrová, 'Postava tuláka, loupežníka a kouzelníka', *Česká literatura*, 32 (1984), 5, p. 452.
74) 'This summer is pretty unremarkable' (Vančura et al., *Poetistická próza*, p. 122.)
75) 'That skill of yours [...] is pretty unremarkable' (ibid., p. 137).

MARKÉTA LAZAROVÁ AND ALCHYMISTA: THE RENAISSANCE CZECH

Rozmarné léto signals a decisive intensification of focus in Vančura's writing on the insipidness of the contemporary Czech character, as incarnated in the petty bourgeois morality and culture favoured by the First Republic establishment. Perhaps reflecting a desire to address his audience more directly, after *Rozmarné léto* Vančura turned to drama. Blahynka describes the resulting plays *Učitel a žák* and *Nemocná dívka*, together with the later *Alchymista*, as a trilogy 'about the Czech national character and its poetry',[1] and this preoccupation continues when he returns to fiction, implicitly in *Poslední soud* and explicitly in *Hrdelní pře*. Vančura's view of Czechness is typical of successive 'generations' of Czech creative artist since at least the 1890s. In his essay on the *fin-de-siècle* in Austria-Hungary, Robert Pynsent comments: 'The Decadents and other young groups were generally critical patriots. The trouble was that criticism grew and grew until there was not much left about the Czechs for those young artists to be patriotic about.'[2] The post-1918 Avant-garde differ only in their apparent faith in the possibility of a recovery.

In works like *Rozmarné léto* and *Alchymista*, Vančura seems pessimistically to question whether the Czech character is capable of embracing the expansive, voracious, intuitive approach to life he advocates. More commonly, however, he presents the current state of Czechness as a temporary deformation caused by centuries of adaptation to western merchant capitalism and burgher mores, suggesting that Czechs retain within themselves the potential for a different way of being that, like Janek the bear, they have merely forgotten. Vančura expresses this view above all through his use of the Czech language. Seemingly indifferent to the prevailing norms and expectations that place implicitly artificial restrictions on the 'life' of the language, Czech from the mouths of his

1) M. Blahynka, *Vladislav Vančura*, Prague, 1978, hereafter Blahynka, *Vančura*, p. 145.
2) R. B. Pynsent, 'Conclusory Essay: Decadence, Decay and Innovation' in R. B. Pynsent (ed.), *Decadence and Innovation*, London, 1989, p. 152.

narrators not only symbolizes a life lived fully, intuitively, voraciously, but also indicates the innate potential of the Czech to shed the prevailing conventions circumscribing his existence and live that life. In *Markéta Lazarová*, he also asserts this potential by confronting the present-day Czechs with their wilder past selves.

Markéta Lazarová, Vančura's sixth novel, marked his belated commercial breakthrough. In a 1998 poll in the Czech weekly *Týden*, asking leading contemporary Czech literary scholars and critics to nominate the most significant Czech novels of the twentieth century, *Markéta Lazarová* came third and was Vančura's highest placed work.[3] This choice might suggest that, for 'specialists', *Markéta Lazarová* represents an acceptable compromise between Vančura's radical treatment of language and narrative in, say, *Pekař Jan Marhoul* or *Pole orná a válečná*, and his more lightweight, popular works like *Rozmarné léto* and *Konec starých časů*, a quintessential expression of his themes and concerns. The novel, after all, bridges the period between the enduring linguistic and narratorial challenges of *Poslední soud* and *Hrdelní pře* and the reader-friendly *Útěk do Budína*. However, the novel, which receives greater attention than any other Vančura novel from both Holý in his monograph and Hodrová in her study of twentieth century literature, undoubtedly attracts the late twentieth-century interpreter because of Vančura's 'game-playing'. His metafictional narrative approach and the blurring of high and popular literary styles, as much as it looks back to Cervantes, Rabelais, Sterne and Gogol, all favourites of the Formalists and their successors, also looks forward to techniques often described as postmodern.

Set at an unspecified time in medieval Bohemia, the novel describes the conflict between a robber tribe led by Kozlík, the king's troops and another robber tribe, led by Lazar. In the savage dispute that follows Lazar's rejection of a request for help against the king made by Kozlík's son Mikoláš, Lazar's fort is burnt down, Lazar is stabbed and his daughter, Markéta Lazarová, who had been destined to become a nun, is taken captive. Mikoláš forces himself on her, awakening in her, first, terrible shame and self-disgust, but then gradually love. In a parallel story, a young German nobleman, Kristián, is captured by Kozlík, who

---

3) In the poll, *Osudy dobrého vojáka Švejka za světové války* (The fortunes of the good soldier Švejk in the world war) by Jaroslav Hašek (1883–1923) came first and *Příliš hlučná samota* (Too loud a solitude) by Bohumil Hrabal (1914–97) second. Vančura had the greatest number of nominated works.

is seeking for information about the whereabouts of the king's men. Pale-skinned and effete, Kristián speaks no Czech, but attracts the attention of Kozlík's wildest daughter, Alexandra. The novel follows Kozlík's doomed resistance to the king's army and the equally doomed fates of the two pairs of lovers.

As Vančura indicates in the dedication to his cousin, Jiří Mahen, the novel draws on the family chronicle of the Vančuras of Řehnice, but it cannot be described as a conventional historical novel in that it does not seek either to educate by striving for factual accuracy or to express 'a profound awareness of man's largest historical situation and destiny'.[4] Hodrová writes: 'its heroes are not "God's fighters", knights or rulers, but people standing in the margin of great history, de facto outside society [...] It is not matters of historical significance that stand at the centre of the action, but purely personal matters of love.'[5] Similarly, in Holý's view, among Czech historical fiction writers Vančura belongs to the tradition not of Alois Jirásek (1851–1930) and his 'magnificent landscape of a classified and spacious History' but of Zikmund Winter (1846–1912) and his 'anti-heroes', arguing: 'Winter's and Vančura's heroes [...] do not live in an ideal History, they do not move in an abstract "world process". They are woven into their everyday world, into battle, work, love, suffering, terror, joy and dreaming.'[6] This feature might suggest that Vančura would concur with Lukács, who, in his 1937 study of the historical novel, asserts that 'the "cult of facts" is a miserable surrogate for [...] intimacy with the people's historical life'.[7] Vančura's preoccupation with marginal figures might even be seen as a manifestation of what Lukács calls 'partisanship with the active man', that is to say, with those whose destiny is 'inwardly connected with the great typical questions of popular life'. These, however, do not seem to be Vančura's priorities in the work.

In *Markéta Lazarová*, Vančura sets the factual and didactic against the creative and playful, in effect paradoxically seeking to teach the reader this perspective in literature and in life. Writing on the rise of the histori-

4) J. Maynard, 'Broad Canvas, Narrow Perspective', quoted in H. Orel, *The Historical Novel from Scott to Sabatini*, Basingstoke, London, 1995, hereafter Orel, p. 4.

5) D. Hodrová, 'Markéta Lazarová' in M. Zeman et al. (eds), *Rozumět literatuře* I, Prague, 1986, pp. 272–73.

6) J. Holý, *Práce a básnivost: Estetický projekt světa Vladislav Vančury*, Prague, 1990, hereafter Holý, *Práce a básnivost*, pp. 125–27.

7) G. Lukács, *The Historical Novel*, translated by Hannah and Stanley Mitchell, New York, 1962, p. 253.

cal romance in late Victorian British literature, Harold Orel notes the shift in emphasis in historical fiction towards escapism, to entertainment that is not necessarily restricted to the reader. Orel writes: 'I would like to stress the element of play, and of good-natured fun, in these historical novels: fun in the plotting for its own sake rather than as a subsidiary aspect of dialogue or character development.'[8] Píša describes the novel as a 'game of the imagination',[9] while Ladislav Štoll wrote of the poet's determination to 'create for himself his own world and his own people according to the law of his artistic, omnipotent will'.[10] Hodrová writes: 'Although we are dealing here with action that is to a certain extent historical [...] this action seems to be created as it were in the process of narration, in the act of speaking before the eyes of the reader.'[11] Vančura seeks to draw the reader's attention away from a pedantic preoccupation with factual accuracy – the problem of Skočdopole and his friends in *Hrdelní pře* – towards intuitive, artistic accuracy. This effort is epitomized by the lines that replace clear specification of the date – 'Popřejte této příhodě místa v kraji mladoboleslavském, za časů nepokojů, kdy král usiloval o bezpečnost silnic'[12] – which, like many other passages in the narration, explicitly engage the reader in the creative process of imagining.

The importance of play in *Markéta Lazarová* is made clear in the dedication. Vančura tells a story he has ostensibly heard from his aunts, describing how the older Mahen, rather like the tailor, Teige, catching birds in 'Čižba' and like Kozlík in *Markéta Lazarová*, used to spend all night fishing, only to throw back anything he caught, 'laughing like one whose whiskers are smeared with honey'. Vančura continues:

Neviděl jsem rovněž smyslu v těchto zoologických zálibách, ale hra mi bývala srozumitelná. Tím lépe. Strop těchto dní je očazen a přichází podzim. Je ovšem zevrubná noc, a na okna mé světnice bubnuje větvoví lesa. Je mi útěchou mysliti na tvoje kousky a rád bych znal veselé dareb-

8) Ibid., p. 3.
9) A. M. Píša, *Třicátá léta*, Prague, 1971, hereafter Píša, *Třicátá léta*, p. 51.
10) L. Štoll, 'Poslední kniha Vladislava Vančury', *Tvorba*, 6 (1931), 43, p. 687.
11) D. Hodrová, *...na okraji chaosu...*, Prague, 2001, hereafter Hodrová, *...na okraji chaosu...*, p. 584.
12) 'Grant this tale a setting in the Mladá Boleslav region during a time of unrest, when the king was striving to make the roads safe' (V. Vančura, *Markéta Lazarová*, Prague, 2004, hereafter Vančura, *Markéta Lazarová*, p. 9).

nosti, jež mi zůstaly utajeny. Žel, můj otec, který by o nich mohl mnohé vypravovati, zemřel. Můj otec, jemuž se tak příliš podobáš! Je mi drahé mluviti právě s tebou, a protože z věcí, jež se tě dotýkají, znám méně, než bych si přál a než mne dostačuje, dovol mi, abych začal o loupežnících, s nimiž máme společné jméno.[13]

Given this slightly melancholy image of the lonely writer on an autumn night, the novel might be described as an example of authorial escapism, an attempt to commune with the spirit of 'merry mischief', the trace that remains of his robber-ancestors in his cousin and in his father and perhaps in him. This spirit seems somehow encapsulated in the motif, seen in 'Cesta do světa' and elliptically in Ramus in *Poslední soud*, of the branch knocking on the window, the world not merely reminding the writer that he is not alone, but calling on him to come out and play.

In this context, *Markéta Lazarová* may be seen as a game, like Mahen's fishing, played for the amusement of the author, which may leave the reader amused or bemused, depending on the extent to which he shares the implied author's perspective. The game is therefore not as innocent as it appears, since it expresses and seeks to awaken in the audience what is implicitly a superior attitude to life, 'humour as a point of view', embodied by the exuberant, provocative narrator, who seems able both to understand the world describe from inside and to rise above it, to sympathize and criticize, mock and mourn. One can sense what Orel terms the 'fun' the author is having in descriptions like that of Mikoláš's vengeful return to Lazar's tribe: 'Pohružuje svůj meč do břicha tu po jílec, tu, kam až zachází naraziv na páteř, rozrušuje kosti a otvírá útroby, stíná.'[14] As Hodrová notes, 'the battle between the royal troops and

13) '[Like my aunts] I could not see the sense in these zoological predilections, but the game used to make sense to me. All the better. The ceiling of those days is black with smoke and autumn is coming. It is, however, a thoroughgoing night, and the branches of the forest are drumming on the window of my room. It is a comfort to me to think of your tricks and I would love to know the merry acts of mischief that have remained a secret from me. Alas, my father, who could have told me much about them, is dead. My father, whom you too much resemble! It means so much to me to talk to you and because I know less of the things that concern you than I would wish and than is enough for me, allow me to begin talking about the robbers with whom we share a common name' (Vančura, *Markéta Lazarová*, p. 8).
14) 'He buries his sword into a stomach here up to the hilt, there until it disappears, having struck against the spine, he jumbles bones and opens bowels, he cuts off heads' (ibid., p. 30).

the robbers is first portrayed from the perspective of the troops, then from the perspective of the robbers'.[15] This also allows him also to describe twice the beheading in battle of Kozlík's eight-year-old daughter, Drahomíř, of which the reader is also forewarned at the beginning of the novel. Hodrová argues that this narratorial self-indulgence disrupts the narrative momentum. However, it may also be seen as a reflection of the reader's self-indulgence, the pleasure of re-reading passages that excite or move. In this way Vančura not only expresses what Blahynka terms his – and indeed the Avant-garde's – 'fascination with kitsch and trash literature',[16] but challenges himself to replicate its effects.

At the same time, however, Vančura evidently enjoys the challenge of imagining convincingly in words the medieval bandits' experience of life, a notion which might equally be applied to his earlier attempts to depict, for example, the lives of Ruthenians or Austro-Hungarian soldiers on the eastern front. None of these portrayals draws on personal experience, but on the accounts of others and the activity of the author's imagination. For Holý, the contribution of *Markéta Lazarová*, together with Durych's Wallenstein trilogies, *Bloudění* (Wandering, 1929) and *Rekviem* (Requiem, 1930), to the development of Czech historical fiction lies precisely in the effort to evoke the atmosphere of the period depicted, as it were, 'for its own sake'. In this context, Vančura's approach more recalls that described by Herbert Butterfield, who writes in 1924:

If a writer wishes to 'work up' a period in order to set a story in it, he will feel history a fetter and every unexpected fact may hamper the story he intended to tell. But if he has steeped his mind in some past age, and has lived in that age, turning it over and over in his imagination, realizing the conditions of affairs and the relationships of men and pondering over the implication of these and so recasting the life of the age for himself, then that particular age and those particular conditions will suggest their own story, and the historical peculiarities of that age will give point to his novel and will become a power.[17]

Markéta Lazarová constitutes a literal injection of blood into bloodless First Republic society and culture, echoing, for example, Jiří Půlpytel's

15) Hodrová, *...na okraji chaosu...*, p. 401.
16) Blahynka, *Vančura*, p. 174.
17) H. Butterfield, *The Historical Novel: An Essay*, Cambridge, 1924, p. 36.

yearning with blood in *Hrdelní pře*.[18] Půlpytel's dispute with Vyplampán, the mercilessly caricatured representative of First Republic establishment sensibilities, is transposed in *Markéta Lazarová* into the narrator's taunting of the implied reader. From his opening address, the narrator establishes that the 'worthless, broken nature of the narrator's contemporaries' will compare unfavourably with the 'bravery of [the robbers'] deeds and the fullness of their passions':[19]

> Stali jste se ze samého uvažování o ušlechtilosti a spanilém mravu našeho národa opravdu přecitlivělí, a když pijete, rozléváte ke škodě kuchařčině vodu po stole, ale chlapi, o nichž počínám mluviti, byli zbujní a čertovští. Byla to chasa, již nedovedu přirovnati než k hřebcům. Pramálo se starali o to, co vy považujete za důležité. Kdežpak hřeben a mýdlo! Vždyť nedbali ani na boží přikázání.[20]

The narrator's 'roughing up' of the reader playfully mimics the experience of Markéta and Kristián, torn suddenly from their 'civilized' way of living by the 'barbarism' of Kozlík's tribe. Kristián is a product of his pampered German aristocratic upbringing and education, his name and his white hands cause hilarity among the robber daughters and his efforts to express his high-flown views about the unjust treatment of Markéta meet with incomprehension: 'Kdo mu však měl odpověděti, Mikoláš? Nikdy mu nepřišlo na mysl, aby užíval jazyka jinak než k rozkazům. Mlčel, jen ať si Kristián žvastá.'[21] Unlike Kristián, Markéta

---

18) In *Učitel a žák*, the bourgeois student Jan expresses disappointment early on that his father died of blood poisoning after pricking his finger on a spindle, arguing that he should have cut off his hand and bled to death.

19) Holý, *Práce a básnivost*, p. 100.

20) 'By the very fact of contemplating the nobility and fair ways of our nation you have become truly over-sensitive, and when you drink, to the cost of the cook you spill water over the table, but the men of whom I am starting to speak were wanton and devilish. This was a band that could only be compared to stallions. They cared very little about the things you consider important. Certainly not a comb and soap! After all they did not even pay heed to God's commandments' (Vančura, *Markéta Lazarová*, p. 9).

21) 'Who did he think was going to answer him? Mikoláš? It had never occurred to him to use his language for anything other than giving orders. He remained silent. Let Kristián babble on if he wants to' (ibid., p. 38). At this point, Kozlík has had Mikoláš and Alexandra chained to Kristián and Markéta for opposing his will. Vančura comically demonstrates how Kristián and Markéta's refined manners distance them from natural behaviour to their own cost in the narrator's description of the suffering they inflict on themselves through their refusal, unlike Mikoláš, to relieve themselves in front of the others.

comes from robber stock, but her experience of life is mediated through religious faith, which is presented in the novel as a cold, fictional dogma that prevents human beings from embracing life. As Götz points out, Mikoláš's deflowering of her exposes her to the warmth of life, making her suddenly and shockingly aware of herself as a living, physical being: 'Jeho ruce jsou palčivé, pod jeho polibky tryská krev, dech pekelníkův žhne a mámí jako pára.'[22] Distraught and suicidal, she nevertheless now shares a 'little robber wildness', and gradually a struggle develops within her between her powerful fear of God and her growing love for Mikoláš.

As the novel progresses, the hypocrisy inherent in so-called 'civilized' ways of life is revealed. Kristián is captured by the robbers while fleeing from the servants of a bishop who hope to take him hostage in order to force Kristián's father to give the money he apparently promised for the building of a monastery, and the whole world from which they and the king's troops come is shown to have been corrupted by money. When Markéta seeks succour from the priory, she is met with the austere pre-scription that she can but seek forgiveness from God. When she fails to renounce her physical love, she is locked in a room without windows. Throughout, the prioress is shown, however, to be suppressing a natural desire to show pity and compassion, and eventually – after praying – she releases Markéta into the world to find out what God's will is for her. By contrast, Kozlík's 'barbaric' tribe, who prefigure the description of the prehistoric Czechs in the first chapter of *Obrazy z dějin* as 'a wild and fecund people',[23] are untainted by hypocrisy or corrupt motives. They act intuitively, with humour, courage, honour and a fierce sense of loyalty and solidarity. Mikoláš is executed alongside his father after a valiant but failed attempt to rescue him from imprisonment. As we also see in the depiction of Kozlík's wife, Kateřina, they love and grieve deeply, accepting what life brings and never turning away from it.

Of the aspects of human existence that interfere with this approach to life, the narrator saves his greatest scorn in the novel for religious faith:

---

22) 'His hands are burning, blood gushes beneath his kisses, the demon's breath scorches and intoxicates like steam' (ibid., p. 34). See Götz, F., *Básnický dnešek*, Prague, 1931, hereafter Götz, *Básnický dnešek*, p. 300.
23) V. Vančura, *Obrazy z dějin národa českého*, Vol. 1, Prague, 1956, p. 10.

Ach, pomatenci! Jakou hrůzou jste zalidnili čas, jakou hrůzu jste vmetli do podvědomí maličkých dítek. Jaké běsnění pochyb! Věčně se budete tázati, proč je kohoutí oko okrouhlé? Proč má chlupáč u vašich nohou vlastnosti psa? Věčně budete obzírati kolébku a hrob? Věčně budete mluviti o tajemství, zanedbávajíce věcí života? Mluvte cokoliv. Nebe je prázdné! Prázdné a prázdné![24]

This passage contains repeated allusions to the major Czech Romantic poem, *Máj* (Spring, 1836) by Karel Hynek Mácha (1810–36), which, in the common interpretation asserted by Vančura here, rejects Christian notions of eternity, describing the after-life as a terrible nothingness. As Holý notes, Markéta's name appears to be an allusion to Goethe's Gretchen in *Faust Part 1*.[25] Gretchen is similarly plunged into torment after betraying her previously virtuous life when she is seduced by Faust, with Mephistopheles' help. Where Markéta fails, Gretchen succeeds in committing suicide, but it is made clear that she is taken up to heaven. In the passage preceding that just quoted, Vančura implicitly also links Markéta to Mácha's Jarmila: 'Nekonečno je prázdné. Nekonečno, ten blázinec bohů, na jehož okrajcích bloudí hvězdička.'[26] The events of *Máj* occur following the deflowering of Jarmila by the father of her sweetheart, who, not recognizing the man who cast him out when he was a child, has murdered him and now awaits execution. The reader is led to believe that, on learning of this, Jarmila throws herself into a lake, a fate suggested by the recurring motif of the falling star, with which Jarmila is associated: 'Klesla hvězda s nebes výše, / mrtvá hvězda, siný svit; / padá v neskončené říše, / padá věčně v věčný byt.'[27] By contrast, Markéta faces neither redemption nor its absence in the next world, but,

24) 'Oh you madmen! What a horror you have filled time with! What a horror you have swept into the subconscious of little children! What a fury of doubts! Will you eternally be asking why the cockerel's eye is round? Why the hairy thing at your feet has the characteristics of a dog? Will you eternally scan the cradle and the grave? Will you eternally speak about mystery, ignoring the things of life? Speak what you like. Heaven is empty! As empty as empty can be!' (ibid., pp. 106–07).
25) See Holý, *Práce a básnivost*, p. 134. In versions preceding the first book publication of the novel, and on the cover of the first edition, she was called Margareta (see Blahynka, *Vančura*, p. 172).
26) 'Infinity is empty. Infinity, that asylum of the gods, at whose edges wanders a little star' (Vančura, *Markéta Lazarová*, p. 106).
27) 'A star fell from the heavens' heights, / a dead star, a livid light; / it falls into infinite realms, / it falls eternally into eternal being' (K. H. Mácha, *Básně*, Prague, 1997, p. 18).

like her namesake Lazarus of Bethany, she is resurrected in this life.[28] This is not, however, a resurrection into a glorious new life, but merely the shedding of previous illusions, a refusal to shelter anymore from life. At the end of the novel, with Alexandra having committed suicide after killing Kristián in a fit of rage, she faces bringing up both her and Alexandra's sons in Kozlík's tribe.

Markéta Lazarová might be described as Vančura's most 'eugenic' novel, even given the apparent extinction of a degenerate humanity in *Pole orná a válečná*. As we have seen in accounts of the portrayal of the robbers or the prioress, to which we might add the depictions of Kristián and his loving father, the characterization in the novel is surprisingly nuanced, reflecting Vančura's implicit belief in an essential humanity that has merely become weakened or suppressed in human beings over time and may only be witnessed in pale imitations. Nevertheless, these pale imitations, like Kristián, are shown to be destined to die out. Despite the rejection of religion in the novel, the strength of Markéta's devotion marks her out for survival. By contrast, Kristián's over-breeding has emasculated him, depriving him of any strength of character or depth of feeling. The narrator comments of him: 'Není mi nejasno, že Bůh zmátl mysl tohoto Kristiána a proměnil ji právě tak, jako hospodář proměňuje kohoutky na kapouny. Kristián jakživ nevěděl, co má udělat. Hned si přál to, hned ono.'[29] At a key moment Kristián chooses to remain with his father, lacking the courage to follow his heart, and the less predictable path of life with Alexandra, and she kills him, enraged by his betrayal.

This 'eugenic' approach finds a metaphor in what Hodrová identifies as 'the peculiar way in which the epic is confronted by the novel' in the work, particularly at the level of character.[30] In her study of twentieth-century literature, Hodrová argues that there is a move in twentieth-century fiction away from what she terms the 'character-definition' towards the 'character-hypothesis'. Defining the latter, she writes:

28) Vančura makes ironic use of the name 'Lazarus', which means 'he whom God has helped' in Hebrew.
29) 'It is not unclear to me that God confused the mind of this Kristián fellow and transformed it just as a farmer transforms cockerels into capons. For as long as he lived Kristián did not know what he ought to do. One moment he wants this, the next moment he wants that' (ibid., p. 81).
30) Hodrová, ...*na okraji chaosu*..., p. 583.

the character-hypothesis is a character viewed not as a totality, a whole complete at the moment of creation and as it were merely transferred to the work, but as a silhouette, a torso, which appears in this indeterminate and fragmentary form in the work and which the author tries (though often there is also an element of pretence here) to reconstruct in the text.[31]

Writing of *Markéta Lazarová*, she argues:

In this novel, the concept of the character-hypothesis, a character created as though before the reader's eyes, comes into conflict in its own way and without doubt intentionally with the desire to create epic heroes, living a full-blooded life of great deeds and grand emotions, in the past generally conceived as a character-definition. In other words, Vančura tries to create striking epic heroes using methods common to self-reflexive fiction, above all through the hypothesizing of character. That is to say – and this is actually quite peculiar – the act of creating full-blooded epic heroes is made public.

To illustrate that this conflict is intentional, Hodrová points out that, of each pair of lovers, one – Mikoláš, Alexandra – is a 'character-definition' derived from epic, while the other – Markéta Lazarová, Kristián – is a 'character-hypothesis' drawn from the modern novel.

In Hodrová's account this conflict emerges simply as a theoretical experiment conducted by the author perhaps as part of his 'game-playing' in the novel. However, in the very last lines of the work, the narrator says, reflecting on the prospects for the lovers' offspring: 'Vyrostli z nich chlapáčtí chlapi, ale, žel, o jejich duši se sváří láska s ukrutností a jistota s pochybnostmi. Ó, krvi Kristiánova a Markétina!' [32] Most strongly of all Vančura's novels, *Markéta Lazarová* expresses a yearning to recover the strength and certainty of the epic. Its assault on contemporary readers' tastes and on the tormented, uncertain Kristián and Markéta constitutes an attack on the modern novel, a rejection of its over-complication, its psychologizing, its emphasis on passivity, contemplation, hesitation and inaction that, in Vančura's view, breed weakness and prevent the

31) Ibid., p. 559.
32) 'They grew up to be the manliest of men, but, alas, love battles with cruelty and certainty with doubts for their soul. Oh, blood of Kristián and Markéta!' (Vančura, *Markéta Lazarová*, p. 132).

human being from realizing himself to the full. In this context perhaps the key line in the novel is the narrator's rhetorical question: 'Nepůsobí tato povídka jako mlat v porovnání s rozkošnou složitostí současné literatury?' [33]

Both Götz and Píša saw in *Markéta Lazarová* a positive development in the relationship between the narrative style and its content. Götz argued that where previously the narrator in Vančura's writing had artificially provided the impetus for the plot, here at last he had 'unleashed in a glorious wave the collective fate of a whole family line in a most dangerous time'.[34] Píša wrote that 'in *Markéta Lazarová* Vančura has found an environment that is absolutely congruent with his imagination and mode of expression'.[35] As noted earlier, in, say, *Pole orná a válečná* or *Rozmarné léto*, the full-blooded narration contrasts with the half-hearted lives it describes, exposing the unsuitability of the epic imagination to the unepic times. In *Markéta Lazarová*, this discrepancy lies not between the narration and the characters, but between the heroes and the reader. This change, however, has the effect of undermining the narrator by drawing attention to his relationship to both character and reader, exposing the 'pretence' of his epic narration. The narrator of *Markéta Lazarová* appears at times to be an eye-witness of the events described, at others a contemporary of his readers. This shifting perhaps reflects his yearning to return to these times. Like Spera in the subsequent *Konec starých časů*, however, he cannot be more than an imitator, aspiring to be like the characters he admires in the style and spirit of his narration, which itself can never be more than a parody.

In *Markéta Lazarová* Vančura in fact diminishes the work of the writer and suggests that there are limits to what language can describe, beyond which lies love. Predicting the readers' reaction to Kozlík's witch-like daughters, the narrator comments: 'Kéž vás příliš nepohorší tato šklebící se krása, snad právě jim bude dáno, aby uzřely boží tvář, a my písaříč-kové možná zahyneme.'[36] Later, describing Kristián and Alexandra, in

---

33) 'Does this story not act like a threshing-floor in comparison with the delicious complexity of contemporary literature?' (ibid., p. 58).
34) See Götz, *Básnický dnešek*, p. 298.
35) Píša, *Třicátá léta*, p. 50.
36) 'Would that this grimacing beauty did not unduly scandalize you. Perhaps to them will be granted a glimpse of the face of God, and we scribblers may perish' (Vančura, *Markéta Lazarová*, p. 21).

a manner entirely consistent with Vančura's advocacy of intuition and his rejection of intellectualization here and elsewhere, the narrator declares: 'Jaká prohra, ó géniové řeči! Ti dva milenci nerozmlouvávali, neboť jeden neuznal mateřštiny druhého, byli němí, a držíce se v loktech, mluvívali jen vzdycháním a polibky a stiskem těla. Jak nevýmluvný je jazyk, jak nevýmluvné je básnictví lásky.'[37] In the introduction to his next novel, *Útěk do Budína*, he draws attention to the unflattering parallels between lovers and writers, who also have lips, but tell stories because they have no one to kiss with them.[38]

In *Markéta Lazarová*, Vančura does not restore the potency of the epic but, with ironically self-deprecating sentiments like these, hopes to recover the spirit of Cervantes, Gogol and those other pioneers of the modern novel whose work appears to feel more keenly than contemporary literature the absence of the epic and more strongly foregrounds, in Lukács's terms, the attempt to restore the epic that must fail until the world itself has been regenerated. Ostensibly describing Mikoláš's attempt to free his father from the king's prison, the narrator refers to the 'nádherné šílenství neúčelného a marného boje'.[39] With this quixotic remark, Vančura once again restates the thankless burden of the Avant-garde writer, condemned to live in transitional times, born too late or too early to have his aspirations realized. By using legends about his family, Vančura lends this predicament a personal dimension, implicitly reflecting in the story that, though he retains something of his ancestors' rebellious spirit, it is confined to the relative feebleness of literary satire.

This sense of failure of expressed more bleakly in Vančura's next historical work, the play *Alchymista*, set in the time of Rudolf II, in which the Italian-born central character, an alchemist and astronomer, Alessandro de Morone, ponders whether to remain in Bohemia.[40] At the end, hav-

---

37) 'What a defeat, oh geniuses of speech! Thee two lovers did not converse, for neither knew the mother tongue of the other, they were dumb, and holding each other at the elbow, they would speak only in sighs and kisses and by pressing their bodies against one another. How ineloquent is language, how ineloquent is the poetry of love!' (ibid., p. 86).

38) See Vančura, V., *Útěk do Budína*, Prague, 1949, p. 8.

39) 'the glorious madness of the pointless battle fought in vain' (Vančura, *Markéta Lazarová*, p. 118).

40) According to Blahynka the play was apparently inspired by a request from Götz, then director of the National Theatre, for an adaptation of Ben Jonson's Jacobean drama of the same name, but ultimately bears no relationship to it (see Blahynka, *Vančura*, p. 187).

ing decided to leave, he declares in terms reminiscent of the narrator of *Markéta Lazarová*: 'Stýská se mi v těch chmurných Čechách, v té zemi bez vzletu a bez lásky, mezi lidmi, již věčně uvažují, kteří se trápí a vedou pro slovíčko války [...] Jste chladní a přísní a žádná vášeň se vás nedotkla, mimo jediné a právě nejzhoubnější, mimo vášeň rozumu. Mě pobláznuje život, vás úvaha.'[41] Critics have tended to see Alessandro as the embodiment of the Renaissance man. Following the play's first performance, Píša noted the recurring theme of the 'conflict of the Renaissance man with the Czech national character' in early Czech twentieth-century drama, citing particularly *Posel* (The messenger, 1907, revised 1922) by Viktor Dyk (1877–1931), *Král Václav IV* (King Wenceslas IV, 1910) by Arnošt Dvořák (1881–1933) and *Nad městem* (Above the town, 1917) by Miloš Marten (1883–1917).[42] Dostál interprets the play as an expression of the 'end of the Avant-garde's dream of the Renaissance man',[43] Alessandro's departure symbolizing the failure of the Avant-garde to realize their aspirations for a new human being, implicitly because such a human being could not prosper in Bohemia. At the same time, however, through Alessandro Vančura also seems to explore the situation of the artist who nurtures these aspirations.

In his politically compromised afterword to the volume of Vančura's collected plays, Mukařovský discourages the reader from identifying Alessandro too closely with the author, unwilling to associate Vančura with such a harsh judgement of Bohemia. Mukařovský compares Alessandro with Megalrogov, the central character in *Konec starých časů*, who appears on a 1920s Bohemian estate claiming to be a White Russian aristocrat fleeing from Bolshevik Russia. For Mukařovský, both are immoral, cynical characters, who nevertheless differ through their greater freedom from the 'brooders and moralists who at the same time thirst greedily for power and are obsessed with eroticism'.[44] Kundera, who highly praises the novel, sees it, in effect like *Alchymista*, as a confrontation

---

41) 'I am homesick in this dreary Bohemia, in this land without flights of fancy and without love, among people who endlessly brood and worry over things and wage wars over a single little word [...] You are cold and severe and no passion has touched you apart from one, the one that is most malign, the passion for reason. My madness comes from life, yours from thought' (V. Vančura, *Hry*, Prague, 1959, hereafter Vančura, *Hry*, p. 209).
42) A. M. Píša, *Stopami dramatu a divadla*, Prague, 1967, p. 203. For a discussion of these works in relation to *Alchymista*, see Blahynka, *Vančura*, pp. 193–96.
43) V. Dostál, *Slovo a čin*, Ostrava, 1972, hereafter Dostál, *Slovo a čin*, p. 77.
44) J. Mukařovský, 'O Vančurovi-dramatiku' in Vančura, *Hry*, p. 390.

of the Renaissance humanist ideal with the shabby contemporary world, epitomized by the relationship between the characters of Megalrogov and the rather squalid librarian-narrator Spera, whom Mukařovský sees as a caricature of Megalrogov's characteristics.[45] Lopatka writes that Spera is 'the shadow of the hero; with a certain delay, with less colour and intensity, with less luck and with a lack of generosity he imitates the hero'.[46] Perhaps, given that Spera is often the mouthpiece of the implied author in the novel, Vančura also sought to acknowledge through this relationship his own subordinate, even parasitic relationship to the writers of the early modern period implicit in *Markéta Lazarová*.

Kundera's interpretation, however, would imply that the Renaissance ideal might itself be a sham. Píša notes the parallels between *Konec starých časů* and Gogol, whom Vančura admired and whose narration, like Vančura's, in its vivacious freedom expresses the life lacked by contemporary humanity, as depicted in his writing.[47] Like Khlestakov in *The Government Inspector* and Chichikov in *Dead Souls*, Megalrogov's function is to expose the empty charade of the world in which he finds himself, where the First Republic *nouveaux riches* play at being nobility, a function he fulfils most effectively because his own existence might also be an empty charade, only better performed. Like the travelling showman Arnoštek in *Rozmarné léto*, discussed below, Megalrogov mirrors his surroundings. By contrast, though Alessandro is also suspected by other characters of being a fraud, rather than preserving any doubt about his apparent superiority, Vančura confirms it when, at the end of the play, Alessandro's mathematical calculation about the timing of a solar eclipse, to which he attributes far more importance than attempts to make gold, is proved right.

In his review of *Konec starých časů*, Píša develops his earlier criticism of Vančura's approach to characterization in *Rozmarné léto*, arguing:

> [characters] are at times flattened into mere puppets of a plot mechanism dashingly set in motion; they lack sufficient internal tension to bear this complex and rich apparatus of twists and tales which then, all of a sudden, dries up. From this arises a sense that the novel is overloaded

45) M. Kundera, *Umění románu: Cesta Vladislava Vančury za velkou epikou*, Prague, 1960, p. 118.
46) J. Lopatka, 'Konec starých časů' [1969] in M. Špirit (ed.), *Tvář: Výbor z časopisu*, Prague, 1995, hereafter Lopatka, 'Konec starých časů', p. 519.
47) Píša, *Třicátá léta*, p. 134.

and long-drawn-out, and in places a feeling of boredom at some of the apparently most exciting episodes, accompanied by an impression that many of these tales and anecdotes are designed to appeal to a somewhat infantile imagination and taste.[48]

Perhaps ironically, given that Arnoštek and Megalrogov are characters in novels, while Alessandro is from a play, the reader of *Rozmarné léto* and *Konec starých časů* has more of a sense of observing the characters, who, as Píša suggests, resemble puppets, distanced, ironized and manipulated by an invisible master. By contrast, the reader or audience of *Alchymista* is drawn into the title character's perception of the world, seeing him as a more fully-fledged human being than the other characters, and challenged to share his more radical and expansive, but not necessarily more comfortable perspective. To this extent, Alessandro seems closer to the implied author of *Rozmarné léto* or *Konec starých časů* than any of their characters.

Alessandro, as an alchemist and astronomer, also embodies the division between what Holý terms 'imagination' and 'work', or between what Vančura describes as the artist's 'defamiliarization' and the scientist's 'automatization' of reality. In an exchange with his patron, Martin Koryčan, Alessandro declares:

Alessandro: Alchymie je moje hra.
Martin: Hra?
Alessandro: Hra. Umění.[49]

Alchemy is equated here with art and both are understood as a game. Citing Rimbaud's 'Alchimie du verbe' in *Une saison en enfer*, as well as examples from Nezval, Blahynka notes the history in literature of alchemy as a metaphor for poetry, often as an expression of the ambiguity of creative activity, which may produce something miraculous, but which the creator feels to be fraudulent. Blahynka draws particular attention to a discussion of the phenomenon published by Šalda in 1931, which he suspects influenced Vančura's work on the play.[50]

48) Ibid., p. 136.
49) 'Alessandro: Alchemy is my game. / Martin: Your game? / Alessandro: My game. My art' (Vančura, *Hry*, p. 162).
50) See Blahynka, *Vančura*, p. 198–99.

Given this understanding of alchemy and poetry, Vančura may be said to be questioning here the activity of 'defamiliarization', as Blahynka suggests in his interpretation of the quarrel between Alessandro and his student, Ondřej Buben. Buben is a purist who believes in the nobility of scientific endeavour and abandons his teacher when he thinks he has betrayed the cause of science by falsely claiming to have forged gold: 'Jsi dobrodruh a hejsek, jsi špatný učitel, jenž si necení ani za mák své práce, máš zřetel leda k rozkoši – tvoje práce leží v sutinách ... Alchymistické umění hraničí s podvodem, pracuje ruku v ruce s chytráctvím a čaruje, místo aby poznávalo.'[51] Blahynka, though seeing more of Vančura in Alessandro than Mukařovský, takes Buben's rejection of Alessandro as an expression of Vančura's rejection of Surrealism, espoused at the time by Nezval, Teige and others: 'Vančura knew about the myriad charms and advantages of alchemy, mixing poetry and the findings of science, he loved the alchemists of the word and image among his friends, but he himself takes a different road, more similar in his play to Ondřej Buben's.'[52] However, as Dostál points out, Buben is jealous of Alessandro, whom he sees as a love rival, and is, moreover, shown not to have understood the extent of Alessandro's commitment to his work. Alessandro claims to have forged gold in order to gain time to complete his work on the solar eclipse, gambling his reputation on the success of his predictions. Though a far from negative character in the play, Buben lacks precisely the open, 'defamiliarizing' imagination to understand Alessandro.

This kind of imagination is what distinguishes Alessandro from nearly all the Czech characters in the play, whose experience of life is circumscribed by their obsessions. Martin Koryčan hopes his investment in Alessandro will bring him fame and wealth, his brother Michael hopes through Alessandro's work to come to know the mind of God, Buben places his faith in science. As Dostál puts it, Alessandro is more interested in the 'gold' of the sun than in material gold.[53] He apparently has no preconceptions about life and resists attachments in life, seeking instead to be liberated into life rather than to shelter from it, to embrace it and

51) 'You are a swindler and a fop, you are a bad teacher who does not value his work in the slightest. You care only about pleasure, your work lies in ruins... The art of alchemy borders on deceit, it goes hand in hand with guile and practises sorcery instead of learning' (Vančura, *Hry*, p. 186).
52) Blahynka, *Vančura*, p. 200–01.
53) See Dostál, *Slovo a čin*, p. 48.

move in harmony with it. He pursues Martin's wife, Eva Koryčanová, because in her alone he senses someone with the comparable courage to love life, the definition of love in Vančura:

Alessandro (pokorně): Vyslovuješ jméno láska jinak než všichni ostatní.
Eva: Hlasitěji.
Alessandro: Beze strachu.
Eva: To dozajista.
Alessandro: Má drahá, má drahá.[54]

In an implicit definition of the 'defamiliarizing' imagination, he tells her: 'Podstata štěstí je proměnlivost, na niž se zhusta naříkává. Zalkl bych se i rájem, jenž trvá, aniž se pohne, jenž opakuje jednu myšlenku, který si vede jako skot a zpívá jako kolovrátek. Zalkl bych se bezvětřím stálosti a nesvobodou, která mluvívá o věrnosti a na obrátku z dobrých milenců udělá stvůry nebo věrolomníky.'[55]

Mukařovský's description of the alchemist as 'immoral and cynical' seems a misunderstanding. Alessandro is not a man without principles, but on the contrary asserts what he, like Vančura, sees as the highest principle of all, that the human being be all he can be. Alessandro's alchemy masks not his lack of seriousness – his charlatanry – but his seriousness, simultaneously distracting attention from his real goal and enabling its achievement. As I discussed in Chapter One, defamiliarization for Vančura functions in the same way. It does not constitute some extraneous linguistic pyrotechnics designed to mask the fact that an author has nothing to say, but distracts from the message of the work, undermining didacticism, while at the same time embodying that message, engaging the reader's imagination in an attempt to liberate him into a more 'epic' way of seeing and living.

54) 'Alessandro (humbly): You utter the word 'love' differently from all the rest. / Eva: More loudly. / Alessandro: Fearlessly. / Eva: That's for sure. / Alessandro: My dearest, my dearest' (Vančura, Hry, p. 183).
55) 'The essence of happiness is changeability, about which people frequently complain. I would suffocate in a paradise that endured without moving, which repeats a single idea, which behaves like cattle and sings like a barrel organ. I would suffocate in the windlessness of permanence and unfreedom which likes to speak of fidelity and in return turns good lovers into monsters or breakers of trust' (ibid., p. 184). This passage curiously prefigures the characterization in unsanctioned literature of the atmosphere in Communist Czechoslovakia in the 1950s and the Normalization.

In Chapter One I noted the decline in demonstrative defamiliarizing language in Vančura's 1930s writing. Beginning most obviously with *Útěk do Budína*, Vančura's work undergoes what Lopatka describes as a 'striking shift from a concentration on expression to an attempt at an entire, would-be realist depiction of a sociological universe'.[56] Holý describes the change as a shift from experiments in complication to 'experiments in simplification'.[57] Perhaps the most obvious change is in the choice of novel types with which he works. In his three major novels of the 1920s, Vančura takes on types of prose at the cutting edge of high literary experimentation in the period, imposing himself on the social novel in *Pekař Jan Marhoul* and the Expressionist novel in *Pole orná a válečná* and in effect creating a novel-length *poéme en prose* in *Poslední soud*. With the parody detective novel *Hrdelní pře* and the historical romance *Markéta Lazarová*, Vančura begins to move towards *Trivialliteratur* novel types, dominated by plot or episode and by an abundance of characters, and seeks less to impose his own style on the type. This move bears out Holý's assertion that Vančura was motivated in the 1930s by a desire to reach a wider readership.[58]

The shift away from ostentatious defamiliarization might be taken as a friendly move towards the reader. However, it is accompanied by a hardening of attitude and tone in Vančura's writing, first signalled by Půlpytel's antagonism, albeit balanced by Lucie's plaintive entreaty to forgive and forget. The assertions in *Nemocná dívka* that 'there is no courage without doubt, no heroism without fear' and in *Poslední soud* that 'every courage has a tiny moment's hesitation' are replaced by the emancipation of Markéta through rape and the scornful condemnation of the alchemist. *Luk královny Dorotky* ends with a 'moral', jocularly parodic in keeping with the style of the collection, but genuine in its sentiments:

Ať se lidé honí po nesmyslech a jalovinách, jednoho dne přijdou přece jen k rozumu. Neočekávejte však, že se to stane z jejich vlastní vůle a jejich přičiněním. Ne! Bude jim to vtlučeno do hlavy. Pak je veta po jejich důstojnosti a věru poznají, že si vedli bláhově, osobujíce si práva na mladé ženy, mladé myšlenky, mladou zem a na vše, co nenáleží starcům či lidem

56) Lopatka, 'Konec starých časů', p. 520.
57) Holý, *Práce a básnivost*, p. 151.
58) See ibid.

obráceným ke zdi. Kteréhosi jitra se probudí a jejich majeteček bude ten tam. Vzbouřil se, prchl, zařídil si život po svém. Mládencům, o nichž si staří pánové myslili, že jsou usmrkánkové, narostla za noc brada, zamilovali se, jsou odhodlaní a sázejí vše na jednu kartu.[59]

From the context, that card is love, the increasingly explicit supreme value for Vančura, though implicitly the card might equally be communism. For Vančura, both are associated with the abandonment of narrow prejudices and preconceptions and the willingness to empathize and to participate in an ever expanding, all-embracing view of life. It is not Vančura's message that has changed, but his method. The move away from ostentatious defamiliarization is a move away from persuasion, from the attempt to win the reader over to a new way of seeing through co-operative work with the author, born perhaps of a frustration with a First Republic reader who has proved stubbornly resistant to his vision, towards Křikava's aggressive intervention, 'banging' the message into people's heads.

Critics have generally attributed the change in Vančura's use of language to changing socio-political circumstances. Hodrová argues that in the 1930s, with the rise of Fascism in Germany and other neighbouring states, Czech writers abandoned the apparently alienating and divisive practice of experiment in favour of unifying Realist approaches. Referring to works by Vančura and Karel Čapek, she argues that 'the novelistic form [...] hardens up in the thirties, that is in a period of social uncertainty and impending catastrophe'.[60] This uncharacteristically absolute assertion, however, fails to take into account, for example, the strong trend of psychological realism in writers like Jaroslav Havlíček (1896-1943), Egon Hostovský (1908-1973) or Václav Řezáč (1901-56), in

---

59) 'Let people run around after silly things and sterile notions, one day they will none the less see reason. Don't expect that it will happen of their own free will and through their own actions. No! It will be banged into their heads. Then their dignity will be done for and they will truly see that they behaved foolishly, claiming for themselves the right to young women, young ideas, a young land and everything that does not belong to old men or people turned to face the wall. One morning they will wake up and their precious property will be gone. It will have risen up, fled and organized life in its own way. Young people, whom old men thought were snotty-nosed children, will have overnight grown beards and fallen in love, they will be determined and stake everything on a single card'. (V. Vančura, *Luk královny Dorotky*, Prague, 1947, p. 183.)
60) Hodrová, *...na okraji chaosu...*, p. 133.

which the theme of personal and social disintegration might also be said to reflect the external threat facing Czech society at the time.

As Blahynka points out, Vančura reflects on this need to change in the short story 'Občan Don Quijote', in which Quixote resolves to tame his eccentricity in the greater interests of the cause.[61] In the story, included in an anthology published in support of the Republican cause in the Spanish Civil War in 1937, Quixote and Sancho Panza, still roaming in present-day Spain, escape from a group of Franco's men, who have hanged a peasant girl for declaring 'Long live Republican Spain', and set off to enlist in the Republican army.[62] Quixote demands to be called comrade: '"Je čas, příteli, abychom nazývali vše pravým jménem." Na ta slova vzhlédl Sancho s podivením na svého pána; zdálo se mu, že jej nepoznává.'[63] Behind the exhortation to support the anti-Fascist cause, given Vančura's consistent identification with quixotic characters in his writing, this statement appears to express the need to relinquish defamiliarization in favour of 'calling things by their proper names'. Blahynka writes: 'Quixote's decision to call things by their proper names and join the fight also expresses Vančura's authorial programme. Beginning with this story about a knight errant in our own times who puts discipline before all else, Vančura's work is subordinated to the needs of the struggle and seeks its freedom in voluntary discipline.'[64]

Blahynka, writing from the Marxist-Leninist perspective, and Hodrová, writing in the spirit of Formalism and its descendants, both agree that Vančura changes in response to the political situation. However, for Blahynka, claiming Vančura retrospectively for the Party line, this development represents in effect an acknowledgement at long last of the internal ideological logic of his writing: 'In "Občan Don Quijote", Vančura does not renounce his "predilections", so often interpreted incorrectly and one-sidedly, but merely thinks them through to their logical conclusion' in 'civically committed literature'.[65] For Hodrová, by

61) See Blahynka, *Vančura*, p. 269.
62) This attempt, at the time of the Spanish Civil War, to claim Quixote as a left-wing revolutionary may also be seen in the contemporaneous poem 'Don Quijote bojující' (Don Quixote the militant) by František Halas (1901–49).
63) '"It is time, my friend, to call everything by its proper name'. At these words Sancho looked up at his master in surprise; it seemed to him as if he did not recognise him' (Vančura, V., *Občan don Quijote a jiné prózy*, Prague, 1961, p. 8).
64) Blahynka, *Vančura*, p. 269.
65) Ibid.

contrast, this change implicitly signifies something of a betrayal of his early method, a turning-away from the internal cultural logic of the century.

Blahynka makes no mention of any implied authorial regret that the time for Avant-garde 'tilting at windmills' must end. A year earlier, in *Jezero Ukereve*, Vančura had expressed a reluctant acceptance that ideals must sometimes be compromised for the greater good through the character of Forde, the doctor treating the sleeping-sickness in Uganda. He is forced temporarily to act in a way that provokes the hostility of those he wants to heal, in particular by collaborating with the colonists who violently suppress the tribesmen's attempts to stop them draining the marshes, where the disease-bearing flies live. In 'Občan Don Quijote', Vančura is alluding not so much to Cervantes's novel, but to the best-known exploration of the Quixote character in Czech literature, Dyk's *Zmoudření Dona Quijota* (Don Quixote comes to his senses, 1913). The play comes from a period when Dyk foregrounds in his work the conflict faced by the artist between his ideals and reality, and seems to renounce the uncompromising idealism of his earlier work in favour of a less romantic, humbler practical engagement. In the play Quixote is forced to abandon his illusions and confront reality. He is introduced to the uninspiring woman whom other characters believe to be the 'real' Dulcinea and, in disappointment but true to his principles, agrees to marry her. On his death-bed, Dyk's Quixote declares: 'Představoval jsem si všechno jinak. Ale nutno smířit se se skutečností a viděti věci, jak skutečně jsou [...] Celá má minulost je jen hloupý a směšný sen. Nyní bude načase bdíti [...] Mé bláznovství mi odpusťte. Bylo tuším nicméně zábavné. Tomu, kdo mnoho bavil, odpustí se mnoho.'[66]

The implied author in 'Občan Don Quijote' does not express such wistful resignation; the story essentially constitutes a rejection of this defeatism. Blahynka is right that Vančura continues to follow the internal logic of his work, not, however, because he straightforwardly embraces the didactic function of literature, but because he continues to strive for the dynamic balance between 'automatizatio' and defamiliarization that underpins all his writing. The story seems at face value an

66) 'I imagined everything differently. But one must reconcile oneself with reality and see things as they really are [...] My whole past life is but a foolish and ridiculous dream. Now it is time to wake up [...] Forgive me my folly. It was, I think, at least amusing. He who has amused many is forgiven much' (V. Dyk, *Dramata a próza*, Prague, 2003, p. 90).

exhortation to the reader to become active in the anti-Fascist cause, but the reader is invited at the same time to read more intuitively, and on discovering the self-reflexive interpretation glimpses the playful, subversive, quixotic Vančura, who has not 'come to his senses'. In a way that foreshadows the subversive strategy of some sanctioned writers in the Communist period, the artlessness of the message is undermined not by an explicit counter-message, but by the artful spirit of the author.

In Chapter One I characterized Vančura's writing in the 1920s as an un-ending struggle to preserve a balance between two contrasting notions of modernity, between the desire to embrace present reality in its frag-mentation and incompleteness and the aspiration to impose an order on that reality, between language tending towards dislocation from reality and language embedded in the everyday, between an art threatening to exist for its own sake and an art in the service of an extra-literary ideol-ogy. His attempts in the 1930s to move from the Avant-garde margins of mainstream literature merely signify an expansion of this struggle from the writing of the left-wing Avant-garde to the whole of literature, reflected in the adoption of styles and techniques from popular literature and the change in the treatment of the implied reader, who may be cast more as an opponent than a 'fellow-traveller'.

In *Markéta Lazarová*, this struggle takes the form of redressing the balance between the novelistic and the epic imagination, and appears directed at a modern literature that Vančura perceives to have accepted and even grown comfortable with a reduced understanding of the human being as weak, limited, even sick. According to Blahynka, 'Vančura wrote *Markéta Lazarová* as a polemic against the feeble contemporary Czech way of living and against literature that possesses similar qualities'.[1] His main target might be thought to be the Symbolist legacy, which the post-1918 Avant-garde perhaps all too vehemently rejected.[2] In his 'Literární

1) M. Blahynka, *Vladislav Vančura*, Prague, 1978, hereafter Blahynka, *Vančura*, p. 173.
2) In his early theoretical articles, Teige reserved his strongest attacks for the Symbolist 'retreat from the world': 'Art for art's sake, born in ivory towers hermetically sealed from life, is simply not art, but merely the pathological product of a degenerating old world, in which the modern human being cannot have the slightest interest' (K. Teige, 'S novou generací (polemické poznámky)' in Š. Vlašín (ed.), *Avantgarda známá a neznámá*, Vol. 1, Prague, 1970, p. 142). Later, however, Nezval, in his 1937 history of modern European poetry *Moderní básnické směry* (Modern poetic trends), placed the post-1918 Avant-garde implicitly in a tradition that emerged from Symbolism.

vyznání', Vančura, acknowledging the attractions of Decadence to his generation in its formative years, writes:

> This new group, which [...] rose up as a reaction to the preceding poetic school, moved our literature a good distance forward along the way. Nevertheless, it was not without flaws and like all revolutions it went to extremes and overdosed on the cure, as they say. [...] A distaste for educative elements and for ideas that the author might share with the wider public led to an overwrought subjectivism in the Decadents, which sought at all costs to distinguish itself from the surrounding world. Poets therefore piled wilfulness on top of wilfulness, rejected any form of tendentiousness and therefore any form of evaluation, and in short became passionate advocates of *l'art pour l'art*. Death, the beauty of fading things, the fire of sin, Satanism, aristocratism, shine, shimmer and inimitability so crazed the minds of poets at that time that they easily renounced reality and truth.[3]

Vančura's criticism of extremism and his implicit call for balance here are revealing, and are reflected in his casting of the novel in *Markéta Lazarová* as a dynamic intermediate stage between the loss of the epic perspective and its recovery. Vančura's perception of an 'unbalanced' literature might, however, be extended beyond the Decadents to include various types of 'psychological' and self-reflexive writing, and also the often journalistic writing favoured by the establishment, limited by the intellectual and material aspirations of the petty bourgeois.

It is not a great leap to see how, later in the 1930s, Vančura might come to connect this debilitating view of the human being propagated in literature with the growing mood of defeatism and despair in the First Republic establishment as the political situation worsened. In February 1938, the month that Vančura first proposed to his publishers the idea of *Obrazy z dějin národa českého*, Hitler declared that the only way of resolving the plight of the Sudeten Germans was to incorporate those areas of Czechoslovakia which they inhabited into the German Reich. Following the meeting in Berchtesgaden on September 15 between Hitler and the British Prime Minister, Neville Chamberlain, the Czechoslovak government was presented with an ultimatum to cede to Germany lands where the majority population was German. The ultimatum was initially re-

3) V. Vančura, *Řád nové tvorby*, Prague, 1972, hereafter Vančura, *Řád*, p. 161.

jected by the Czechoslovak government, but Britain and France brought pressure to bear on the president, Edvard Beneš, and the terms were accepted on September 21, prompting the resignation of the government and mass demonstrations in Prague and elsewhere. When Hitler then called for Czechoslovakia also to yield to the territorial demands of Hungary and Poland, the new Czechoslovak government announced a general mobilization, suggesting that Czechoslovakia was preparing to defend itself. After some hesitation by Britain and France, however, on September 30 the Munich agreement, enshrining all Hitler's demands, was signed by the heads of government of Britain, France, Germany and Italy and accepted by Beneš, who emigrated soon after. Amid widespread dismay in Czechoslovakia, the terms of the agreement were implemented in the ensuing weeks and augmented in November 1938 by the First Vienna Arbitration, which ceded land in Slovakia and Ruthenia to Hungary.

Parallels with Beneš seem to be invited by the depiction in the first volume of *Obrazy z dějin národa českého* of the tenth century Bishop of Prague, Vojtěch (St Adalbert), who, unable to contend with the realities of life, ultimately cannot bear to watch the bloodshed and misery in Bohemia and leaves for Italy, intending to travel on to the Holy Land. His story recalls that of Josef Danowitz in *Pole orná a válečná*; indeed, Vojtěch, a Slavník, also comes from a prominent noble family. Initially, the narrator appears moved by his spirituality, but gradually he becomes critical of his detachment from the joys and woes of terrestrial existence, the fate from which Markéta Lazarová was rescued:

Ten však kdo se napil ze studnice osamění, ten, kdo zahlédá všude nicotu, ten, kdo zří jen lebky pod spanilými tvářemi, ten, kdo poznává nezměrnou slávu zmaru, ten se nikdy nerozveselí [...] Věci, nádhery, věci světského zdaru, věci pozemské slávy jsou mu uzavřeny na zámek, jehož klíček se ztratil [...] Nevěřil, že hlína a prach, z nichž bylo zhněteno tělo, jsou k obrazu božímu? Nevěřil, že z dotyku tvůrcových rukou ulpělo na té hlíně něco tak vznešeného a líbezného, že to nikdy nemá býti přehlédnuto? [...] Byla mu snad odepřena moudrost, jež sluje láska živá a jež se schyluje k lidem chybujícím.[4]

4) 'However, he who has drunk from the well of solitude, he who sees worthlessness everywhere he who sees only skulls beneath fair cheeks, he who knows the untold glory of destruction, he will never cheer up [...] The things, the wonders, the things of worldly achievement, the things of terrestrial glory are locked away from him and the key has

Later, in Volume Two, one might equally see an allusion to the failure of foreign allies abroad to support Czechoslovakia in the account of Pope Gregory X's decision not to support the Bohemian warrior king Přemysl Otakar II's claim to the imperial throne. The vacillating Gregory's thoughts are conveyed in the form of a prayer, from which he emerges as motivated by cowardice and fear.[5]

Obrazy z dějin národa českého emerges in effect as an attempt to counter the atmosphere of defeatism and despair. Holý writes: '*Obrazy* is an act more cultural and political than literary. With it Vančura wanted to serve the need of the time to raise national self-confidence, to see the contemporary period as a short and merely transitional episode in the broad panorama of past events, to awaken "the awareness of interconnectedness" and hope for the future.'[6] As Seifert describes in his memoirs, Vančura conceived the project as a collective effort, an expression of Czech unity and solidarity, with different chapters to be written by different authors, on the basis of the latest research, in collaboration with Marxist historians.[7] Among the writers mentioned as potential contributors were Seifert, Nový, Jaromír John (1882-1952) and Josef Kopta (1894-1962).[8] Milada Součková (1898-1983) and Jiří Mařánek (1891-1959) are credited with contributing to respectively the first and third chapters of the first volume. Vančura, however, eventually took on the task himself, after 'some authors pulled out, while others let him down and did not deliver their chapters or could not take them beyond an initial outline'.[9] The

been lost. [...] Did he not believe that the clay and dust from which the body was kneaded are in God's image? Did he not believe that the touch of the Creator's hand on that clay left something so sublime and lovely that it should never be overlooked? [...] Perhaps he had been denied that wisdom known as living love which leans towards those who err' (V. Vančura, *Obrazy z dějin národa českého*, Vol. 1, Prague, 1956, hereafter Vančura, *Obrazy* 1, p. 158).

5) See V. Vančura, *Obrazy z dějin národa českého,* Vols.II and III, Prague, 1981, p. 242. Hereafter Vančura, *Obrazy* 2.

6) J. Holý, *Práce a básnivost: Estetický projekt světa Vladislav Vančury*, Prague, 1990, p. 145.

7) These historians, Václav Husa, Jaroslav Charvát and Jan Pachta, were prominent members of the Historická skupina, responsible for the historiographical periodical *Dějiny a přítomnost*, published by Družstevní práce. Seifert recalls how, in 1976, the families of these historians launched an unsuccessful court case, arguing that their contribution had not been fully recognized (see J. Seifert, *Všecky krásy světa*, Prague, 1999, pp. 124–25.)

8) See ibid., p. 121.

9) L. Vančurová, *Dvacet šest krásných let*, Prague, 1974, p. 137. Seifert recalls how he and Nový persuaded Vančura that he was the only person capable of doing the project justice.

first volume was published in the German-administered Protectorate of Bohemia and Moravia in December 1939.

Holý is not alone in seeing *Obrazy z dějin národa českého* as somehow exceptional to Vančura's work, to be judged less according to literary criteria than his earlier work, yet this point of view seems fundamentally to undermine what Vančura seeks to achieve with them. In *Obrazy z dějin národa českého* Vančura in fact fights against the subjugation of literary criteria to others in the period, in an attempt to preserve the 'normality' of literature and the literary process at an abnormal time. In this sense Vančura remains true in *Obrazy z dějin národa českého* to the principles that govern all his writing. Kožmín, indeed, suggests that Vančura makes a partial return in *Obrazy z dějin národa českého* to his 1920s techniques, to enhance the 'density of the content'.[10] Grygar argues more unequivocally that *Obrazy z dějin národa českého* 'constitute both artistically and in terms of philosophy and worldview a synthesis of Vančura's previous work'.[11] In an article first published in *samizdat* in 1981, the medievalist Jan Lehár criticizes interpreters, perhaps like Blahynka, who, 'pat Vančura on the back, seeing in [...] *Obrazy* a turning away from autonomous literary creation towards ideology and tendentiousness'. In Lehár's view, 'Vančura remained in *Obrazy* faithful to himself and to his conception of literature',[12] by which he means that Vančura's concerns remain strictly formal. Most recently Milan Jankovič has written: 'In the breadth of the historical action that they capture, the wealth of life situations, human character types and fates depicted, and last but not least in the dynamism of the stylistic transformations of the narrator, [*Obrazy*] represents the culmination of the author's previous creative searching.'[13]

Lehár bases his assessment on an examination of one of the best-known episodes in *Obrazy z dějin národa českého*, portraying Cosmas (c.1045–1125), the first chronicler of Czech history, and his relationship with two other monks, Bruno and Šebíř, whose names Vančura takes from the dedication in Cosmas's chronicle and transforms into characters. For Pavel Eisner, writing as Jaroslav Dlouhý, the episode constitutes the

10) Z. Kožmín, *Styl Vančurovy prózy*, Brno, 1968, p. 149.
11) M. Grygar, 'Vladislav Vančura' in J. Mukařovský, (ed.), *Dějiny české literatury* IV, Prague: Victoria, 1995, hereafter Grygar, 'Vladislav Vančura', p. 327.
12) J. Lehár, *Studie o sémantizaci formy*, Prague, 2005, hereafter Lehár, *Studie*, p. 140.
13) M. Jankovič, 'Rytmičnost v próze' in M. Červenka, M. Jankovič, M. Kubínová, M. Langerová, *Pohledy zblízka: zvuk, význam, obraz*, Prague, 2002, hereafter Jankovič, 'Rytmičnost v próze', p. 168–69.

'key not only to Vančura's aesthetics, but also to his philosophy of the word and of literary creation'.[14] In the episode, Šebíř presses a reluctant Cosmas to include in his chronicle material relating to the Sázava monastery, founded in 1032 and thought to have retained elements of the increasingly 'suspect' Slavonic rite despite Bohemia's close ties with Rome, even after the Great Schism of 1054, until its dissolution in 1097. Josef Žemlička writes:

> It is difficult to prove but also to disprove the role of vanishing Church Slavonic traditions in the emergence of the Benedictine Sázava monastery, established through the combined efforts of the duke and the hermit Prokop. Even though the Sázava monks kept the Roman liturgy and merely used the Slavonic tongue, they constantly had to defend themselves against accusations of 'un-Roman' deviations.[15]

Šebíř also challenges Cosmas's view that pagan stories are corruptions of stories from classical literature. Though Lehár points out the boldness of Vančura's treatment in the face of the uncertainty of historians and notes likely recent sources for his thinking, he does not see in this treatment the 'communication of messages' about the status of folk culture or the question of a western or eastern cultural orientation:

> The twin lines of narration – about Cosmas, Božetěcha [his wife], Šebíř and Bruno, bathed in the light of an education that raises unconscious being up to individualized life, and about the adventures of vagrants, chewing over old tales, who are borne on the current of a simple, sheer existence – converge towards the emerging Chronicle without heading for any kind of resolution [...] Each of the two lines of action and each of the characters represents a specific compositional principle; from their development in time and space arises form that is not static, but dynamic, and from this form arises a reality that is not unequivocal, but ambiguous.[16]

Critics have traditionally seen the portrayal of Cosmas as an authorial autostylization. Karel Polák wrote in 1940 that Cosmas was 'more

14) J. Dlouhý, 'Logofág Kosmas', Kritický měsíčník III (1940), 4, p. 166.
15) J. Žemlička, Čechy v době knížecí (1034–1198), Prague, 1997, p. 379.
16) Lehár, Studie, p. 139.

true to Vančura than to historiography', describing him as 'Vančura himself, the true Vančura, Vančura in 1939'.[17] The narrator writes: 'Kosmas byl obdařen znamenitou chutí k jídlu a se stejnou ochotou zasedal k všelijakým spisům latinským. Jedl, co mu dali, ale pokud jde o čtení, byl vybíravý a měl zálibu jen v tom, co bylo naplněno nějakým zvláštním kouzlem. Spisy koktavé a otáčející se na jediném místě nemiloval.'[18] A convivial old man, lively in mind and body and often depicted on horseback, he loves the challenge and charm of putting things into words. On one occasion, after a successful negotiation with a Moravian duke, Cosmas longs to talk and share the experience with a friend: 'Seděl na koni, klátil se se strany na stranu a smál se, přemýšleje o slovních obratech a hříčkách, kterých užil v hádce.'[19] Lehár's interpretation, however, leads the reader away from the straightforward 'resolution' of Cosmas's identity in Vančura, encouraging him instead to see Vančura divided across the three 'bookworm'-monks. From this perspective, their relationship can be seen as a new dramatization of the conflict within Vančura the writer between the objective and subjective, between the desire to 'automatize' and to defamiliarize. This conflict is perhaps reflected in the narrator's comment that 'Kosmova mysl nevynikala pevností a byl tak trochu nestálý'.[20]

In 'Kosmas' this conflict is reflected in the problem of how to balance attested fact with the work of both his own imagination and the popular imagination over the centuries. In a stylized 'interview' with himself, published in 1939 to publicize the first volume, Vančura comments: 'History is a great science, I tremble with respect before it, but what is the use of it all, when human cognition grasps only fragments of life. It seizes on records and known facts, puts them into context, confers an order of significance on them and, when all is said and done, interprets them

17) Polák, K., 'Vladislav Vančura: *Obrazy z dějin národa českého*', *Kritický měsíčník* III (1940), 3, p. 186.
18) 'Kosmas was blessed with a remarkable appetite for food and would sit down with the same enthusiasm to all kinds of Latin works. He ate whatever he was given, but as far as reading is concerned, he was choosy and only things that were filled with some kind of peculiar magic took his fancy. He had no love for works that stuttered or went round and round in circles' (Vančura, *Obrazy* 1, p. 219).
19) 'He sat on his horse, rocking from side to side and laughing as he thought over the turns of phrase and word play he had used in the dispute' (ibid., p. 249).
20) 'Cosmas's mind was not distinguished by its dependability and he was just a little inconstant' (ibid., p. 229).

like a story-teller.'[21] Vančura's comments reflect his enduring Bergsonian attitude to the limitations of positivist scientific methods and the place of artistic intuition in grasping reality. Coincidentally, this problem is also raised by the German left-wing, at one time Expressionist doctor-writer, Alfred Döblin (1878–1957), in his 1936 essay 'Der historische Roman und Wir', in which he writes:

> The present-day novel, not only the historical, is subject to two currents – the one derives from the fairy tale, the other from the report. Their source is not the ether of aesthetics, but the reality of our life. Within ourselves we incline towards both currents to a greater or lesser extent. But we are not deluding ourselves if we say: the active progressive circles are taking today to the report, while the serene and satisfied go over to the fairy tale [...] The novel is caught up in a struggle between the two tendencies: fairy-tale constructions with a maximum of elaboration and a minimum of material and novel constructions with a maximum of material and a minimum of elaboration.[22]

As we have seen, for Vančura, the 'active, progressive' writer's task is implicitly to prevent the eradication of literature by the report, while seeking a balance between the two tendencies that Döblin describes. In his view, expressed in the story 'Samotný chlapec' in *Amazonský proud*, 'thinking that creates, folly and the happiest love are the unrecognized masters of the world'.

In 'Kosmas' the two extremes are represented by Bruno and Šebíř, men who, according to the narrator, were destined to be the best of friends, but were caught on either side of a power struggle between the duke and the bishop and driven apart. Bruno spends his time copying sacred texts: 'Vzhledem k píli a k učenosti byl mu [...] svěřen zápis důležitých událostí do kapitulních annalů. Činil to jazykem chudobným. Činil to jazykem bez síly, bez zaujetí, suše, přesně, latinou osvědčenou, větami otřelými a slovy, která kulhají jako křapavé babizny a ďáblové s jednou tlapou a jedním paznehtem.'[23] He avoids secular things and

21) Vančura, *Řád*, p. 141.
22) Quoted in G. Lukács, *The Historical Novel*, translated by Hannah and Stanley Mitchell, New York, 1962, p. 273.
23) 'Given his diligence and his learnedness, he was [...] entrusted with the task of recording important events into the Annals of the Chapter. He did this in an impoverished

Old Slavonic texts like the plague. By contrast, Šebíř's love of literature is undiscriminating: 'prudká a silná láska k písemnostem ohlušila i jeho církevní horlivost – nerozeznával věci kanonické od věcí pochybených.'[24] He tells Cosmas: 'jsou dva zdroje našich vědomostí. A prvý, lepší a zajímavější, vyvěrá z lidské paměti.'[25]

As one might expect, Cosmas seems more drawn to the merry Šebíř than to the bony, pedantic Bruno; in their contrasting characters they together recall Vančura's reported description of his parents. Cosmas reconsiders his attitude to pagan texts and agrees to retain the section in his chronicle about the Sázava monastery, provided no monk from there is ever found to be uncultured and of low character. At the end, however, Cosmas reconciles the two men and the reader's perception of them is somewhat altered. Bruno secretly slips a copy of his Annals of the Chapter into Cosmas's bag in a tacit expression of support for his chronicle. Šebíř, on the other hand, encounters a monk from the Sázava Monastery who reflects Cosmas's fears and has to remove the pages about the monastery from the chronicle, though Cosmas allows him to keep them for himself. From this interpretation Cosmas emerges as not so much an autobiographical Vančura as an implied authorial Vančura, a representation of his ideal of the writer who succeeds in bringing opposites together and restoring harmony between them.

In this context Cosmas emerges as, in effect, a model of the Avant-garde writer as Vančura implicitly defines him in his early 1920s writing, a chronicler of the 'process of becoming', standing between the past and the future, striving endlessly to balance the collective desire to 'automatize', to establish and reiterate such shared, attested foundations as historical facts or linguistic conventions, and the individual desire to 'defamiliarize', destabilize those foundations and assert an individual vision. Like the Avant-garde writer in Píša's description, quoted in Chapter Two herein, the chronicler must 'study the collective human being as he passes from darkness to light', yet is not destined to join him there.

language. He did this in a language without strength, without enthusiasm, drily, precisely, in competent Latin, using hackneyed phrases and word that hobbled like gossipy old hags and devils with one paw and one claw' (Vančura, *Obrazy* 1, p. 230).
24) 'A fierce, powerful love for the written word even drowned out his ecclesiastical zeal – he could not differentiate between things of the canon and things on which doubt had been cast' (ibid., p. 228).
25) 'There are two sources of our knowledge. And the first, the better and the more interesting one springs from human memory' (ibid., p. 249).

This emphasis on the struggle rather than the outcome is reflected in the narrator's description of Cosmas's thoughts as he watches workers in Prague repairing a bridge: 'Vlekli těžká břevna, valili kmeny jako v dětských hrách a Kosmas cítil rozmar a tíhu i smysl a marnost počínání, které je nádhernější než samo dílo.'[26] Cosmas relates their work to his own, seeing the bridge over the river as a metaphor for his chronicle as a bridge over time and between times. Through Cosmas's empathy with the labourers, Vančura reasserts the identification made in his early 1920s writing between the efforts of the writer and worker, for both of whom, as the contrast between the making of bread and bread as a commodity in *Pekař Jan Marhoul* reflects, the process of creation is more important than the finished product.

Vančura, however, does more here than merely reiterate the early principles of the post-1918 Avant-garde. The emphasis on 'how' rather than 'what', on the spirit with which one approaches life, rather than on what one achieves, acquires a more concrete, universal meaning in the socio-political context faced by the implied reader. The identity between writer and worker similarly becomes less a statement of the Avant-garde's connection with the proletariat, and more a reflection of a broader unity between people, a glimpse of the empathetic collectivity to which Vančura aspires. In the same way, the chronicler is more than just a synonym for the Avant-garde writer. With *Obrazy z dějin národa českého*, Vančura seeks to raise the contemporary Czech nation up from its sense of isolation and despair by contextualizing its plight, connecting the present-day reader with those of his ancestors who also endured terrible times, which the nation always came through in the end. At the same time, however, he also rescues himself from his own isolation, conjuring a community from across the ages, connecting himself with kindred spirits among the chroniclers of the past.

As we have seen from Vančura's apparent depiction of Cosmas in his own image, he enjoys creating identifications between himself and those he sees as predecessors. According to the detailed synopsis left by

26) 'They dragged the heavy planks and rolled the tree-trunks like children playing games and Cosmas felt the frivolity and the burden, the purpose and the futility of their activity, which is more glorious than the finished world itself' (Vančura, *Obrazy* 1, p. 265). Vančura also uses the word *nádherný* in the narrator of *Markéta Lazarová*'s description of the sheer magnificence of Mikoláš's futile attempt to rescue his father, a remark that might also be read self-referentially as a comment on the fate of the Avant-garde writer.

Vančura at his death, the unfinished Volume Three would have recreated the life of Dalimil, that is to say the author of the chronicle mistakenly attributed to Dalimil, up to the point where he begins writing his chronicle.[27] Since his chronicle covers the same period as the first three parts of Vančura's chronicle, the two men would have thus been brought together across the centuries, not in a final unity, but in an infinite cycle where as one finishes, the other begins.[28] Grygar also notes the importance as a source of the sophisticated Latin chronicle, *Chronicon Aulae Regiae*, written by monks, the abbot Ota and then Peter of Zittau (c.1260–70–c.1339), at the Cistercian monastery in Zbraslav, where Vančura lived and wrote his own, new Zbraslav Chronicle.[29] The fact that Vančura keeps this connection playfully implicit perhaps reflects his desire to be identified, above all, with the humorous outlook of these men, 'the elevated stand-point of poets' that preserves balance in the face of life's sorrows, though few would argue that *Obrazy z dějin národa českého* compares with their medieval counterparts in this respect.

Obrazy z dějin národa českého does mark a return to his 1920s writing in the dominant emphasis on awakening the self-awareness of the collective, contrasting with the emphasis, most notable in *Markéta Lazarová*, on awakening the self-awareness of the individual human being. The contemporary Czech nation as implicitly characterized in *Obrazy z dějin národa českého* may be compared to the unrealized collectivity of the oppressed proletariat in 'Býti dělníkem' and the oppressed peasantry in *Pole orná a válečná*. As in his earlier work, notably *Poslední soud*, in the more novelistic episodes in *Obrazy z dějin národa českého*, like 'Kosmas' or 'Několik

27) The chronicle, initially known as the Boleslav Chronicle, became known as the Dalimil Chronicle through the erroneous identification of the author as Dalimil Mezeřický, canon of the Boleslav Church, who is given as a source by Václav Hájek z Libočan (?–1553) in his *Kronika česká* (Bohemian chronicle, 1541) (see the historical notes by Zdeněk Kristen in B. Havránek and J. Daňhelka (eds.), *Nejstarší česká rýmovaná kronika tak řečeného Dalimila*, Prague, 1957, hereafter *Dalimil*, p. 237).

28) This identification is no doubt intensified for Vančura by the historical parallels between the publication of his own chronicle and the publication of the first printed edition of the so-called Dalimil Chronicle in 1620, in an attempt to galvanize support for the Czech estates in their opposition to the Holy Roman Emperor, Ferdinand II's claim to the Czech throne. This opposition, widely but inaccurately understood, at least since the National Revival, as Czech resistance to German aggression, was crushed at the Battle of White Mountain that year, leading to the absorption of the kingdom of Bohemia into the Habsburg Empire.

29) See Grygar, 'Vladislav Vančura', p. 327.

příběhů z doby, kdy se v Čechách zakládala města' (Some stories from the time when the towns were being founded in Bohemia), Vančura depicts heterogeneous collectives of non-conformists from different educational and social backgrounds, whose intuitive sense of community prefigures the collective to come.

In the opening chapter, 'Stará vlast' (The old motherland), Vančura depicts the ideal collective he imagines as once existing among the prehistoric Slavs, who, in an echo of the fourteenth-century so-called Dalimil chronicle, the first to be written in Czech, are shown living in happy anarchy as they may one day again: 'Společná práce vnukala jim povědomí rovnosti a tak Slovanům nikdo nevládl, ale všichni mluvili o věcech společných a každý sám sebe spravoval.'[30] At the end of the chapter, however, amid reports of new peoples arriving from the east, a Slav is depicted as he prepares to cross a river into the lands that will become his new home: 'Jímá ho bázeň, neboť řeka burácí. Proudy hučí po skaliskách, vlna za vlnou se valí, mělčinou, krajem v šíř a šíř oblohy, kde ostříž rozepjal svá křídla, v šíř a šíř země, kde za třemi proudy leží nová vlast, v šíř a šíř času, v němž duní války, i pád, i slavná vzkříšení.'[31] His trepidation reflects that, on entering the river, he is leaving the time-lessness of his forest existence and entering the turbulence of historical time.

The presentation of historical time as a time of conflict reflects the Hegelian model of dialectical progression that Marx developed, in which opposites are confronted and synthesized, giving birth to new conflicts until eventually timeless paradise is restored. This dialectical progression is reflected in *Obrazy z dějin národa českého* most obviously in the conflicts

---

30) 'Communal work imbued them with an awareness of equality and thus no one ruled the Slavs, but all spoke about communal matters and each man governed himself' (Vančura, *Obrazy* 1, p. 10). In Chapter Two of the Dalimil chronicle, the reader learns that the Czechs owned property in common and had no judges because they did not do harm to one another. Vančura, however, omits to mention that, according to Dalimil, they also practised polygamy.

31) 'Fear grips him, for the river is in torrent. Streams rush down the rocks, wave rolls after wave, through the shallows, through the countryside into the wide open sky, where the hawk spread its wings, into the wide open lands where, beyond three streams lies a new motherland, into a wide open time where the clamour of wars, of decline and glorious resurrection, can be heard' (ibid., p. 22). The Slav might be assumed to be a Czech from the allusion in the passage to the Czech national anthem: 'Voda hučí po lučinách / Bory šumí po skalinách' (Water rushes through the meadows / Pine groves rustle on rocky outcrops).

between the old and the new, between paganism and Christianity at the time of Wenceslas I, or between agriculture and the trades and the new mercantilism in the twelfth and thirteenth centuries. It manifests itself in the life of the collective in the repeated cycles of division and coming-together that implicitly continue to the present day. Indeed, the narrator seems to allude to divisions prevailing at the time of writing in his description of disunity among the Slavs at the time of the emergence of Great Moravia: 'jenom rozličné chtění jim bránilo, aby se semkli v nesmírnou moc. Žel, nebylo mezi nimi jednoty. Někteří se přidržovali starých mravů a jiní bažili po novotách.'[32] The Slav's entry into the river might, however, also be compared to the rising of the 'Amazonian current' in 'Ráj', which energizes the somnolent, unproductive twin paradises of male and female, bringing them together in a dynamic relationship through which the story – and history – is born. Though Vančura's work is predicated on an ultimate healing of division and the culmination of historical time in a new and lasting order, in practice he appears paradoxically to idealize more this time of conflict, of struggle and suffering and momentary joys, because it is the time when things are created. Associating the rhythms of Vančura's prose with an implicitly Bergsonian 'pulsation of life', Jankovič writes:

> The polyphony of the stories and characters created in *Obrazy* is the polyphony of the human being, for whom the narrator speaks. It is the polyphony of human possibilities, will and desire, longing and dreaming, strength and weakness, courage and cowardice, glory and suffering, the polyphony of contradictory human qualities and deeds, which in accordance with the author's conviction [...] co-create the current of life, a current that does not cease, that is continual creation.[33]

As a reflection of his desire to heal division and build a stronger sense of collectivity, in *Obrazy z dějin národa českého* Vančura emphasizes tolerance, equality and solidarity over the rough, expansive, combative approach to life embodied by Kozlík's tribe in *Markéta Lazarová*. This distinction between the two works, however, also betrays the difference between

32) 'only diverse desires prevented them from uniting to form an enormous power. Alas, there was no unity among them. Some abided by the old ways while others hankered after novelty' (ibid., p. 41).
33) Jankovič, 'Rytmičnost v próze', p. 170.

his implicit literary targets in each case. While in *Markéta Lazarová* he is preoccupied with a literature that he perceives as deforming the human being by encouraging weakness, in *Obrazy z dějin národa českého* he is more concerned about literature that, in the service of chauvinist nationalist ideologies, encourages belligerence and aggression.

Vančura's position is encapsulated in his treatment of Soběslav II, who reigned from 1173 to 1178. He was nicknamed the 'duke of peasants' because he lacked support among the nobility and knights. In the episode entitled 'Selské kníže' (The peasant duke), Vančura controversially suggests that Soběslav espoused the ideal of a collective without hierarchy, with an intuitive understanding of its freedom, declaring: 'chci a toužím navždy spojiti své konání s konáním svého lidu. Chci se přiodíti vznešeností, která není podle jména, ale podle skutků a podle prací. Velmožové jsou jako stíny v mých myšlenkách, a jako smeť letí po větru; lid chci však milovati.'[34] Imprisoned by his brother to prevent him from taking the throne, Soběslav does not despair: 'věřil v jakousi sílu, která se nepodobá síle známé a která nespočívá ani ve vojště, ani v zákonu psaném, ani v právech, ani v držení moci, ale která je pokorná a čekající, a která je nesličná a bez slávy, a která jednoho dne přece změní tvář země.'[35] In the context, this faith seems to be Christianity, but for the implied author it is communism.

Vančura's Soběslav differs radically from the Soběslav introduced at the beginning of Chapter Sixty-Eight of the Dalimil Chronicle:

> Po královi syn jeho Soběslav knězem bieše,
> ten, kteréhož Němce uzřieše,
> k sobě přivésti kázáše a nos jemu uřezáše
> řka: "Němče, po světu nesleď,
> v své zemi mezi svými seď!
> Po dobrés od svých nevyšel,
> pověz, proč mezi cizie přišel."

---

34) 'I want and yearn to unite forever my actions with the actions of my people. I want to adorn myself in a majesty that derives not from name but from deeds and from labour. Noblemen are like shadows in my thoughts and like a speck of dust fly with the wind; my people, however, I want to love' (ibid., p. 313).

35) 'he believed in some kind of strength which was not like any known strength and which did not reside either in armies or in the written law or in rights or in the holding of power, but which was humble and latent, and which was plain and without glory, and which one day would nevertheless change the face of the earth' (ibid., p. 309).

Jiní, kněžě vidúce,
kdež uzřiechu Němcě jdúce,
jako na vlka voláchu,
uši a nosy jim řězáchu.
Ktož mu německých nosóv sto přinesieše,
ihned jemu sto hřiven střiebra dadieše.[36]

Vančura's omission of this kind of rhetoric at a time when it might have seemed apposite may be seen as a deliberate attempt to distance *Obrazy z dějin národa českého* from the shrill anti-German nationalism, prominent in Czech right-wing literature and the press in the 1930s, which constituted merely a hollow imitation of its German counterpart, offering only the illusion of strength. Practising the lack of prejudice he implicitly preaches, Vančura's treatment of Germans in *Obrazy z dějin národa českého* is surprisingly measured given his subject matter. The tenth-century first bishop of Prague, the Saxon monk Dietmar, is shown to have learned Czech and called Bohemia his homeland. The narrator notes: 'zdála se biskupovi česká země býti zemí míru a cítil, že ji miluje z celé síly své duše.'[37] The most memorable negative character in the work is not a German, but a Flemish merchant in 'Několik příběhů z doby, kdy se v Čechách zakládala města'. This section, despite its title, most closely resembles a popular historical novel in its use of fictional figures to characterize the period, its sharply delineated positive and negative characters and its dramatic, emotive plot-line. The misery that the Flanders merchant consciously and inadvertently inflicts on the family of the Bohemian blacksmith serves as a metaphor for the divisive, destructive effect of the medieval commercialization of Prague by traders from the West, strongly recalling the references to the eradication of artisans in the story 'Houpačka' from *Amazonský proud*.

36) 'After the king his son Soběslav became duke / he who, if he caught sight of a German / would order that he be brought before him / and cut off his nose / saying: "German, don't wander about the world / stay among your own in your own land! / You have not left your own kind with good intentions / Tell me why you have come among foreigners." / Others, on seeing what the duke had done/ whenever they caught sight of a German going by / shouted as if they had seen a wolf / and cut off his nose and ears./ Anyone who brought him one hundred German noses / was at once given one hundred talents of silver.' (*Dalimil*, p. 118.)
37) 'the Bohemian land seemed to the bishop to be a land of peace and he felt that he loved it with all the power of his soul' (Vančura, *Obrazy* 1, p. 144).

Obrazy z dějin národa českého, moreover, does not include any material from the *Rukopis královédvorský* (Queen's Court Manuscript, 1817) and *Rukopis zelenohorský* (Green Mountain Manuscript, 1818). These manuscripts, apparently dating respectively from the late thirteenth and tenth centuries, were 'discovered' at a time when, across Europe, nations were seeking for early written evidence of their cultural maturity and Czech scholar-patriots were growing unaccountably anxious about the absence of ancient Czech texts. In the nineteenth century, the sincerity of one's Czech patriotism became linked with one's belief in their authenticity, not least after studies were published in German in the 1850s demonstrating that they were forgeries. In 1886-88, the findings of these studies formed the basis of a 'battle' over the Manuscripts between intellectuals espousing essentially two distinct versions of patriotism: one focused on the past, emotional and mythopoeic, the other aspiring to objectivity and modernity. In the 1930s, when most academic opinion was satisfied of the Manuscripts' inauthenticity, the debate was rekindled by František Mareš (1857-1942), a prominent academic and leading figure on the Czech right, in a series of studies, including *Marnost bojů proti Rukopisům* (The futility of battles against the Manuscripts, 1933) and *Strach z pravdy* (Fear of the truth, 1937), that sought to restore the Manuscripts as an article of faith in Czech patriotism. In a further example of the intolerance that Vančura implicitly resists in *Obrazy z dějin národa českého*, Mareš was also a central figure in the 1934 campaign to force the German University in Prague to return the insignia to the Czech University, a campaign that was condemned by Communist intellectuals as radicalizing students towards Fascism.

This context may explain the narrator of *Obrazy z dějin národa českého*'s occasional explicit rejection of certain stories or ideas that have not been reliably documented, a stance that might otherwise seem paradoxical given his own use of embellishment and invention. For example, in his account of Břetislav I, who ruled from 1034-1055, Vančura describes how the duke meets a fisherman at Děvín, on the Danube, who catches a cross in his nets with the words inscribed on it in Church Slavonic: 'Jsem východ i západ. Jsem čas míjející i ten, který přichází.'[38] Břetislav believes that this is a sign from God and that the fisherman has been sent by an

---

38) 'I am the east and the west. I am the time that is passing and that which is coming' (ibid., p. 181).

apostle. The narrator, however, comments: 'Podobné myšlenky nemají místa ve vážném vypravování, a jestliže se tu a tam přece vyskytnou, je to jen proto, aby ukazovaly k zadumání Břetislavovu a k jeho touze. Jsou plané, není o nich zmínky v zápisech.'[39] By explaining how these ideas should be received by the reader, the narrator implicitly seeks to differentiate between the use of legends as evocative metaphors and their misuse as 'facts' in the service of a broader ideological campaign.

He expresses this point of view in a different way in his re-evaluation of the traditional characterizations of Ludmila, the reputedly Christian grandmother of St Wenceslas, and his reputedly pagan mother, Drahomíra, who apparently ordered her murder in 921. The narrator's central point here is that little for sure is known about them. He suggests, however, that Ludmila was just as fearsome as her rival, and vaguely implies that she owes her pious, peace-loving reputation as St Ludmila to the German-led myth-making of Roman Christianity. He similarly resists the saintly image of Wenceslas in an effort to render him more human and less distant in the imagination:

Jako se přiházívá, stavěl snad i jemu ďábel do cesty přerůzná pokušení, jako se přiházívá, byl snad i on zraňován hříchy, jako se přiházívá, byl snad i on přinucen státi pod znamením své doby a země, ale vypravování, v jehož věrnost přemnozí uvěřili, spatřuje jej kráčet od věku chlapeckého až po samu smrt mučednickou k bráně svatosti bez uchýlení.[40]

This subversion of well-established legends may be seen as a non-linguistic form of 'defamiliarization', introducing conflict and movement, disturbing the comfort and passivity of the implied reader and forcing his active engagement.

In 'Býti dělníkem', Vančura had condemned those who measure for breaking life up. In *Obrazy z dějin národa českého*, this division is implicitly nurtured by nationalist ideologies that seek to bind nations on the basis

39) 'Such ideas have no place in a serious narration, and if they none the less do appear here and there, this is only to draw attention to Břetislav's melancholy and to his yearning. They are sterile, there is no mention of them in the records' (ibid.)
40) 'As tends to happen, perhaps the devil set the most varied temptations in his path too; as tends to happen, perhaps he too was wounded by sins; as tends to happen, perhaps he too was forced to stand beneath the sign of his times and his land; but in stories, in whose veracity too many have believed, he is seen marching from his boyhood years through to his martyr's death towards the gate of sainthood without deviating' (ibid., p. 92).

of moral or genetic superiority over common enemies. In their place, as Holý indicates, Vančura asserts the 'awareness of interconnectedness' ('vědomí souvislostí'). This notion, taken from the title of an earlier essay, is explained in the context of the relationship between the individual and the collective in an apostrophe about the relationship between the ruler and his people, inspired by the life of Břetislav I:

> Neboť co jest kníže? Pán lidí ochotných a pranic více. Může vytáhnout do pole, může rozhodovat o věcech práva, vládne, rozkazuje, žene se jako proud nějakým řečištěm, ale to řečiště je závora i příčina jeho běhu. A jako je vztah mezi řečištěm a proudem, tak jsou podobné vztahy mezi konáním člověka jediného a činy lidí ostatních, neboť žádnou bytost a žádnou sílu nelze odděliti od společných věcí života.[41]

In this metaphor, which recalls the reference in the 1918 version of 'Ráj' to the river current that constantly finds its level (see Chapter Four), the river current represents total, chaotic freedom, the undirected movement of time, while the river bed represents a model of apparently constant, timeless order. Life emerges as and through the constant interrelationship between the two. Implicitly the total individual freedom that a ruler like Břetislav believes he exercises is an illusion provoking conflict and despair. In Vančura's view, for individual human beings to be freed of this illusion they need to recover their awareness of their interconnectedness, which is not a source of despair, but of hope, since it gives shape to individual freedom and guarantees it.

This metaphor of the river and the river-bed resonates with Kožmín's assertion that language in Vančura's writing is presented as simultaneously 'entirely open to human interventions' and 'a collection of very strict laws that must not only be respected but exploited precisely as the sources of human freedom' (see Chapter One). In *Obrazy z dějin národa českého*, the 'false monk', Bernard of Burgundy, asked why he sings in a muddle of different languages, replies: 'Proud, který je uzavřen v lidském

---

41) 'For what is a duke? A master of willing people and not a thing more. He can march into battle, he can decide on matters of law, he governs, he gives orders, he rushes like a current through a river-bed, but that river-bed marks the limit of and reason for the course he takes. And as the river-bed is related to the current, so are the actions of an individual human being and the deeds of all other people related, for no being and no force can be separated from the shared things of life' (ibid., p. 193).

srcdi, mě má, abych otvíral ústa, a dává tryskati mému hlasu.'[42] The desire to pour forth language is compared here to a current of water and appears intimately connected with the 'current of life' flowing through the human being. The narrator comments similarly of Cosmas and his friend Šebíř: 'Zdálo se jim, že kdesi uvnitř jejich bytostí leží vřeténko slov či nekonečné řeči, jež může obsáhnout vše, co je hodno lásky a co rudne vášněmi a co se rdí citem a co zní skutky. Zdálo se jim, že svět vypravuje a že oni jsou ústy toho světa.'[43] As Vančura suggests in his ironic comments about the writer, notably in the introduction to *Útěk do Budína* but also, for example, in his portrayal of Spera, the librarian-narrator of *Konec starých časů*, the impulse to write constitutes a vicarious substitute for the impulse to enter and embrace life fully, but both are expressions of the 'current of life' coursing through the human being. Like the individual life, literature also emerges as a negotiation between the activity of the imagination and the collective that receives and gives shape to its creations.

The notion of the 'interconnectedness' of individual human lives might be seen as an attempt to replace divisive nationalism with some kind of internationalism, a reminder of the essential humanity shared by all human beings that nationalism distorts and denies. In his memoir about Vančura, Bedřich Fučík describes how, in 1934, a meeting of intellectuals co-ordinated by Šalda to establish an anti-Fascist consensus broke up after Vančura rejected its nationalist basis, arguing that in future people would adopt communism.[44] This perspective is evident in the treatment of the Flanders merchant, who is depicted negatively not because of his nationality but because he represents the incursion into Bohemia from the West of early mercantile capitalism, the amoral pursuit of wealth and status. The narrator of *Obrazy z dějin národa českého* also seems attracted to the absence of nationalism in Bishop Dietmar: 'Skutečnost, že se narodil v zemi jiného jazyka, neměnila mnoho na [jeho] příchylnosti [k Čechám], neboť mužové těch starých dob neměli citu, který by věci

42) 'The current that is enclosed within the human heart makes me open my lips and lets my voice gush forth' (Vančura, *Obrazy* 2, p. 83).
43) 'It seemed to them that somewhere within their beings lay a small spindle of words or endless language that could contain everything that is worthy of love and that reddens with passion and that blushes with emotion and that resounds with brave deeds. It seemed to them that the world was telling stories and that they were the mouthpieces of that world' (Vančura, *Obrazy* 1, p. 253).
44) B. Fučík, *Čtrnáctero zastavení*, Prague, 1992, p. 130.

podobných přesněji rozlišoval. Pokud jde o národnost, věřil biskup, že je jeho povinností býti římským knězem. Mluvil latinsky, osvojil si jazyk český a užíval ho s radostí učeného člověka.'[45]

This interpretation is, however, complicated by the metaphorical relationship in the work between the 'current of life' and the 'current of language' flowing through all human beings. As Dalimil indicates in the first chapter of his chronicle, which retells the story of the Tower of Babel, though human beings are united by language, they are divided by languages, which for Dalimil form the basis of nationhood. Vančura seems to return to this conception in *Obrazy z dějin národa českého*. Early on, describing how the Frankish king, Louis II, subjugates Great Moravia, the narrator notes that German, for unknown reasons, did not displace the Slavonic language and therefore, implicitly, Slav nationhood was preserved: 'Bylo ustanoveno v tajemství příběhů, jež se řídí silami povědomými i silou skrytou, aby řeč, která je dechem národů, byla zachována slovanskému lidu.'[46] In the conclusion to Volume One, which reflects on the chaos and weakness that followed the exiling of Soběslav but appears simultaneously to address the circumstances faced by the implied reader, the narrator says:

Zdálo se, že lid právě se seskupující bude roztříštěn. – Ale duch, který tkví ve věcech života a který sám je život, skytl mu mocnější sílu, než skýtá troubení k bitvám; a vztahy a společenství práce a společenství jazyka a to, co neumírá, a to, co věčně bude opravovati zrady a omyly vládců, učinily jej pevným. Učinily jej národem.[47]

45) 'The fact that he had been born in the land of another tongue did not change anything much about [his] inclination [towards Bohemia], for men of those old times did not possess the sentiment that would more precisely differentiate between such things. As far as nationality was concerned, the bishop believed that his duty was first and foremost to be a Roman priest. He spoke Latin, but he learned Czech and used it with the pleasure of an educated man' (Vančura, *Obrazy* 1, p. 145).
46) 'It was ordained in the mystery of stories, which is governed by known forces and by a hidden force, that the language, which is the breath of nations, would be preserved for the Slavonic people' (ibid., p. 49).
47) 'It seemed that the people just assembling would be scattered. But the spirit that rests in the affairs of life and is itself life afforded them a greater strength than is afforded by clarion calls to battle; and the relationships and the community of labour and the community of language and that which does not die and that which will forever mend the treachery and errors of rulers made them steadfast. They made them a nation' (ibid., p. 355).

This spirit (*duch*) recalls Hegel's notion of *Geist*, but it is also associated explicitly in the quotation with the 'current of life' and etymologically with the 'breath' (*dech*) of the nation, reflecting that a nation lives through and is sustained by its language. For Vančura, the multitude of languages represents – or could represent – not the division but the diversity of humanity, comparable to the heterogeneous collectives he gathers in his work or the heterogeneity of his linguistic style. As we have seen, his understanding of unity is not uniformity, but a community that tolerates non-conformity like the river-bed tolerates the twists and turns of the current. In this sense, the languages of different nations constitute their individuality, their eccentricity, their spirit, which does not threaten, but rather reflects the nature of the human collective.

Those, like Vančura, within the Czech post-1918 Avant-garde who believed in what Calinescu terms the 'independently revolutionary potential of art' and rejected the subordination of art to a particular ideology nevertheless saw an intimate connection between the renewal of art and the renewal of the human being. Indeed the release of art from its traditional didactic function implicitly reflected the emancipation of the human being from passive obedience to restrictive norms into an active, creative relationship with life. The Avant-garde writer in theory realized in literature what would one day be realized in life, that is to say an open, empathetic, intuitive, joyful, communal attitude to life that for these writers reflected nothing more than the true nature of the human being, unencumbered by the debilitating inherited traits of the present, dying civilization. This view of art and of the human being and of the relationship between them remains unchanged in *Obrazy z dějin národa českého*, where the attempt to preserve normality in the writing and judgement of literature serves as a metaphor for the preservation of normality more generally in human behaviour. Only, where this attempt was once presented as the preserve of the Avant-garde, in *Obrazy z dějin národa českého* it is implicitly shown to be the task of all literature.

The Czech inter-war writer most widely read by both Czech and foreign readers remains Karel Čapek. In both *Hrdelní pře* and *Luk královny Dorotky*, Vančura, a regular attender at Čapek's Friday evening gatherings of 'interesting people', appears to mock him as the embodiment of what he perceives as the First Republic establishment's modest, mediocre conception of art and of the human being and its espousal of pragmatism over principle. In the story 'Usmívající se děvče', the narrator says with Půlpytel-like sarcasm: 'Je však naší povinností mluvit o skutečnostech tak, jak si toho žádají pravidla hledící k umění vypravěčskému. Na štěstí je naše doba osvícená a nesedne na lep hňupům. Mezi stem se u nás najde sotva jediný, kdo by se dal nachytat na něco jiného než na dobrou filosofii pragmatickou.'[1] In an article written in 1977 defending Čapek's pragmatism against what he perceives as Vančura's elitism, Aleš Haman argues that, while Čapek adopts the 'stance of a proper democrat and humanist', Vančura adopts the 'stance of romantic aristocratism, scorning the filth and mud of the earth-bound [*přízemnost*] and setting nobility of spirit and strength of passion against parvenu arrogance and narrow-minded hypocrisy. It is the stance of a man stricken with creative thirst, raising himself up from the prose of life to the absolute values of art'. For this reason, claims Haman, Vančura's work remains a 'matter for literary gourmands and specialists'.[2]

In the introduction to a 1990 Čapek reader in English translation entitled *Toward the Radical Center*, Peter Kussi, essentially echoing Haman's view of Čapek, writes: 'Philosophically as well as politically, Čapek was

---

1) 'It is, however, our duty to speak about facts as the rules pertaining to narrative art demand. Luckily our age is an enlightened one and will not get taken for a ride by idiots. Out of a hundred people you'll barely find one who would fall for anything other than good pragmatic philosophy' (V. Vančura, *Luk královny Dorotky*, Prague, 1947, p. 53.)
2) A. Haman, *Východiska a výhledy*, Prague, 2002, p. 287.

a man of the centre, but not in the sense used by hostile critics. The centre he was aiming for was not a lukewarm middle ground between extremes. It was a radical centre, radical in the original sense of the word: at the root of things.'[3] Kussi further associates this 'radical centre' with a pluralist outlook and with the advocacy of reason and 'common sense'. In his review of this volume, Alfred Thomas, pondering the meaning of Kussi's deliberate oxymoron, argues that Čapek 'subordinates the ambiguities of art' to an understanding of the human being that amounts to a 'reassuring philosophical and ethical schema'. Thomas continues: 'In this sense, the "radical centre" is not simply an alternative to political extremism in a Europe on the brink of barbarism; it can equally be seen as a haven from epistemological uncertainty, a mythic space where the monist dictates of metaphysical truth and the ambiguities engendered by art may be seemingly reconciled.'[4] For Thomas, what Kussi terms the 'radical centre' proves simply a repetition of the common retreat in Czech literature into extra-literary truths.[5]

Despite the nebulousness of the term, it strikes me that, artistically, if anyone represented the 'radical centre' of Czech literature in the interwar period, it was not Čapek, but Vančura. The line from W.B.Yeats's 1919 poem 'The Second Coming' - 'Things fall apart, the centre cannot hold' - has become something of a short-hand for the cultural mood which Modernism appeared to reflect and respond to.[6] As Vančura depicts vividly in the contrasting frame stories of *Dlouhý, Široký a Bystrozraký*, that response seemed a paradoxical combination of the enthusiastic embrace of chaos and the anxious attempt to establish a new order. Malcolm Bradbury and James McFarlane write:

Modernism was in most countries an extraordinary compound of the futuristic and the nihilistic, the revolutionary and the conservative, the naturalistic and the symbolistic, the romantic and the classical. It was a

---

3) K. Čapek, *Toward the Radical Center: A Karel Čapek Reader*, edited and with an introduction by Peter Kussi, Highland Park, NJ, 1990, p. 13.
4) A. Thomas, 'Toward the Radical Center: A Karel Čapek Reader', *Slavic and East European Journal*, 36 (1992), 4, p. 521.
5) Indeed, Kussi unwittingly reflects this unhappy conflation by blurring an original use of the notion of the 'radical centre' in an artistic context with its more familiar association in political jargon with the search for a 'third way' between right and left.
6) See, for example, M. Bradbury and J. McFarlane (eds), *Modernism: A Guide to European Literature 1890-1930*, Harmondsworth, 1991, p. 26.

celebration of a technological age and a condemnation of it; an excited acceptance of the belief that the old regimes of culture were over, and a deep despairing in the face of that fear; a mixture of convictions that the new forms were escapes from historicism and the pressures of the time with convictions that they were precisely the living expressions of these things.[7]

As I argued in Chapter Two, Vančura's writing, neither embracing totally the absence of centre nor attempting to establish a centre that could hold, strives instead to remain at the centre of these two contradictory impulses, perhaps in the hope that their interaction might recover a lost unity, the 'root of things', but mainly to prevent one impulse coming to dominate over the other until such time as that unity is recovered. This danger is reflected in the two key metaphors for this 'centre' in Vančura's writing, the human being and the literary work, both of which are threatened by deformation through the pressure to conform, or disintegration through the absence of any ordering principle. This 'centre' does not, therefore, constitute a retreat from the 'ambiguities engendered by art' – what Holý calls 'the Čapeks' humility in the face of reality'[8] – but the dynamic embodiment of them. By definition, it is not a stable place, but more recalls the interaction between the current and river-bed described in *Obrazy z dějin národa českého*, with the current as capable of bursting its banks as the river-bed of absorbing the current.

Vančura's writing may also be seen as central in that it constitutes something of an encyclopedia of the patterns of thought and style prevalent in Czech inter-war literature. Holý describes how, at the end of the 1920s, Vančura may be said to move in all or none of the directions adopted by other artists, listing among his examples Proletarianism, Surrealism, Existentialism, Ruralism and Catholicism,[9] but the heterogeneity consonant with his conception of the centre is evident in his writing much earlier. At the same time, Vančura's shift from the centre of Avant-garde disputes in the 1920s to the centre of the division between 'high' and popular literature in the 1930s might either reflect, as Hodrová argues, the declining radicalism of Czech literature, perhaps

7) Ibid., p. 46.
8) J. Holý, *Práce a básnivost: Estetický projekt světa Vladislav Vančury*, Prague, 1990, p. 39.
9) Ibid., p. 83.

as the political situation worsened, and the shift of the 'radical centre' to a more conservative position, or Vančura's desire to take his struggle for a balanced understanding of literature and the human being out of the margins of the Avant-garde and into the mainstream.

I describe Vančura in the title as the 'heart of the Avant-garde' because he seeks to remain at the centre of existence understood as a living, evolving organism, working constantly to sustain a healthy equilibrium. Repeatedly in his writing the heart – tolerance, empathy, love, but also courage, hearty eating and intuitive harmony with the rhythms of nature – longs to overrule the head. (Others can decide which organs are represented by other members of the Avant-garde.) One can only speculate whether, had Vančura lived, he would have acquiesced to abandoning this 'centre', either following Mukařovský and Nezval in finding ignominious accommodation with the post-1948 Stalinist regime, or falling silent, like Olbracht, or dying prematurely in despair, like Teige, or the poet Konstantin Biebl (1898–1951), who committed suicide. In his memoirs, Seifert implies that Vančura's response would have been different. Convinced of accounts that Vančura remained brave and noble at the moment of execution, he recalls how Vančura had once unsuccessfully tried to teach him to swim and to ride a bicycle and comments: 'neither did Vladislav Vančura at that time manage to teach me that great human gesture that is courage at all times and in all circumstances, even when death itself is approaching.'[10] In any event, despite the claims of some critics, the immediate legacy of Vančura's writing lay not in the literature that placed itself in the service of the post-war Communist regime, but in the literature, sanctioned and unsanctioned, that tried to resist its static, prescriptive, normative views, presenting an image of an innately imperfect, troublesome human being perpetually torn between order and freedom, who responds to oppression with subversion in an effort to preserve balance, a human being for whom another name cannot be found.

10) J. Seifert, *Všecky krásy světa*, Prague, 1999, p. 126.

BIBLIOGRAPHY

Primary Sources

Vančura, Vladislav, *Amazonský proud* - *Pekař Jan Marhoul* - *Pole orná a válečná* - *Poslední soud*, Prague: Lidové noviny, 2000.

Vančura, Vladislav, *Hrdelní pře anebo Přísloví* (third edition), Prague: Odeon, 1979.

Vančura, Vladislav, *Hry*, Prague: Československý spisovatel, 1959.

Vančura, Vladislav, K. Konrád, J. J. Paulík, *Poetistická próza*, Prague: Lidové noviny, 2002 (This volume contains *Dlouhý, Široký, Bystrozraký* and *Rozmarné léto*.)

Vančura, Vladislav, *Konec starých časů* (third edition), Prague, Družstevní práce - Melantrich - Svoboda, 1947.

Vančura, Vladislav, *Luk královny Dorotky* (fourth edition), Prague: Družstevní práce - Melantrich - Svoboda, 1947.

Vančura, Vladislav, *Markéta Lazarová* (nineteenth edition), Prague: Maťa, 2004.

Vančura, Vladislav, *Nemocná dívka*, Prague: Plejada, 1928.

Vančura, Vladislav, *Občan don Quijote a jiné prózy*, Prague: Československý spisovatel, 1961.

Vančura, Vladislav, *Obrazy z dějin národa českého*, Vol. 1, Prague: Československý spisovatel, 1956.

Vančura, Vladislav, *Obrazy z dějin národa českého*, Vols.II and III, Prague: Československý spisovatel, 1956.

Vančura, Vladislav, *Řád nove tvorby*, edited by Milan Blahynka and Štěpán Vlašín, Prague: Svoboda, 1972.

Vančura, Vladislav, *Rodina Horvatova*, Prague: Evropský literární klub, 1938.

Vančura, Vladislav, *Tři řeky*, Prague: Československý spisovatel, 1958.

Vančura, Vladislav, *Útěk do Budína* (sixth edition), Prague: Družstevní práce - Melantrich - Svoboda, 1949.

Secondary Sources

Bergson, Henri, *Creative Evolution*, translated by Arthur Mitchell, New York: Henry Holt & Co., 1911.

Bergson, Henri, *Laughter: An Essay on the Comic*, translated by Cloudesley Brereton and Fred Rothwell, New York: Macmillan, 1911.

Blahynka, Milan, *Vladislav Vančura*, Prague: Melantrich, 1978.

Bradbury, Malcolm and McFarlane, James (eds.), *Modernism: A Guide to European Literature 1890–1930* (second edition), Harmondsworth: Penguin, 1991.

Bürger, Peter, *Theory of the Avantgarde*, translated by Michael Shaw, Minneapolis: University of Minnesota, 1984.

Butterfield, Herbert, *The Historical Novel: An Essay*, Cambridge: Cambridge University Press, 1924.

Calinescu, Matei, *Five Faces of Modernity*, Durham: Duke University Press, 1987.

Čapek, Karel, *Toward the Radical Center: A Karel Čapek Reader*, edited and with an introduction by Peter Kussi, Highland Park, NJ, 1990.

Čelovský, Boris, *Řešení české otázky podle německých dokumentů 1933-1945*, Ostrava: Sfinga, 1995.

Čep, Jan, *Rozptýlené paprsky*, Prague: Vyšehrad, 1993.

Chvatík, Květoslav, *Od avantgardy k druhé moderně*, Prague: Torst, 2004.

Dostál, Vladimír, *Slovo a čin*, Ostrava: Profil, 1972.

Dyk, Viktor, *Dramata a próza*, Prague: Lidové noviny, 2003.

Erenburg, Il'ia, *A vse-taki ona vertitsia*, Dresden: Helikon, 1922.

Fraenkl, Pavel, 'Rozmarné léto', *Rozprávy Aventina* II (1926-27), p. 118.

Fučík, Bedřich, *Čtrnáctero zastavení*, Prague: Melantrich – Arkýř, 1992.

Fučík, Bedřich, *Kritické příležitosti I*, Prague: Melantrich, 1998.

Fučík, Bedřich, *Setkávání a míjení*, Prague: Melantrich, 1995.

Fučík, Julius, *Stati o literatuře*, Prague: Svoboda, 1951.

Götz, František, *Básnický dnešek*, Prague: Václav Petr, 1931.

Götz, František, *Jasnící se horizont*, Prague: Václav Petr, 1926.

Götz, František, *Literatura mezi dvěma válkami*, Prague: Československý spisovatel, 1984.

Grygar, Mojmír, 'Vladislav Vančura' in Mukařovský, J., (ed.), *Dějiny české literatury* IV, Prague: Victoria, 1995, pp. 310-28.

Grygar, Mojmír, *Rozbor moderní básnické epiky: Vančurův Pekař Jan Marhoul*, Prague: Academia, 1970.

Hájková, A., Závodský, A., Galík, J., *Tři studie o Vladislavu Vančurovi*, Olomouc: Filosofická fakulta UP, 1970.

Hájková, Alena, *Humor v próze Vladislava Vančury*, Prague: Academia, 1972.

Halas, František, *Imagena*, Prague: Československý spisovatel, 1971.

Haman, Aleš, *Východiska a výhledy*, Prague: Torst, 2002.

Havránek, Bohuslav and Daňhelka, Jiří (eds.), *Nejstarší česká rýmovaná kronika tak řečeného Dalimila*, Prague: Československá akademie věd, 1957.

Hodrová, D., 'Markéta Lazarová' in Zeman, Milan et al. (eds.), *Rozumět literatuře I*, Prague: Československý spisovatel,1986, pp. 272-79.

Hodrová, Daniela, *...na okraji chaosu...*, Prague: Torst, 2001.

Hodrová, Daniela, 'Postava tuláka, loupežníka a kouzelníka', *Česká literatura* 32 (1984), 5, p. 443-59.

Holý, Jiří, *Práce a básnivost: Estetický projekt světa Vladislav Vančury*, Prague: Československý spisovatel, 1990.

Hora, Josef, *Poesie a život*, Prague: Československý spisovatel, 1959.

Jankovič, Milan, 'Rytmičnost v próze' in Červenka, Miroslav, Jankovič, Milan, Kubínová, Marie, Langerová, Marie, *Pohledy zblízka: zvuk, význam, obraz*, Prague: Torst, 2002, pp. 163-204.

Koutská, Ivana and Svátek, František (eds.), *Politické elity v Československu 1918-48*, Prague: Ústav pro soudobé dějiny AV ČR, 1994.

Kožmín, Zdeněk, 'Jazyková charakteristika postav v díle Vladislava Vančury' in *Sborník vědeckých prací vyšší pedagogick školy v Brně, 5: O literatuře*, Prague: Státní pedagogické nakladatelství, 1958, pp. 89-182.

Kožmín, Zdeněk, *Styl Vančurovy prózy*, Brno: Universita J.E.Purkyně, 1968.

Králík, Oldřich, 'Příspěvek ke studiu Vančurova stylu', *Slovo a slovesnost*, 5 (1939), 1, pp. 65-78.

Kučerová, Hana, '*Poslední soud* jako syntéza Vančurovy tvorby dvacátých let', *Literární archive PNP*, 10 (1978), pp. 21-44.

Kučerová, Hana, 'Vančurův umělecký vývoj v prvních letech poválečných', *Česká literatura*, XX (1972), 6, pp. 496–521.

Kundera, Milan, *Umění románu: Cesta Vladislava Vančury za velkou epikou*, Prague: Československý spisovatel, 1960.

Lehár, Jan, *Studie o sémantizaci formy*, Prague: Karolinum, 2005.

Lukács, Georg, *The Historical Novel*, translated by Hannah and Stanley Mitchell, Harmondsworth: Penguin, 1962.

Lukács, Georg, *History and Class Consciousness*, translated by Rodney Livingstone, London: Merlin, 1971.

Lukács, Georg, *The Theory of the Novel*, translated by Ann Bostock, Cambridge, MA: MIT Press, 1971.

Lukeš, Emil, 'Vančurova Pole *orná a válečná*: K otázce kompozice, syžetu a ideového smyslu', Acta Universitatis Carolinae 1973: Philologica 3–4, *Slavica Pragensia XVI*, 1975, pp. 69–80.

Mácha, Karel Hynek, *Básně*, Prague: Český spisovatel, 1997.

Mahen, Jiří, *Měsíc* (third edition), Brno: Jota, 1997.

Malevich, Oleg, *Vladislav Vanchura*, Leningrad: Khudozhestvennaia Literatura, 1973.

Moretti, Franco, *Modern Epic*, translated by Quintin Hoare, London, New York: Verso, 1996.

Mukařovský, Jan, 'Doslov' in Vančura, V., *Poslední soud*, Prague: Československý spisovatel, 1958.

Mukařovský, Jan, *Studie II*, Brno: Host, 2001.

Mukařovský, Jan, *Studie z estetiky*, Prague: Odeon, 1966.

Mukařovský, Jan, *Studie z poetiky*, Prague: Odeon, 1982.

Mukařovský, Jan, *Vančurův vypravěč*, Prague: Akropolis, 2006.

Neumann, S. K., *Stati a projevy IV*, Prague: Odeon, 1973.

Nezval, Vítězslav and Teige, Karel, *Manifesty Poetismu*, Prague: Odeon, 1928.

Nezval, Vítězslav, *Dílo* Vol. XXIV, Prague: Československý spisovatel, 1967.

Nezval, Vítězslav, *Moderní básnické směry* (third edition), Prague: Československý spisovatel, 1969.

Nezval, Vítězslav, *Z mého života* (third edition), Prague: Československý spisovatel, 1965.

Nový, K., 'Rozhovor', *Panorama*, 14 (1936), 4, pp. 56–57.

Orel, Harold, *The Historical Novel from Scott to Sabatini*, Basingstoke, London: Macmillan, 1995.

Peroutka, Ferdinand, *Sluší-li se býti realistou*, Prague: Mladá fronta, 1993.

Pešat, Zdeněk, 'Vladislav Vančura a počátky socialistické literatury: Příspěvek k analyze literární avantgardy', *Česká literatura*, IX (1961), 4, pp. 477–95.

Pinthus, Kurt, *Menschheitsdämmerung: The Dawn of Humanity*, translated by Joanna M. Ratych, Ralph Ley and Robert L. Conard, Columbia, SC.: Camden House, 1994.

Píša, A. M., *Dvacátá léta*, Prague: Československý spisovatel, 1969.

Píša, A. M., *Stopami dramatu a divadla*, Prague: Československý spisovatel, 1967.

Píša, A. M., *Třicátá léta*, Prague: Československý spisovatel, 1971.

Pohorský, Miloš, *Portréty a problémy*, Prague: Mladá fronta, 1974.

Polák, Karel, 'Vladislav Vančura: *Obrazy z dějin národa českého*', Kritický měsíčník, III (1940), 3, p. 186.

Pynsent, Robert B., 'Conclusory Essay: Decadence, Decay and Innovation' in Pynsent, Robert B. (ed.), *Decadence and Innovation*, London, 1989, pp. 111–248.

Rutte, Miroslav, *Jaro generací*, Prague: F. Topič, 1929.

Rutte, Miroslav, *Nový svět: Studie o nové české literatuře 1917–19*, Prague: Aventinum, 1919.

Šalda, F.X., *Kritické glosy k nové poesii české*, Prague: Melantrich, 1939.

Seifert, Jaroslav, *Všecky krásy světa* (fourth edition), Prague: Eminent, 1999.

Sezima, Karel, 'Z nové tvorby románové III: Surrealisté', *Lumír*, LVI (1930), pp. 195–99.

Sokel, Walter H., *The Writer in Extremis: Expressionism in Twentieth Century German Literature*, Stanford: Stanford University Press, 1959.

Špirit, Michal (ed.), *Tvář: Výbor z časopisu*, Prague: Torst, 1995.

Steiner, Peter, *Russian Formalism*, Ithaca, London: Cornell University Press, 1984.

Štoll, Ladislav, 'Poslední kniha Vladislava Vančury', *Tvorba*, 6 (1931), 43, p. 687.

Thomas, Alfred, 'Toward the Radical Center: A Karel Čapek Reader', *Slavic and East European Journal*, 36 (1992), 4, pp. 520–21.

Urban, Milo, *Živý bič*, Bratislava: Perfekt, 2003.

Urx, Edo, *Básník v zástupe*, Bratislava: Slovenský spisovatel, 1961.

Václavek, Bedřich, *Kritické stati z třicátých let*, Prague: Československý spisovatel, 1936.

Václavek, Bedřich, *Od umění k tvorbě*, Prague: Odeon, 1928.

Václavek, Bedřich, *Tvorba a společnost*, Prague: Československý spisovatel, 1961.

Vančurová, Ludmila, *Dvacet šest krásných let* (second edition), Prague: Československý spisovatel, 1974.

Vladislav Vančura mezi dramatem a filmem: Sborník materiálů z vědecké konference v Opavě, v září 1971, Opava: Slezské muzeum – Památník Petra Bezruče, 1973.

Vlašín, Štěpán et al. (eds.), *Avantgarda známá a neznámá*, Vol. 1, Prague: Svoboda,1971.

Vlašín, Štěpán et al. (eds.), *Avantgarda známá a neznámá*, Vol. 2, Prague: Svoboda, 1972.

Vlašín, Štěpán et al. (eds.), *Avantgarda známá a neznámá*, Vol. 3, Prague: Svoboda, 1970.

Vodička, Timotheus, *Stavitelé věží*, Tasov: Maria Rosa Junová, 1947.

Vyskočil, Albert, *Kritikova cesta*, Brno: Vetus Via, 1998.

Žemlička, Josef, *Čechy v době knížecí (1034–1198)*, Prague: Lidové noviny, 1997.

INDEX

RAJENDRA A. CHITNIS

VLADISLAV VANČURA:
THE HEART OF THE CZECH AVANT-GARDE

Published by Charles University
in Prague, Karolinum Press
Ovocný trh 3, 116 36 Praha 1
Prague 2007
Vice-Rector-Editor prof. PhDr. Mojmír Horyna
Cover and Layout by Zdeněk Ziegler
Typeset by MU typografické studio
Printed by tiskárna Nakladatelství Karolinum
First Edition

ISBN 978-80-246-1456-4